Explorations in Practical Theology

Bridging the Divide Between Faith Theology and Life

The Church in Oceania

edited by Anthony Maher

ATF Theology
Adelaide
2015

Text copyright © 2015 remains with the authors and for the collection with ATF Theology. All rights reserved. Except for any fair dealing permitted under the Copyright Act, no part of the publication may be reproduced by any means without prior permission. Inquiries should be made in the first instance with the publisher.

A Forum for Theology in the World
Volume 2, Issue 2, 2015

A Forum for Theology in the World is an academic refereed journal aimed at engaging with issues in the contemporary world, a world which is pluralist and eucumenical in nature. The journal reflects this pluralism and ecumenism. Each edition is theme specific and has its own editor responsible for the production. The journal aims to elicit and encourage dialogue on topics and issues in contemporary society and within a variety of religious traditions. The Editor in Chief welcomes submissions of manuscripts, collections of articles, for review from individuals or institutions, which may be from seminars or conferences or written specifically for the journal. An internal peer review is expected before submitting the manuscript. It is the expectation of the publisher that, once a manuscript has been accepted for publication, it will be submitted according to the house style to be found at the back of this volume. All submissions to the Editor in Chief are to be sent to: hdregan@atf.org.au.

Each edition is available as a journal subscription, or as a book in print, pdf or epub, through the ATF Press web site — www.atfpress.com. Journal subscriptions are also available through EBSCO and other library suppliers.

Editor in Chief
Hilary Regan, ATF Press

A Forum for Theology in the World is published by ATF Theology and imprint of ATF (Australia) Ltd (ABN 90 116 359 963) and
is published twice or three times a year.
ISSN 1329-6264

ATF Press
PO Box 504
Hindmarsh SA 5007
Australia
www.atfpress.com

Subscription Rates 2015

Print	On-Line	Print and On-line
Aust $65 Individuals	Aus $55 individuals	Aus $75 individuals
Aus $90 Institutions	Aus $80 individuals	Aus $100 instiutions

It has been said that Catholicism is the 'sleeping giant of pastoral and practical theology'. This volume shows the giant has risen from its slumbers, gracefully active, creatively and sensitively dancing, building bridges between disciplines, doctrine and lived communal experience. The collection displays the vitality of the particular church in Oceania whose voices have much to teach local churches everywhere, not least the value of pastoral and practical theology. The book is a serious contribution to the shaping of Catholic and Christian culture. (Professor Gavin D'Costa, Religion and Theology, Bristol University, UK)

This volume breaks new ground in providing a deeply contextual work of practical theology from Oceania. The essays move across key topics—mission, worship, place, youth, women, ministry in a decentered society—as they engage with Indigenous cultures and envision the future of the church 'down-under'. The volume presents a dialogical practical theology that is open to wisdom from all sources and seeks mystical-political transformation. *Explorations in Practical Theology: the Church in Oceania* is a much-needed contribution to the international conversation in practical theology and to the global church. (Associate Professor Claire Wolfteich, Co-Director, Center for Practical Theology, Boston University, USA; President of the International Academy of Practical Theology.)

This is a *must* read for practical theologians *everywhere*. Though the focus of authors is on theological reflection within the context of Oceania, there is an engaging, even unique, freshness in the manner in which they choose their topics and develop their insights. Their articles are case studies of *how* dialogue should occur. At the same time, I sense the humbling pain they feel as they yearn to bridge the ever-widening gaps between Gospel values and the different cultural realities that concern them. It is this pain, born of love of Jesus Christ, that gives every article an authentic quality. For these reasons practical theologians in every part of the world have much to learn from them". (Gerald A Arbuckle, SM, Consultant Anthropologist and Co-director, Refounding and Pastoral Development Unit, Sydney.)

This is a splendid example of what the editor terms 'theological integration'. We are indebted to Anthony Maher for bringing together this wide-ranging collection: it bridges many divides—especially between theology and pastoral communication, and between the Christians of Oceania and the larger church. An essential point of reference. (Professor Anthony Kelly CSSR, Australian Catholic University, Member of the International Theological Commission (2004–2014.)

The Church in Oceania: Bridging the Divide between Faith, Theology and Life offers a timely overview of the rich tapestry of practical theology in Oceania. Many of its defining features, born of the special characteristics of the region, are woven together beautifully: a rootedness in space and place, a respect for the many cultural heritages of the region, lack of sentimentality towards ecclesial privilege, together with rigorous engagement with the sources and resources of Christian tradition. The result is a vision of the discipline that deserves to be highly valued by its desired audiences of church leaders, laity and theological educators. (Elaine Graham, Grosvenor Research Professor of Practical Theology, University of Chester, UK)

This is an exciting ecumenical book of essays from diverse theologians dispersed throughout Oceania. Their writings are the mature distillation of their deliberations when they first met in 2014 as the *Association of Practical Theology in Oceania*. They venture well beyond the derivative thought of scholars schooled in Europe and the USA. They are well grounded in this part of the world, and they are not swamped by the big local Catholic and Australian players. They are bold enough in each other's company to provide us with stimulating images for a grounded practical theology, including 'the church of the verandah' and the call to practice 'slow church' for an ancient land; we need a Christianity unfolding with the pace of the place. (Frank Brennan SJ AO Professor of Law, Australian Catholic University)

It is possible to engage in contextual theologizing without doing practical theology. But practical theology can only be done as contextual theology. This is a book that articulates practical theology at its best and so is strongly contextual in every way. It is rooted in the experience of the church in Oceania; the result of a rich theological imagination of its contributors; it is respectful of and faithful to the Christian Tradition. While it is contextual, however, the essays here have not been written in isolation, but are developed in a fruitful dialogue with the church catholic. Because of such catholicity, other contextual practical theologies can be enriched and challenged, and can greatly profit from this book. (Steve Bevans SVD Professor Emeritus, Catholic Theological Union, Chicago, USA)

This book is dedicated to
a humble priest and a good man

Gerard Hall SM

Inaugural Fellow of APTO

Forum for Theology in the World Vol 2 No 2/2015

Contents

Acknowledgements   ix

Introduction
    Anthony Maher   xi

1. Pastoral-Practical Theology: An Impression from Oceania
    Anthony Maher   1

2. 'The Primacy of the Pastoral': Bridging the Divide between Faith, Theology and Life in the Ecclesiology of Yves Congar
    Anthony Maher   27

3. 'I thank my God about you always' (1 Cor 1:4): Pauline Insights Toward Pastoral Theologies of Location for the Churches of Oceania Today
    Catherine Playoust   49

4. A Missional Church in Process and Willing to Learn
    Neil Darragh   73

5. 'Re-placing the Church': Challenges and Prospects for Christianity Down-Under
    Stephen Pickard   87

6. Challenges and Prospects for Christianity Down-Under—A Response to Stephen Pickard
   Gerard Kelly   101

7. Hunger Games: Addressing the Young Catholic Slide to the Periphery
   Chris Duthie-Jung   107

8. Creating Spaces between: Women and Mission in Oceania
   Katharine Massam   123

9. Aboriginal Cultures and a Spirit of Place: Ancient Origins and Twenty-first Century Relevance
   Kathleen Butler-McIlwraith   135

10. 'They asked for bread and you gave them a stone, for fish a snake': The Future of Worship in Oceania.
    Gerard Moore   151

11. Everywhere and Nowhere: Experiencing God in a Decentered Context
    David Ranson   165

12. Are there Really Angels in Oceania? Forging a New Mysticism of Place, Time and History Through Dialogue Among Oceanic Peoples and Traditions
    Gerard Hall   181

Contributors   197

Acknowledgements

This is a collaborative work of theological integration; the work of many minds and hearts striving collectively to bridge the divide between theology and pastoral ministry. This book would not have been possible without the generosity of colleagues writing both the APTO conference papers and subsequent chapters. I am particularly grateful to my colleagues from the Catholic Institute of Sydney, Gerard Kelly and David Ranson for their support with the conference and this book. My sincere thanks go to each of the ten authors for their expertise and graciousness; with regard to the dawning potential of the church in Oceania, I have learnt a great deal from each of them. I wish also to thank the APTO executive, Zach Duke and John Collins for their great support and encouragement with the conference. Thanks must also go to my colleague at CIS, Angelina Tropeano, for her exemplary patience and meticulous attention to detail in reading the proofs. I am indebted to Gerard Hall not only for his insightful reading of the manuscript, but also for his contagious enthusiasm in daring all at APTO to become more than we are. I am sincerely grateful to Mervyn Soares, founder of The LMent, graphic design, and Hilary Regan of ATF Press, for their skills and creativity in bringing this book to press. Finally, I must offer a heartfelt note of love and gratitude to my unflappable wife Lesley Maher and our four gregarious children: Harry, Grace, Fred and Fin.

Forum for Theology in the World Vol 2 No 2/2015

Introduction

This collection of essays represents the culmination of an ambitious project that sought to engage the theological academy with a practical ecclesial task, namely to support efforts to bridge the divide between faith, theology and life. Arguably such a divide serves to exacerbate the marginalisation of Christianity within Western culture. Two consequences of this developing reality, experienced by most Christian denominations, are the steady decline in ecclesial practice and essentially the growing perception of ecclesial irrelevance in issues of critical public debate. Spiritually minded people in Western societies seem to believe, but don't belong, while the 'turn to the subject', so evident in the growing antipathy towards religious institutions, affirms the necessity for theology to be fully attuned to culture.

Pope Paul VI drew our attention to the concern with regard to 'the split between the Gospel and culture', which he understood to be 'without doubt the drama of our time. . . . [Thus every] effort must be made to ensure a full evangelisation . . . of cultures'.[1] In a similar manner, Pope John Paul II declared, 'I have considered the church's dialogue with the cultures of our time to be a vital area, one in which the destiny of the world at the end of the twentieth century is at stake'.[2] Further, Pope John-Paul II insisted that 'authentic inculturation of the Christian faith is grounded in the mystery of the Incarnation'.[3] More

---

1. Paul VI, Apostolic Exhortation, *Evangelii Nuntiandi* (1982), 25. Cited in Gerald A Arbuckle, *Culture, Inculturation, Theologians: A Postmodern Critique* (Collegeville: Liturgical Press, 2010), xix.
2. John Paul II, Letter to Agostino Cardinal Casaroli, *Osservatore Romano* (28 June 1982), 7. Cited in Arbuckle, xix.
3. John-Paul II, Apostolic Exhortation, *Ecclesia In Oceania*, (2001), 46.

recently in *Evangelli Gaudium,* Pope Francis highlights the immense significance of culture, believing it is imperative to evangelise culture in order to inculturate the Gospel. Vatican Two's pastoral constitution, *Gaudium et Spes,* particularly focused upon the imperative of Gospel / culture synthesis, an endeavour that requires theologians to be skilled in 'reading the signs of the times', so that the church, 'ordered to the care of souls',[4] might enter into 'authentic dialogue with the world'.[5] Such endeavour requires the combined efforts of the theological academy including the human sciences.[6]

The chapters presented here, through the matrix of pastoral-practical theology, first appeared as conference papers for the 2014 gathering of the *Association of Practical Theology in Oceania* (APTO). In celebrating the tenth year of this ecumenical conference, APTO invited academics from across the theological spectrum, together with a broad range of ministry practitioners, to engage in an experiment in pastoral-practical theology, from their own disciplinary perspective, in order to make a collective response that would enhance an ecclesial sense of place and purpose in Oceania.

Although undoubtedly shaped by diverse methodologies and multifaceted inter-disciplinary dialogical partners, pastoral-practical theology is intrinsically a unifying discipline. Informative for our undertaking, Kathleen A Cahalan refers to the task of integration as, 'the bringing together of distinct entities or parts and in the process

---

4. David Schultenover, 'From the editor's desk', in *Theological Studies,* 76/2 (2015): 241.
5. William W Neher and Paul J Sandin, *Communicating Ethically* (Boston: Pearson, Allyn and Bacon, 2007), 85–103. For a seminal definition of church, informative for this current work, see Denis Edwards, *Called to be Church in Australia* (Homebush: St Paul's Publications, 1987).
6. For example see the profound work over many decades of the anthropologist Gerry Arbuckle, *Earthing the Gospel: An Inculturation Handbook for Pastoral Workers* (Eugene: Wipf and Stock, 2001); *Grieving for Change: A Spirituality for Refounding Gospel Communities* (Homebush: St Paul's Publications, 1991); *Healthcare Ministry: Refounding the Mission in Tumultuous Times* (Collegeville: Liturgical Press, 2000); *A Preferential Option for the Poor: An Application to Catholic Health and Aged Care Ministries in Australia* (Deakin West: Catholic Health Australia, 2007); *Culture, Inculturation, and Theologians: A Postmodern Critique* (Collegeville: Liturgical Press, 2010); see also the application of Eric Erikson and Urie Bronfenbrenner to education and youth ministry, in Anthony Maher and Bob Hanley, *Educating Hearts: Seven Characteristics of a Good School* (Homebush: St Paul's Publications, 2013), 27–42.

the creation of something new that exceeds the sum of its parts.⁷ Encouraged by such insight, the APTO 2014 conference sought to dialogue with various theological concerns including scripture, tradition, experience, doctrine, history ethics, spirituality, reason and so on, around the common focus of normative Christian praxis.⁸

In presenting an argument to 'the Church, the university and the world', Gavin D'Costa claims that 'Christian culture and civilisation are at stake if we do not attend to the nature of the university, a major institution that fosters the cultural and intellectual life of nations and trains the intelligentsia of the ecclesia'.⁹ In an important argument in favour of inter-disciplinary collaboration which moves far beyond the theological academy and includes all areas of human knowledge, he states provocatively that unless, a 'marriage of the disciplines' takes place 'the enterprise of a Catholic university is doomed'.¹⁰ In a thesis that resonates with the thought of Congar, and perhaps most pressing for D'Costa, is the call from pastoral-practical theologians to transform the curriculum so that the Christian vision can illuminate every aspect of created reality, both natural and cultural. D'Costa insists, 'without curriculum changes, Christian intellectual culture will continue to be impoverished'.¹¹ Those who advocate the integration of theological education, recognise along with Saint Bonaventure, [the inadequacy of] reading without repentance, knowledge without devotion, research without the impulse to wonder, prudence without the ability to surrender to joy, action divorced from religion, learning sundered from love, intelligence without humility, study unsustained by divine grace, thought without the wisdom inspired by God.¹²

---

7. Kathleen A Cahalan, 'Integration in Theological Education', in *The Wiley-Blackwell Companion to Practical Theology*, edited by Bonnie J Miller-McLemore (Malden: Wiley-Blackwell, 2012), 386–395, 386.
8. Randy L Maddox, 'The Recovery of Theology as a Practical Discipline', in *Theological Studies*, 51 (1990): 650–72, 665.
9. Gavin D'Costa, 'Theology: The Church at the Heart of the Christian University Proclaiming the Word of God', in *Theology in the Public Square*, 215. See also Gavin D'Costa, *Vatican II Catholic Doctrines on Jews and Muslims* (Oxford: Oxford University Press, 2014).
10. D'Costa, 'The Marriage of the Disciplines: Explorations on the Frontier', 178.
11. D'Costa, 'Theology: The Church at the Heart of the Christian University', 216.
12. Saint Bonaventure, *Itinerarium Mentis in Deum in Prologus*, 4 cited in D'Costa, 218.

The current work of theological collaboration is less ambitious, but may represent a movement towards the university of the future, the stakes are high, and although dramatic, we agree with D'Costa that 'education is central to the development of civilisation and if the church fails to transform education at every level, then the future of the church and the world are in deep trouble.'[13]

In general, within Oceania, 'practical' theology seems to be considered as a largely Protestant pursuit, and although Stephen Pattison asserts that Catholicism is the 'sleeping giant of pastoral and practical theology', in the context of Oceania, pastoral-practical theology is not widely acknowledged or embraced in Catholic ecclesial or academic institutions.[14] Kathleen A Cahalan's observation with regard to the North American ecclesial milieu has considerable resonance in Oceania, she writes, 'claiming a vocation and a disciplinary identity as a practical theologian is not without its problems in the Catholic context'. The challenging environment is further complicated by the geographical isolation of Oceania.[15]

Out of the midst of all these great challenges, perhaps one of the most encouraging developments in theology in the past sixty years is the emergence from the global south of liberation perspectives, and in deference to this line of reasoning and the persuasive arguments of scholars such as Congar and D'Costa, the current work seeks to raise a clarion call to attract the support of three essential

---

13. D'Costa, 'Theology: The Church at the Heart of the Christian University', 218. See also Neils Henrik Gregersen, 'J Wentzel van Huyssteen: Exploring Venues for an Interdisciplinary Theology', in *Theology Today*, 72/2 (2015): 141–159.
14. Stephen Pattison, 'Foreword', in *Keeping Faith in Practice: Aspects of Catholic Pastoral Theology*, edited by James Sweeney, Gemma Simmonds, and David Lonsdale (London: SCM Press, 2010), ix.
15. Whilst over five million people self-describe as Catholic in Australia (2011 census), only around thirteen per cent attend church services on a regular basis. The percentage of Catholics who attend Mass every week has been falling steadily since it peaked in the mid-1950s, see Bob Dixon, 'Why Catholics Have Stopped Going to Mass, Final Report', Pastoral Projects Office, Australian Catholic Bishops Conference. Lord Carey, the former Archbishop of Canterbury, believes that 'the Church of England is 'one generation away from extinction . . . unless more is done to attract new worshipers then every one of the forty-three church of England dioceses across the world could be wiped out within twenty-five years.' Keynote speech, Holy Trinity Church, Shrewsbury, Shropshire Churches Conference, 2013.

ecclesial constituencies within Oceania: first, to ecclesial bishops in Conference, that they be inspired by the example of Pope Francis to read more contextually the signs of the times; to the laity, that they may be encouraged to develop further their crucial role in building the kingdom through informed participation in Christ's mission, and in the process, avoid what John Henry Newman described as a church, in which the educated classes will terminate in indifference and the poorer in superstition. And finally, to our colleagues within the theological academy, that they may continue to embrace the 'capstone' dimension[16] of pastoral-practical theology and strive collaboratively to reconnect theology to the lived life of faith, *theologia* in its fullest sense.

Towards Integration in Theological Education

Pope Francis is convinced that Vatican II tried to overcome the 'divorce between theology and pastoral ministry, between faith and life.' Theology, he believes, should not be at odds with the lives of real people, 'doctrine is not a closed system devoid of dynamics but able to raise questions, doubts, inquiries'. The Pope teaches that 'Christianity is a living doctrine called Jesus Christ . . . without encountering families and the people of God, theology runs the great risk of becoming ideology'. Francis maintains that 'If we want to take seriously the principle of the Incarnation', theology must seriously consider the hopes, dreams, struggles, problems, worries and questions of ordinary people.[17]

A leading practical theologian in North America, Claire Wolfteich, reminds us that the project of practical theology 'should be understood as a dialogical contribution to a large discussion'.[18] Thus each chapter in this work seeks to dialogue with pastoral-practical

---

16. See Les Ball, *Transforming Theology: Student Experience and Transformative Learning in Undergraduate Theological Education* (Preston: Mosaic Press, 2012), 'Integrative Learning', 124–147, 143.
17. Pope Francis, address delivered to mark the 100th anniversary of the foundation of the faculty of theology at the Catholic University of Argentina and the fiftieth anniversary of the close of the Second Vatican Council. Posted by Carol Glatz, 5 September 2015. www.catholicherald.co.uk/news/2015/09/05.
18. Claire E Wolfteich, *An Invitation to Practical Theology* (New York: Paulist Press, 2014), 329.

theology, bringing particular expertise to bear upon our task of renewing an ecclesial sense of place and purpose in Oceania. We hear from biblical scholars, missiologists, educationalists, systematic theologians, liturgists, pastoral and practical theologians, together with experts in youth ministry, feminist studies, spirituality and indigenous culture and spirituality. As Wolfteich outlines in her *Invitation to Practical Theology*, 'dialogue with systematic and moral theologians', as well as other members of the academy, 'is vital for the flourishing of practical theology'.[19]

The authors of this work represent various voices of *The Church in Oceania*; together they contribute diverse traditions and methodologies to enhance an ecclesial sense of place and purpose in Oceania. The first essay in the collection, dialogues with the global reality of pastoral-practical theology; in the process Anthony Maher outlines a 'mode of operation' for pastoral-practical theology, primarily through the matrix of five broad characteristics. In the second chapter, drawing upon the French *ressourcement* theologian Yves Congar, Maher gives an insight into the challenges facing the church in secular culture, and suggests *pace* Congar, that the 'primacy of the pastoral' is an essential guide for true and false reform in the church. Congar argued that the church had become detached from society and reality, a small, pure, right-minded sect or party, disincarnate, empty of human blood. The attitude of the church in opposing modern life has excluded faith, Congar insists; faith must be considered in its *totality*: it must have a concrete meaning beyond its theological sense as a virtue of the intelligence alone.

Maher revisits the depths of Congar's prophetic ecclesiology, so evident at Vatican II, and argues that we must again fill our world with signs of faith, or, just as truly, with the presence of faith. Faith must again become humanly present like Christ. A policy of presence, not a policy of prestige of some sort of ecclesiastical imperialism, but a policy of the presence of faith in everything that is human . . . to manifest the total value of faith with regard to the totality of human life. Maher shows that Congar's message for today is clear: our signs of faith must both be dynamic and express a totality of life, one that is inclusive, open to the world, while true to its original message. Catholicism has to learn to be non-discriminatory in its outlook on

---

19. Wolfteich, *Practical Theology*, 9.

life, and perhaps more than anything else in its morals, practice and theological formulation.

The biblical scholar *Catherine Playoust* examines how the earlier Christian communities developed ways to speak theologically, transcending physical separation, allowing those who were in Christ, members of Christ's body, to understand the same ecclesial location of faith. Playoust shows compellingly that the letters of Paul represent experiments in new community; revealing Paul's strategies to shape the Christian communities along specific lines and to negotiate difference. In detecting other voices and perspectives, to whom Paul wrote and communicated, Playoust highlights how we might gain further insights into community identity and practice around the memory of Jesus.

Playoust alerts us to the New Testament texts as a witness to various experiments in shaping or reshaping community, and advises that it would be unwise to imagine that we could adopt the Pauline strategies wholesale. Rather, she suggests that in the light of our own experience, they may provide insights into our own church structures and circumstances. In inviting us to enter into other experiences of God, not to apply the bible to current problems, but rather to understand something of the experience, and therein have our own vision for the present and future reinvigorated. Playoust explains that it is not possible to discover a blueprint for the church today. Instead, those who wish to serve today's churches of Oceania, by discerning an ecclesial sense of place, must do so not only in the light of scriptures but out of knowledge and love of the particular church they serve.

Perhaps one of the most rewarding aspects of Playoust's fascinating contribution to this study is her inclusivist methodology with regard to all the members of the Pauline community, not only its leaders. Thus she can say that Paul's strictures about conformity and insistence on the community over the individual would be excessively harsh and ultimately unproductive. Those whom one is supervising, Playoust insists, need room to breathe and experiment, lest they fail to develop their gifts and to discover new ways to act in an ever-changing environment. By the principle of subsidiarity, local groups need some degree of autonomy, so that they do not constantly reach outside themselves for advice and so that decisions are not made for them centrally without due consideration of the needs of the specific place.

Neil Darragh writes out of the ecclesial context of Auckland, and explores the realities of a missional church to argue that the mission of the church is the well-being of God's people. Darragh investigates the integration of internal church ministry with outward-facing mission in the world. A local church with an outward focus into the wider society may need to adjust its traditional patterns of leadership to fit a contemporary outward focus. Its resources for making such an adjustment include: New Testament perspectives on ministry, traditional patterns of church leadership, church traditions on social justice, models of collaborative ministry, the experience of other church denominations and secular models of social organisation.

Darragh understands that the church is for the reign of God and that missiology precedes and influences ecclesiology. He focuses primarily upon contemporary secular models of organisation and the resources that a local church might draw upon to renew itself as a more authentic missional church. Central for ecclesial renewal, Darragh, argues, are new models of leadership that grow out from active participation of all members of the church. Outlining the core values for the practice of public participation, Darragh concludes that these values can stimulate ecclesiology and missiology and hence work to restore an ecclesial sense of place and purpose.

The theme of the APTO 2014 conference was in part inspired by *Stephen Pickard*, who writes convincingly on the theme of 'recovering an ecclesial sense of place down-under'. Such a desire demands that practical theology should be contextual. Pickard draws attention to the need for a slow church. He argues that *place* and *pace* are the twin co-ordinates for ecclesial *presence*. Pickard contends, wisely, that if the coming church is to be truly *present* in contemporary society, two things are required: (a) a church so *placed* that it can be found and (b) one that moves at a *pace* that is not easily missed in the busyness of life. Place, pace and presence he argues are interwoven aspects relevant to the church's recovery of its place in the world. To speak of 're-placing' the church is not a matter of 'with what', but a question about 'where' and 'how' might a new ecclesial form of life contribute to the enrichment of wisdom in God's world.

Pickard understands that the quest for an ecclesial sense of place in Australia is in its infancy, and requires a movement beyond a colonial preoccupation with space to a more relational approach to place. The process of adaptation and enculturation involves pitching the tent; dwelling in, rather than peering into the world beloved of God. Pickard writes on the importance of 'retrieving veranda as ecclesial place': a veranda ecclesiology may challenge Christians to see church without walls, to become an outward-looking and open community, actively engaged with society and its concerns. Pickard encourages us to imagine a church as an open sanctuary offering safety, nourishment and energy for work. Furthermore, a Christian sensibility, fuelled by an incarnational theology, has resources to overcome the latent pressure of colonial conquest and recover a deeper sympathy with indigenous ways of community and gospel. Reconciliation will include a kenotic listening by European diaspora (Anglo-Saxon and New Zealand Pakeha) to the first inhabitants. Indeed it is hard to conceive how we shall truly construct a 'home' church, without recovering something elemental about the body of Christ as a reality deeply rooted in the place of our habitation.

Offering a critique of certain modes of ecclesial community which appear to represent little more than 'lifestyle enclaves', Pickard reminds us that 'companionship' is a form through which ecclesial presence is ignited and expands into full-orbed ecclesial practices. Companionship is a bedrock condition without which the church cannot be the church. Companionship truly acknowledges otherness, recognising and welcoming difference; it can't be rushed rather it has an emergent gift-like character that continually surprises and lures us towards each other and God. The slow church coming, Pickard sees, will be the kind of church which is formed and nurtured through intricate and complex webs of companionship. It will be a church which lives with a certain restraint and reserve regarding its own claims to place and temptations to self-promotion; a church capable of weaving together place, pace and presence into companionship with our neighbour and the risen Lord.

In his response to Stephen Pickard, *Gerard Kelly* highlights the potential of Australian art and poetry to assist us in becoming more attuned to place and pace, together with the growing realisation that a single expression of this place and of our relationship to it is no longer possible. Kelly also pedestals the church to be a place of intersection between the geographical location and an inner, spiritual realm, one that has been nourished by the word of God and enlivened by the Spirit. Kelly adds a further crucial dimension to our consideration of place when he observes the significance of 'another place': place is never simply the place where I am now; Christians come to Australia from the four-corners of the earth and bring their cultures and traditions of Christianity with them. So the bigger question is, according to Kelly: how might there be an Australian church? How might all of our Christian traditions from elsewhere become a church for this place? For Kelly, the challenge is whether or how the one Christian church will find a variety of expressions precisely because of the intersection with other places.

In offering an important caveat to calls for contextualisation, Kelly raises a concern with regard to the relationship between a local church and the universal church, hinting at some of the dangers associated with a church that becomes too enclosed within its own sense of place. Thus Kelly reminds us of the necessity of local church dialoguing with something beyond itself. Indeed, according to Kelly, a strong sense of the local should not cut us off from the church in other places. In fact, it should contribute to the life of these other local churches. Finally, Kelly links Pickard's notion of companionship as a bedrock condition of 'church to be church' to the question of the Eucharist. Kelly highlights the emergence in recent decades of a close connection between Eucharist, communion and local church. A communion ecclesiology signifies a community of the baptised, one that recognises a eucharistic community is not a self-selecting group, rather it is a group gathered by God.

A eucharistic community is a place where reconciliation is visible, one that recognises that diversity truly manifests the kingdom of God. If our gatherings for the Eucharist are self-selecting, then, Kelly believes, we may not be much different to the Corinthians whom Paul scolded for being driven by factions. The body of Christ is not discerned in such gatherings. The point of the eucharistic gathering is that it is *not* a gathering of people who have a natural affinity. This is where we see the importance of place. The eucharistic community is the place where the gospel of God—this gospel of reconciliation—is made real and visible.

Seen through an Aboriginal lens and showing the continued relevance of *The Dreaming* as an explanatory mechanism in Aboriginal cultures, *Kathy Butler-McIlwraith* delineates the ways the term has been defined and identifies examples that reveal the contemporary relevance of The Dreaming. Offering an insight into Aboriginal cosmology and the connection to *place,* Butler-McIlwraith discusses how The Dreaming explains the formation of the landscape, the inter-connected creation of animals and humans, together with a great variety of laws and customs of the kinship system. Significantly Butler-McIlwraith highlights the complexity of Indigenous belief systems, which, in contrast to models of Western monotheism, are constructed as fluid in a temporal sense (past, present and future), and manifestly different to the hegemonic Judeo-Christian linear time that most people are familiar with.

Butler-McIlwraith maintains that the concept of The Dreaming needs to be lived in the local context to be understood; to understand we are challenged to become involved in The Dreaming within the local area where we live. In this sense non-Indigenous people become part of the ongoing Dreaming where our place may be construed as cultural participant or cultural impediment. This means listening to Dreaming stories and considering their historical, cultural, political and structural implications, Dreaming stories are still being created and today encompass pan-Indigenous relevance. Most notably, Butler-McIlwraith challenges non-Indigenous peoples to dare to dream as she posits that National Dreaming cannot be exclusively limited to Indigenous participation and must have the potential to enfranchise a national reconciliatory position.

Katharine Massam reminds us that historians are fundamentally storytellers; highlighting four particular stories of 'women in mission', Massam critiques the 'power of space "between" conventional categories'. Focusing upon the significance of place and space, Massam considers, from an historical perspective, the significance of creating spaces between women and mission in Oceania. Massam discusses how intersectionality feminist and post-colonialists scholars have engaged in analysis of categories, gender, class, race, to open up discussion of 'identity', recognising in the process that the power is in the 'between'.

In considering the significance of sacred space and place for non-Indigenous people, Massam draws attention to sacred space as 'storied', carrying memory, such places are not chosen, but instead choose us. In challenging the assumption that faith can only be transported to Australia, 'brought in pots', Massam extends an invitation to consider how the heritage of faith can be read in context around us, drawing upon what we have brought, but also on what we find. Massam argues persuasively that it is not possible for the place not to make a difference, and encourages people of faith to claim the reality of connection to place. In drawing close to Butler-McIlwraith, Massam moves away from the notion that 'white man got no dreaming', and instead encourages all Australians to pay attention to the spirituality of place and our own response to that located sense of the sacred. In acknowledging a sense of place and placelessness, the in-between pilgrim people may begin to recognise more clearly the holy ground on which we already stand.

Chris Duthie-Jung draws upon painstaking qualitative research, and his extensive experience of youth ministry, to explore the faith connections of young 'Pakeha' Catholics in New Zealand. He argues that recent research continues to indicate that the Catholic parishes in Australia and New Zealand are less and less 'home' to the young Catholics of European descent. While church leaders wrestle with issues of 'who should receive communion?', and while a refreshingly new papal response adopts mercy as its focus, the vast majority of the young watch from the fringe seemingly wondering, 'Who really cares?'. Duthie-Jung concludes that they are the children of the Catholic disappeared—the children of parents who largely disconnected in recent decades, maintaining a cultural Catholicity but avoiding communal and personal faith commitment.

Duthie-Jung moves on to explore some of the 'signs and calls' in the contemporary experience, which he argues, indicates that although young Pakeha Catholics generally hold a Catholic religious worldview, it is a 'customised' version, whilst their personal Catholic identity appears nominal. In positing a number of considerations for further discussion, Duthie-Jung highlights the difficulties around religious language and suggests a need for deeper contextualisation as a means to reconnecting young people with their faith tradition. In stressing the potential of religious experience to resonate with young people's lives, Duthie-Jung calls for an identification of what are essential meanings and beliefs in Catholicism and a letting-go of the inculturations of previous cultures. Central to youth ministry in contemporary culture, and building upon the cultural anthropology of Gerry Arbuckle, Duthie-Jung maintains there is a real need to radically re-image ecclesial structures, representing a paradigm shift, understood as a restructure of our whole pastoral system, a fundamental 'refounding' of the church.

In reflecting upon the future of worship in Oceania, *Gerard Moore* discusses the effect on peoples and cultures of liturgical and theological paradigms which have been imposed without regard to the contextual and indigenous roots of South Pacific and Australasian communities. Such imposition was further complicated by multifaceted theological debates with regard to scripture, sacraments and tradition which formed the substance of Catholic and Protestant antagonism. Moore expertly draws our attention to what he calls three sub-cutaneous 'heresies': (i) the scriptures as 'bible'; (ii) the sacraments as fixed; (iii) the question of tradition. Much of this 'European' debate was around authoritative interpretation of scripture, while Moore emphasises the primary repository of Word is not script, which is visual, but actualising memory, which is oral and corporeal, held in communities of narrative, dance, song and dreams.

The presentation of the Word of God as a Western script, albeit translated, led to Christians prizing the written text over oral tradition. Bringing a book to Tonga, Samoa and Parramatta was to bring a quintessential reminder of the differences between European and Indigenous societies, showcasing the superiority of the one while reminding all that access to knowledge and power was restricted to the 'educated'. Moore argues that a fixation with the Bible as the sole source of revelation meant there was little missionary interest in evaluating local custom and belief for signs of the ongoing presence of the Spirit. Theologically, this excluded indigenous culture and faith from contributing to the interpretation of revelation, impoverishing the breadth of current Christian thought and understanding.

In presenting the sacraments as fixed, two or seven, the missionaries, according to Moore, lost sight of the sacramentality of faith itself along with the profound expressions of sacramentality across Oceania. Moore argues the number of sacraments is not closed, while the language of sacramentality is ritual, thus each culture is a sacramental expression of humanity in grace. Perhaps most crucial in the context of Oceania is the way in which the land itself is demarcated and often sacred, indeed the way in which the 'land' is an expression of sacramentality. Sacraments acquire their ecclesial authority when they arise out of a community of critical practice. Indigenous Christianity for example wishes to engage the sacramentality of the faith in ways far transcending the limitations of the two or seven rites and practices. In seeking fresh dialogue between church and indigenous peoples with regard to liturgy and sacraments, beyond pen, script and book, in discovering new understandings of the way the sacred is found in creation, Moore contends, there is much to be learnt from the peoples of Oceania.

David Ranson presents a timely and poignant exposition of the tension between place and 'no place', showing that experience is a tension of both emplacement and displacement. *Place* he believes can never fully contain our experience, especially our experience of God, as we are sent forth from the place of our experience, beyond it, to take with us something that affects every new place in which we find ourselves. Ranson draws our attention to the fact that we live in an age of displacement, occasioned, first of all, because we increasingly bear the outcome of widespread patterns of modern migration, primarily as a consequence of violence and economic injustice; and secondly, because of the experience of dislocation inherent to the emergence of post-modernity.

The apparent freedom of Western culture, occasioning a rather superficial celebration of diversity, comes at the cost of a type of fragmentation, allowing a situation of disconnection to develop that diminishes relationships and that potentially creates for us a radical insecurity. Ranson critiques the consequences of this dislocation for our sense of church, he asks: 'What are the implications for our way of being church in this context?' Drawing upon the thought of Michel de Certeau, Ranson considers the church's displacement from the centre of society and the dilemma of the modern Christian who experiences a corresponding loss of place within a secularised context. Out of the ruins of such experience and pointing to the examples of the saints, such as Ignatius of Loyola and Teresa of Avila, Ranson calls for a 'conversion response' from the modern-day Christian, one that is quintessentially mystical, a response relative to an 'Unnameable' one who calls us to conversion.

Ranson understands the sense of loss, as the once firm Christian ground gives way and points to a new opportunity for the church in Oceania, something that begins anew: 'an in-fancy.' The empty tomb gives rise to a new beginning, 'a siteless site . . . requiring a new language to be born', one capable of shaping tradition. For de Certeau, such mystical discourse lends itself to social practice that is, itself, subversive, acting as critique to accepted norms of behaviour. Thus, the mystic, both in language and in practice, critiques the status quo, calling it beyond its innate tendency to complacency, and ossification and to be surprised by the potential within a new rupture, a new beginning.

Gerard Hall concludes our explorations of the church in Oceania by leading the call for a new mysticism of place, time and history through dialogue among all Oceanic peoples and traditions. Crucially Hall insists that practical-mystical-prophetic theology is not an otherworldly disengagement from social concerns, rather he advocates, that if practical theology is to play its role in the recovery of an ecclesial sense of place and purpose in Oceania, then it needs to give impetus to an understanding of religious experience, or what Hall refers to as a new mysticism of place, time and history. Hall challenges theology to be openly inculturated, a process by which Christian faith is genuinely incarnated in a particular culture, transforming it into a new creation. Hall is hopeful that an Oceanian practical theology will be sensitive to these and similar issues in seeking a mystical and prophetic way forward for our lands, seas and peoples.

Hall remains inspired by the visionary insights of Raimon Panikkar and his call for depth-dialogue among traditions, which he argues, has become the existential imperative of our times. The goal of such dialogue is the creation of a 'new innocence', 'new myth', 'new praxis' and/or a 'new mystical way' of thinking, acting and being which celebrates one's identity in relationship with, rather than in opposition to, other traditions. Capable of adopting a 'cosmotheandric confidence', and drawing upon present experience, the people of Oceania are, Panikkar believed, in a privileged situation to be catalysts to a new culture and civilisation. In critiquing the dominant Western approach to reality, Hall reminds us that human knowledge is not simply reducible to the intellect but needs to include sense perception and mystical experience. Such knowledge is sensory, affective, aesthetic, practical, and capable of exhibiting its own kind of life-celebrating intelligence. Integral to this 'cosmotheandric experience' is the need to awaken to 'the voice of the Spirit who inspires dreams and sacred stories' and reconnects us to 'the sacredness of nature'.

Hall speaks of a new kind of consciousness deeply embedded in the biocosmic spiritualities of Indigenous traditions especially in their appreciation of the sacredness of the earth, their sense of the interrelationship of all realities, one is not separate from this reality since there is no *one*—nor for that matter no *other*—separable from creation and the natural world. In calling upon the angels of interreligious and intercultural dialogue, particularly Indigenous traditions, Hall is prophetically emphasising an experiential awareness of the whole, a spiritually heightened, 'total experience of the human being', which, in theological terms, is a genuinely mystical experience of the divine mystery within the cosmos.

Each essay in this work of theological integration represents a reading of the 'signs of the times', an attempt to bridge the divide between faith, theology and life. Perhaps the strongest sentiment that emerges from our authors is the collective call for a contextual theology of *place,* one that engages on a fundamental level with the indigenous peoples of Oceania. Each essay outlines a hope-filled ecclesial vision of reality, allowing the reader to discover the truth contained in George Tyrrell's maxim: 'that the deposit of faith is latent in the collective mind . . . but not in each singly, let them meet and talk it over, and all know at the end what none knew wholly at the beginning.'[20] Arguably such collective endeavour will enhance our sacramental vision of reality, lighting the way for the church of Oceania into the future.

---

20. George Tyrrell (London: Longmans, Green and Co, 1904), 'The Mind of the Church', *The Faith of the Millions II*, 174.

1
Pastoral-Practical Theology: An Impression from Oceania

Anthony Maher

A Mode of Operation

This chapter offers a *mode of operation* for pastoral-practical theology through the medium of five indispensable characteristics, each emphasising the importance of the 'turn to experience', as a source, along with scripture and tradition for theologising. Agreement on a definition for pastoral or practical theology oscillates down the decades; it remains a work-in-progress, both within the church and the wider global theological academy. The focus of this chapter is not to debate definitions of pastoral-practical theology, but rather to explore some of the essential elements of the discipline. Whilst writing out of the Catholic tradition, I feel drawn to the mystical, eschatological and possible non-'practical' sensibilities that resonate with the designate 'pastoral'. Although, I concede, in most academic circles this particular nomenclature is presently not in vogue. Indeed, Wesley Carr warns of the overuse of the term 'pastoral', indicating that the word has become 'broken-backed' through being 'indiscriminately applied' and often used to obfuscate issues, 'avoid hard decisions or to escape the charge of unclarity'.[1]

Furthermore, current thinking seems to suggest that the term 'pastoral' carries overtones of: shepherding the docile uneducated flock; a male dominated clerical culture; and myopic focus on internal structures. Such an approach is more in tune with the deductive theology of the 1950s. It is not unreasonable to argue that pastoral theology appears in general to be experiencing a period of

---
1. Wesley Carr, *Handbook of Pastoral Studies* (London: SPCK, 1997), 9.

academic insomnia, faculty and disciplinary identity-crisis and even ecclesial inertia. Today most theologians who work in the discipline traditionally known as 'pastoral' theology consider themselves to be 'practical' theologians. Therefore, in view of the above and by way of *détente*, this chapter will adopt the nomenclature 'pastoral-practical' theology. Following some brief soundings from the literature, copious in the North American context but rather sparse elsewhere, the chapter will posit five essential characteristics that may serve our task of bridging the growing chasm between faith, theology and life in Oceania.

The Jesuit philosophical-theologian Bernard Lonergan identified 'Eight Functional Specialities of Theology': research, interpretation, history, dialectic, foundations, doctrine, systematics and communications.[2] Significantly for our endeavours here, Lonergan described how the eighth and final stage of theological activity, the area he called 'Communications', and what we most likely understand as pastoral-practical theology:

> [Communications] is of major concern for it is in the final stage that theological reflection bears fruit. Without the first seven stages, of course, there is no fruit to be borne. But without the last, the first seven are in vain, for they fail to mature.[3]

Mindful of Lonergan's 'Eight Functional Specialties', it is reasonable to argue that pastoral-practical theology is not simply an appendage to theological activity, rather pastoral-practical theology is a disciplined attempt within the Academy to bridge the divide between faith, theology and life, particularly the lived experience of marginalisation and suffering. Such understanding leads Nancy Eiesland to reflect that 'pastoral and practical theology shades off into liberation theology whenever the ordinary lived experience involved is seen as caught up in the processes by which the large-scale distribution of power and opportunity in a society [and church] is arranged'.[4]

---

2. Bernard Lonergan *Method in Theology* (London: Darton, Longman and Todd, 1972), 355.
3. Lonergan, *Method in Theology*, 355.
4. DF Ford and M Higton, *Modern Theologians' Reader* (Malden: Wiley-Blackwell, 2012), 248; and Nancy Eiesland, *The Disabled God: Towards a Liberatory Theology*

Practical theology emerged in the university in the late eighteenth century as a distinctive theological discipline among both Protestant and Roman Catholic faculties, such as in Vienna in 1774 and Tübingen in 1794. Central to this development was Friedrich Schleiermacher (1768–1834), who sought to uphold and unite the developing fields of what he termed philosophical, historical and practical theology within the modern university. Instead, Bonnie Miller-McLemore argues, a set of secular disciplines emerged, which exacerbated the separation of systematic theology from the lived life of faith. This led the Dominican Yves Congar to conclude in the 1930s that theology had become disincarnate, devoid of human life.[5] Theology was no longer all-embracing but 'was reduced to one of the so-called fields that have come to be called the "four-fold", that is Bible, church history, theology/ethics, and the practical/ministerial field'.[6]

Don S Browning maintains that 'practical theology moves from descriptive theology and its formation of questions, back to historical theology, systematic theology (and theological ethics) and finally to strategic or fully practical theology'.[7] For Browning, 'to think and act practically in fresh and innovative ways may be the most complex thing that human beings ever attempt'.[8] The distinguished former Dean of Yale Divinity School, Thomas Ogletree, argues: 'practical theology is not one of the branches of theology; the term practical theology characterises the central intent of theology treated as a whole.'[9] While the Jesuit theologian Karl Rahner, arguably the most influential Catholic theologian of the twentieth century, did much to break new ground in practical theology in the Catholic tradition, and laid the foundations for moving the discipline away from the past myopic focus on clericalism, Rahner understood practical theology

---

    of Disability (Nashville: Abingdon Press, 1994).
5. See Chapter Two, 'Yves Congar and the First Principle of Reform: The Primacy of the Pastoral'.
6. Mary McClintock Fulkerson, 'Systematic Theology', *Practical Theology*, edited by Bonnie J Miller-McLemore (Malden: Wiley-Blackwell, 2012), 361.
7. Don S Browning, *A Fundamental Practical Theology* (Minneapolis: Fortress Press, 1991), 139.
8. Browning, *Fundamental Practical Theology*, 7.
9. Thomas Ogletree, 'Dimensions of Practical Theology: Meaning, Action, Self', in D Browning, *Practical Theology: The Emerging Filed in Theology, Church and World* (San Francisco: Harper and Row, 1983), 83–101, 85.

to be 'an original science . . . responsible for a theological analysis of the present situation in which the church is to carry out the special self-realisation appropriate to it at any given moment.'[10]

Rahner considered practical theology to be the scientific organisation of the church's reflection upon mission. Rahner gave further impetus to our endeavours when he insisted that 'practical theology consists in theological reflection upon the entire process by which the church as a whole brings her own nature to its fullness in the light of the contemporary situation of the world.'[11] Rahner argued that 'practical theology's subject-matter is everyone and everything in the church . . . not only those holding office.'[12] Rahner understood clearer than most the importance of synthesis in theological method. Thus, he explained, practical theology is concerned with asking what God is doing in the church and the world. Rahner also claimed, with particular relevance to our explorations, that the church 'cannot fulfil its task without giving serious attention to the other theological disciplines and the human sciences.'[13] For Rahner:

> Practical theology is that theological discipline which is concerned with the church's self-actualisation here and now—both that which *is* and that which *ought* to be. This it does by *theological* illumination of the particular situation in which the church must realise itself in all its dimensions.[14]

In referencing the seminal work of Pattison and Woodward,[15] Eric Stoddart is persuasive when he argues that clear boundaries for

---

10. Karl Rahner, 'Practical Theology within the Totality of Theological Disciplines', in *Theological Investigations,* Volume IX, translated by Graham Harrison (New York City: Herder and Herder, 1972), 102–104.
11. Karl Rahner, *Theological Investigations,* translated David Burke (New York City: The Seabury Press, 1977), Volume X, 350. Here Rahner considers 'caritas as a science', 369ff. For a systematic discussion of the term 'pastoral' in the context of *Gaudium et spes,* see Rahner, Volume X, 293–298.
12. Karl Rahner, *Practical Theology within the Totality of Theological Disciplines* (London: Darton, Longman and Todd, 1972), 102.
13. Rahner, *Theological Investigations,* translated by David Burke (New York City: The Seabury Press, 1977), Volume X, 350. Here Rahner considers 'caritas as a science', 369ff. For a systematic discussion of the term 'pastoral' in the context of *Gaudium et spes,* see Rahner, Volume X (1973), 293–298.
14. Rahner, *Practical Theology,* 102.
15. James Woodward and Stephen Pattison (editors) *The Blackwell Reader in Pastoral*

pastoral theology are 'unnecessary . . . and not useful.'[16] Stoddart states the obvious: pastoral care is no longer the preserve of clergy. Neither is the task of pastoral-theological activity around vocation, formation, counselling, ethics, doctrine, liturgy, spirituality, family relations, sexuality, disability and so forth, the preserve of a 'class' or 'type' of person. Such a desideration in the Catholic tradition, particularly around boundaries, remains contested, evidenced by the political or ideological interlocution arising from Pope Francis' (2015) Synod on the Family.

Stoddart highlights the pressing concern with regard to normalcy and loyalty to traditions. He claims that drawing together current thinking on pastoral theology 'eschews the limiting of *pastoral* to ecclesial contexts and instead, advocates the more encompassing interests of pastoral-practical theology.'[17] Stoddart argues that pastoral-practical theology is discomfiting 'because it complexifies experience, practice and doctrinal traditions . . . [and] as a discipline [it does not] look for one correct interpretation but, enquires how and why interpreters arrive at different understandings.'[18]

Illustrating from his own pastoral context in central Africa, I recall the Jesuit Peter Henriot outlining a memorable insight into the task of pastoral-practical theology:

> A young man was walking besides a fast flowing river, when he was disturbed by the frantic screams of a woman: 'My baby is drowning in the river! Please someone help, he is heading for the water fall.' The young man without a thought for his own safety courageously jumped into the river and managed to rescue the baby returning him to his mother.
>
> The following day the young man was again walking beside the river and to his horror he heard two women screaming:

---

and Practical Theology (Oxford: Blackwell Publishers, 2000).
16. Eric Stoddart, 'Current Thinking in Pastoral Theology', in *The Expository Times*, 123/7 (2012): 323–333, 323.
17. Stoddart, 'Current Thinking', 323.
18. Stoddart, 'Current Thinking', 123. See also Ormond Rush, *Still Interpreting Vatican II* (Mahwah: Paulist Press, 2004) 1–68, and the hermeneutical triad of author, text and receiver, and Ormond Rush, 'Ecclesial Conversion After Vatican II: Renewing "The Face of the Church" to Reflect "The Genuine Face of God"', in *Theological Studies*, 74 (2013): 785–818.

'My baby is in the river and heading for the falls, please help!' Once more the young man jumped into the river, and although exhausted, he somehow managed to save the two children and returned them unharmed to their mothers.

The third day, three babies were in the river and in trying to save all three, tragically two were lost.

On the fourth day there were four babies in the river, five the following day, and so on . . .

Finally, the young man persuaded the villagers to go 'up river' and discover the source of the problem; only then could it be understood and possibly resolved.[19]

Applying Henriot's lesson to our own context, we suggest that pastoral-practical theology must be engaged in the practice of 'going up river', and in constantly seeking to discover, what is going on in the ordinary lives of people, in the lived life of faith, and most crucially from a pastoral-practical perspective, what needs to be done for the temporal and eternal 'care of souls.'

To write and think in pastoral-practical theology is to practice pastoral-practical theology. In support of the *Missio Dei*, pastoral-practical theology is, as Peter Ward perceptively explains, 'the practice of reason as a spiritual discipline that mediates the divine presence'.[20] In synthesising the mystical dimension of faith with the political reality, David Ranson, drawing on the thought of Charles Péguy, shows how the 'two cities of Augustine are subject to *la mystique*' and how 'the spiritual is achieved through the secular'.[21] It is '*la mystique* which nourishes *la politique. Mystiques* are 'the creditors of the

---

19. Frans Wijsen, Peter Henriot, Rodrigo Mejía; Joe Holland, *The Pastoral Circle Revisited* (Maryknoll: Orbis Books, 2005); and Peter Henriot, *Social Analysis: Linking Faith and Justice* (Maryknoll: Orbis Books, 1983).
20. Pete Ward *Participation and Mediation: A Practical Theology for the Liquid Church* (London: SCM Press, 2008), 101; and Stoddart, 'Current Thinking', 329.
21. David Ranson *Between the 'Mysticism of Politics' and the 'Politics of Mysticism'* (Adelaide: ATF Theology, 2014), 26–27. See also Anthony Maher, 'Tyrrell's Ecclesiology: Mysticism Contra Realpolitik', in *George Tyrrell and Catholic Modernism*, edited by Oliver P Rafferty (Dublin: Four Courts, 2010), 76–93.

policies'. Ideal and aspiration, though, have become hijacked by *politiques*. 'The ecclesial ramifications of this, according to Péguy, have been catastrophic.'[22]

> That is why the factory is still closed to the church, and the church to the factory. She [the church] acts as, and is, the official formal religion of the rich . . . And she will not reopen the factory doors, she will not reopen the way to the people except by bearing the cost of a revolution . . . and call a spade a spade, a temporal revolution for eternal salvation . . . that is why our socialism was not so stupid after all, and why it was profoundly Christian.[23]

Ignacio Ellacuría, the martyred Jesuit President of the University of Central America, called a spade a spade: he insisted that the principle subject of study of the university was *la realidad nacional*, the national reality; science must be taught from the position of the national reality, philosophy, history, theology and so forth. To reflect this objective, modern-day Jesuits define their mission as the service of faith, which necessarily includes the promotion of justice and the inculturation of the gospel and its values.

Pastoral-practical theologians are called to teach the local and national reality, including the local and national ecclesial reality. While aspiring to be respected members of the academy, pastoral-practical theologians must also embrace the goals of higher criticism, applying the micro-scope of criticism to church and society. Dean Brackley offers a timely caveat to awaken the university faculty to the danger of studying the literature of our academic field, while neglecting the social and ecclesial reality.[24] Pastoral-practical theology can and should hold itself to a comprehensive set of academic standards beyond either the modern pure-reason paradigm of the Enlightenment or pseudo-Catholic fundamentalism. Brackley insists,

---

22. Ranson, *Between the 'Mysticism of Politics'*, 27.
23. Charles Péguy, *Temporal and Eternal*, translated by Alexander Dru (London: The Harvill Press/New York City: Harper, 1958; Liberty Fund, 2001). Cited in Ranson, *Between the 'Mysticism of Politics'*, 27.
24. Dean Brackley SJ, *The Jesuit University in a Broken World* (San Salvador: Universidad Centroamericana 'José Simeón Cañas', 2005), 2–3.

> We do need to master 'the literature' of our disciplines, but not simply for itself. We study the literature in order to learn about reality and about life . . . every scholar knows how a reductive focus on dominating the literature of ever-narrower sub-specialties can keep us from understanding reality. When that happens, the literature dominates us.

Ellacuría courageously taught *la realidad nacional*, focusing upon the social reality. He led the theological exploration 'up river', and as a result, highlighted how institutional structures work and how they also fail the most vulnerable.

Articulating the local and national reality within the context of Oceania is complicated; there are many fields and realities. Specialisation is also necessary. Drawing upon the work of Brackley, it is possible to extrapolate a finding that deficient Western political cultures, social and ecclesial, foster an air of self-serving expediency; when it becomes 'convenient' not to teach the local and national reality, and to ignore almost completely the global reality, allowing a situation to develop, the dominant political hegemonies collude, in order to protect the status quo. Within Oceania and the wider global context many examples are apparent: neglect of Indigenous rights; environmental degradation; injustices associated with the façade of 'free-market' economics, a political paradigm that Bob Geldof poignantly described as 'a pornography'. Analysis of the national reality awakens us to the fact that we accept a political system that sanctions poverty, oppression and increasing dislocation: three billion of the world's population living below the poverty line and, according to a conservative World Bank estimate, 1.3 billion people living in extreme poverty on less than $1.25 per day.[25]

Five Essential Characteristics of Pastoral-Practical Theology

In drawing together five essential characteristics for this project, in no sense do I understand the compilation to be exhaustive, or prioritised in a particular order, whilst recognising the significance of *place* and

---

25. For a development of this discussion see Anthony Maher, 'The Emerging Role of the Laity: Tensions and Opportunities', in *Compass*, 40/1 (2006): 17–23.

the work of pastoral-practical theologians in Oceania, I begin with a brief discussion of the significance of context.

a. Contextual theology as a theological imperative

Scholars such as Bonnie Miller-McLemore believe that pastoral-practical theology has more affinity with what some Catholics consider to be contextual theology or local theology.[26] Contextual theology recognises the importance of *place* and strives to articulate the *will to meaning* that derives from the subsequent 'acknowledgement' of place. Once we feel secure in our own context, our own moccasins, we become authors of our own liberating theology, a theology whose context is also ecclesial and called to hold in tension the local and universal dynamic.[27] Within the context of Oceania, Neil Brown was one of the first theologians to articulate that:

> The inner gift of God that forms the central impetus of life in the Christian community is always an experience interpreted within a particular context. The word of God is addressed to each person within a system of meaning and value that constitutes a pattern of life. If the dialogue is to be genuine, the message needs to be assimilated by each community, using all the cultural resources at its disposal.[28]

Contextual theology as a methodological imperative remains a central aim of pastoral-practical theology, as, collectively, we strive to understand the importance of place cognisant of, but not limited to: geographical location (Oceania), social status, gender, education, politics, historical consciousness, spirituality, culture and so-forth. All of these insights and contexts shape our psychological horizon,

---

26. Bonnie J Miller-McLemore, *Christian Theology in Practice* (Grand Rapids: Eerdmans, 2012), 104. See also Paul Duane Matheny, *Contextual Theology: The Drama of Our Times* (Cambridge: James Clarke & Co, 2012) and Peter C Phan, *Christianity with an Asian Face* (Maryknoll: Orbis, 2003).
27. Stephen Pickard, *In-Between God, 'Recovering an Ecclesial Sense of Place Down-under'* (Adelaide: ATF Theology, 2011), 133–152 and chapter five above.
28. Neil Brown, 'The Task of Theology in Australia', in *Essays in Faith and Culture* (Manly: Catholic Institute of Sydney, 1979), 1. See also Denis Edwards, 'Australian Local Church as Sacrament of God's Saving Action in this Land', in *Called to be Church in Australia* (Homebush: St Paul's Publications, 1987), 55–80.

forming a sense of belonging, identity, theology and ultimately our humanity.[29]

In a seminal contribution to theology, Stephen Bevans rightly asserts:

> There is no such thing as 'theology'; there is only contextual theology: feminist theology, black theology, liberation theology, African theology and so forth. Doing theology contextually is not an option, nor is it something that should only interest people from the Third World . . . The contextualisation of theology—the attempt to understand Christian faith in terms of a particular context—is really a theological imperative. As we understand theology today, it is a process that is part of the very nature of theology itself.[30]

In seeking to follow the edict of *Gaudium et Spes* to dialogue with the world, pastoral-practical theology employs deductive reasoning (a particular world-view), understanding scripture and tradition alongside the contemporary experienced reality in Oceania—a third *locus theologicus*, as a primary theological resource. Stephen Bevans explains that 'today we speak of theology as having three sources or *loci theologici*: scripture, tradition and present human experience or context'.[31] In process, therefore, pastoral-practical theology is concerned to overcome the isolation of deductive theology from the community of lived faith and the current reality that professionalisation and departmentalisation has fostered. A potential hazard that pastoral-practical theology is not immune from, particularly as adherents of practical theology strive for acceptance within the theological and wider science-economics orientated university.

---

29. Anthony Maher and Bob Hanley, *Educating Hearts: Seven Characteristics of a Good School* (Homebush: St Paul's Publications, 2013), 27–42.
30. Stephen B Bevans, 'Contextual Theology as a Theological Imperative', in *Models of Contextual Theology* (Maryknoll: Orbis Books 2002), 3–15, 3. See also Bevans, 'What has Contextual Theology to Offer the Church of the Twenty-First Century?', in *Contextual theology for the Twenty-First Century*, edited by Stephen B Bevans and Katalina Tahaafe-Williams (Eugene: Pickwick Publications, 2011), 3–17; see also Stephen B Bevans and Roger P Schroeder, *Prophetic Dialogue: Reflections on Christian Mission Today* (Maryknoll: Orbis Books, 2011).
31. Bevans, *Models*, 4.

Holding the current academic context in tension with ecclesial mission, while resisting popular, often antagonistic media-driven polarisation, requires the judgment of Solomon. Relevant and contextual theological activity needs the reflection and the breadth of all persons involved in Christian praxis in order to preserve its vitality and wholeness; it needs to be dialogically ethical, inclusive and proudly ecclesial in its processes. Writing in the Oceania ecclesial context, Ranson further assists our task when he seeks to build bridges between the contemporary 'great divide' between spirituality and religion. Ranson highlights six dimensions or insights for our task of overcoming the separation between faith, theology and life. First, religion needs to be *deconstructed*, that is, 'ready to be scrutinised for its mixed motivations and agendas'. Second, religion 'needs evidently to be both *mystical* and *political*': mystical, 'disclosing a spiritual experience that has immediacy and a deeply experiential quality to it'; political, meaning 'the capacity to effect change in society'. Being political, 'religion retains its public character'.[32] Third, a religion seeking to engage with contemporary culture will be '*sacral*', 'loyal to the world', ready to listen and to 'recognise in that which is finite, the pull to infinity'. Fourth, religion will be characterised as '*communal*'; fifth, as '*resourceful*', and; sixth as '*poetic* rather than didactic in its discourse'.[33]

The Marist priest, scholar and former President of APTO, Gerard Hall, allows significant insight into the 'state' of theology, in particular practical theology, in the context of Oceania. Hall raises an important issue for our discussion when he indicates that in his view 'typically theology in Oceania is marked by a focus on ministry and pastoral formation ... but that this has little to do with practical theology ... moreover, the type of theology ... reflect[s] something of the colonial cringe.' Hall insists that 'there was little if any attempt to provide a method whereby theology and culture would be brought into mutually critical engagement'.[34] Thus given the context of theology's

---

32. David Ranson, *Across the Great Divide: Bridging Spirituality and Religion Today* (Strathfield: St Paul's Publications, 2002), 47–49. See also David Ranson, 'The Priest as Spiritual Leader', in *The Paschal Paradox* (Strathfield: St Paul's Publications, 2009), 91–104.
33. Ranson, *Across the Great Divide*, 47–53.
34. Gerard Hall, 'Defining History and Context in Guild and Global Setting Regional Developments: Australia and Oceania', in *Companion to Practical Theology,*

isolation from society and the academy, little attention was given to its public role.

With optimistic reference to the new style of doing theology that emerged out of Vatican II, one with a particular focus upon liberation and giving primacy to praxis, context and culture, Hall indicates the necessity of the peoples of this region to recognise the potential of escaping from the European and colonial past and to begin to articulate anew Oceanian methods, models and liberating hermeneutical approaches to theologies. 'The next phase of this movement requires', according to Hall, 'sustained focus on practical-political issues with the aim of developing specific theologies of resistance and hope'.[35]

> Not simply 'adapting' the gospel to cultures, but bringing gospel and cultures into critical engagement. In particular, post-colonial contextual theologies critique the once-assumed identification of gospel with European cultural forms.[36]

A further pioneering practical theologian writing in Oceania, whom we should mention, although he was primarily trained in the United States, is Terry Veling, one of the few theologians in the region who also self-describes as a practical theologian.[37] While explaining that 'practical theology [like the church], is not a thing', resonating with Congar's ground-breaking imperative, Veling gives us a helpful insight into what practical theology is seeking to reclaim in Oceania, namely, 'a certain reinstatement of theology into the weave and fabric of human living, in which theology becomes a practice or way of life.'[38]

---

edited by Bonnie J Miller-McLemore (Malden: Wiley-Blackwell, 2012), 544–554, 547.

35. Hall, *Companion to Practical Theology*, 548.
36. Hall, *Companion to Practical Theology*, 548. See also the seminal work of the cultural anthropologist Gerald A Arbuckle, for example, *Catholic Identity or Identities? Refounding Ministries in Chaotic Times* (Collegeville: Liturgical Press, 2013).
37. Terry Veling, 'Catholic Practical Theology: Reflections on an Emerging Field', in *Compass*, 2 (2011): 35–39. See also Terry Veling, *The Beatitude of Mercy* (Mulgrave: John Garratt Pub, 2010); Terry Veling, *For You Alone: Emmanuel Levinas and the Answerable Life* (Eugene: Cascade Books 2014).
38. Terry Veling, *Practical Theology: On Earth as it is in Heaven* (Maryknoll: Orbis Books, 2005), 3; and for a detailed survey of the literature with regard to a definition for practical theology, 19–22.

Veling writes unpretentiously as an Australian and with an authenticity that is grounded in the experience of ordinary family life. He is drawn to 'practical' theology because 'it seemed to give me a place to hang my hat'.[39] Like many of us in this discipline Veling is uncomfortable with the term 'practical.' In his comprehensive recourse to the literature, Veling offers multiple definitions of practical theology; perhaps the one that resonates most, and receives international acclaim for contextual relevance, originates with James Woodward and Stephen Pattison, who understand:

> Practical theology [to be] a place where religious belief, tradition, and practice meets contemporary experiences, questions, and actions and conducts a dialogue that is mutually enriching, intellectually critical, and practically transforming.[40]

Drawing upon the seminal work of Thomas Groome, one of the leading scholars in the field of Catholic pastoral theology in the United States, Veling sees that theology is usually divided into two parts, the 'systematic theology' and the 'pastoral theology', the former being generally considered theoretical, and the latter being where we apply our learning to ministry in the world. Veling and Groome thus concur that such a paradigm 'presumes a one-way relationship between theory and practice with theory always the point of departure; theory is something from "outside" to be applied and practice something to receive it'.[41]

Typically in Oceania, systematic theology organises the theological disciplines into theory and practice: systematics currently dominates the region's schools of divinity and university theology faculties, particularly within the Roman tradition, influenced by an antiquated form of the *ratio studiorum*, which regulates pastoral-practical theology to the periphery, in effect to little more than Canon Law.

---

39. Terry Veling, 'Reflections on an Emerging Field', in *Compass*, 2 (2011): 35.
40. James Woodward and Stephen Pattison (editors), *The Blackwell Reader in Pastoral and Practical Theology* (Oxford: Blackwell Publishers, 2000), 7. And Veling, *On Earth as it is in Heaven*, 20.
41. Veling, *On Earth*, 5 and Thomas Groome, 'Theology on our Feet: A Revisionist Pedagogy for Healing the Gap Between Academia and Ecclesia', in *Formation and Reflection: The Promise of Practical Theology*, edited by S Mudge and JN Poling (Philadelphia: Fortress Press, 1987), 57.

From such restrictive practice derives generational meaning, thus career-minded lay scholars must shy away from pastoral-practical theology, often ignoring contemporary local cultural contexts, and efforts to heal divisions in academic-ecclesial theology.

In the context of Oceania, Veling's work is significant, as he builds upon the work of a number of influential thinkers to make the argument that 'we cannot separate knowing from being, thinking from acting and theological reflection from pastoral and practical involvement'.[42] Theology should be practiced, Veling argues, in the world, attending to life itself: Martin Heidegger thus spoke of the 'forgetfulness of being . . . [and that] we have forgotten that "Being" carries the resonance of a verb rather than the "thingness" of a noun'; Veling also draws on the thought of Rowan Williams, suggesting that 'life is not very systematic . . . a religious discourse will not move too far from the particular.' Paulo Freire reminds us that [theological] knowledge comes from living in the real world, and 'the danger with intellectual systems is their tendency to confuse thought with existence.' Gustavo Gutiérrez stresses our need to learn that theology is always addressed to a particular situation in life and 'that nothing that is genuinely human is alien to the gospel . . . on the contrary, the human story is the very 'site' of God's revelation'; Martin Buber, in referencing prayer, suggests that 'when we pray, we don't remove ourselves or our lives from our prayer, rather we bring our very lives to our prayer'; not even prayer should remove us from life, rather, 'when we pray we "yield" or refer our life to God'.[43]

Veling draws closest perhaps to the thought of Emmanuel Levinas, and profoundly encapsulates what we might consider to be the *reason d'être* of the pastoral–practical theologian: 'life is *vocational*, it addresses me. It calls out to me . . . it asks me to respond.'[44] Pastoral-practical theology is then an invitation to venture up river, following a critique of the (i) national reality (ii) application of critical [specialised] analysis, (iii) theological reflection upon scripture, tradition and lived experience, and then, finally, (iv) we make an incarnate response to the contemporary reality.

---

42. Veling, *On Earth*, 6.
43. Veling, *On Earth*, 9–10.
44. Veling, *On Earth*, 10.

b. Ressourcement for aggiornamento—scripture and tradition

A second characteristic is the combination of the methodological concepts of *Aggiornamento* (updating or renewal) and *Ressourcement*, to draw upon the centrality of Scripture and Tradition. Pastoral-practical theology is called upon to be inherently transformative in pastoral ministry and public theology and thus relies upon an understanding of *Aggiornamento* to bring tradition into the present context. Returning to the sources of the Christian faith does not mean returning to the past (historical-positivism), but rather, renewing pastoral practice through *ressourcement* of the tradition.

Thomas C Oden reminds us of the importance of not losing touch with our historical identity. He describes himself as a proponent of paleo-orthodoxy, essentially to distinguish his work from that of neo-orthodoxy, as he draws upon the profundity of the classical Christian tradition, chiefly the Patristic Fathers. *Ressourcement* pioneered by scholars such as Congar brings historical-consciousness to bear on questions of pastoral significance. Oden, while engaging in a form of *Ressourcement*, insists that pastoral care must 'find its own ground and possibility', and not allow 'contemporary psychotherapies to define what pastoral care is.' Oden believes contemporary pastoral care exhibits 'a vague absentmindedness', and has fallen into a 'pervasive amnesia towards its own classical pastoral past.'[45] Oden rightly asks, 'in what sense pastoral theology is and remains theology?' Such questions, which we might direct to all aspects of pastoral ministry, must be instructed by the tradition in an attempt to recover the classical understanding of pastoral theology. Oden highlights: Cyprian's writings on the virtues; Tertullian's reflections on the soul; Chrysostom and Ambrose on the priesthood; Augustine on happiness, admonition and even grief counselling. At the centre of this classical tradition, Oden duly affirms the seminal *Pastoral Care* of Gregory the Great.[46]

Pastoral-practical theology has an *aggiornamento* agenda: it is called to read the signs of the times. *Aggiornament* requires courage

---

45. Thomas C Oden, 'Recovering Lost Identity', in DF Ford and M Higton, *Modern Theologians Reader*, 248–253, 250.
46. Oden, 'Recovering Lost Identity', 249. See also Thomas C Oden, *Pastoral Theology: Essentials of Ministry* (San Francisco: Harper and Row, 1982).

and pastoral creativity on the part of the ecclesial officials and theologians, of the sort evidenced by John XXIII's call for a new Pentecost at the Second Vatican Council and Francis' desire to hold 'a non- judgmental' Synod on the Family. Of greater significance for the future church will be the reception of the *sensus fidelium*, as a locus for reading the signs of the times, one becoming ever more consistent with the pastoral nature of *aggiornamento*. As a leading Australian theologian, Ormond Rush, suggests, 'the past is a norm for judging the present … [but] the present [also] becomes a norm for judging the past' and moving pastorally oriented towards dialogue with contemporary culture.[47] Such a desideratum may be understood as a concern not only to norm orthodoxy but also to focus upon the sincerity of orthopraxis—Christian 'right' action in the world.

Reading the signs of the times becomes a hermeneutical lens for pastoral and practical theology. Oden rightly suggests that Christians need to build upon the wisdom of the tradition, particularly the early church, undertaken most fruitfully from the perspective of pastoral-practical theology through dialogue and integration with contemporary scholarship including, as (we have) suggested, both the historical-critical method and the human sciences.

c. The integration of theological activity

Attentive to Lonergan's 'Eight Functional Specialties of Theology', the third characteristic underpinning pastoral-practical theology is the integration of theological activity, including theological education for ministry, to assist efforts to read the 'signs of the times' and make an appropriate response to bridge the divide between faith, theology and life. In seeking to understand the contemporary divide, Mary McClintock Fulkerson takes us back to 'Kant's eighteenth-century critique of orthodoxy's claim to God knowledge', and the subsequent division which became embedded in '*theologia* as both science and *paideia*'.[48] The modern university, Fulkerson argues, demoted theology as the queen of sciences, and, in following reason-based science, created a divide between faith, theology and life, exacerbated by 'what came to be called the clerical paradigm' which, arguably, had

---

47. Ormond Rush, *Still Interpreting Vatican II*, 80–81.
48. Mary McClintock Fulkerson, 'The Modern University and Theological Education', *The Wiley–Blackwell Companion to Practical Theology*, 357–366, 360.

the long-term consequence of disconnecting human knowledge and experience from theology.⁴⁹

The current work pedestals theological integration in our time of profound post-modern fragmentation. Cahalan holds that 'there should be no surprise that theological educators are clamouring after the elusive ideal of integration (capstone) as a solution for how to connect and transform the disparate parts of ministerial education into a whole.'⁵⁰ Thus the endeavour of integration of theological activity is emerging as an essential characteristic of practical theology, and serves to underpin our efforts in this work to augment an ecclesial sense of place and purpose in Oceania.⁵¹

Therefore, in building upon epistemological and existential pursuits, the current work challenges *all* theology, to be practical, to bear fruit through challenging the artificial divisions imposed by modern university thinking, particularly professionalisation, departmentisation and today, in a post-modern context, fragmentation, leading to other potential issues that grow out from isolation. Elaine Graham, Claire Wolfteich, Bonnie Miller-McLemore and Kathleen Cahalan, together with other feminist pastoral-practical theologians, draw upon communal insights and apply hermeneutical principles of critical engagement with the dominant epistemological world-view. In this turn to experience, pastoral-practical theologians source the depths of the whole community for theological reflection. Eric Stoddart understands more recently this turn to experience as the authoritative starting and returning point for pastoral-practical theological reflection has matured through its encounter with so many disciplines and cultural realities.⁵²

d. An incarnational spirituality

The Incarnation is both a human and a divine reality. Pastoral-practical theology deals with the human experience of the divine, an incarnational spirituality is thus integral to pastoral-practical theology.

---

49. Fulkerson, 'The Modern University', 360.
50. Kathleen A Cahalan, 'Integration in Theological Education', *The Wiley–Blackwell Companion to Practical Theology*, 386–395, 386.
51. Les Ball, *Transforming Theology: Student Experience and Transformative Learning in Undergraduate Theological Education* (Preston: Mosaic Press, 2012), 14ff.
52. Stoddart, 'Current Thinking.'

Pastoral-practical theology has a distinctive incarnational character: an incarnational spirituality expresses how God is (*in-carno*—in fleshed) at work in the world. While an incarnational vision has the potential to shape the character of pastoral ministry to reflect core Gospel values. Karl Rahner taught that 'the devout Christian of the future will either be a "mystic", one who has experienced "something", or [s]he will cease to be anything at all'.[53] Rahner maintained that all theology is anthropology, and so the mystical is discovered in ordinary life, in the ordinariness of a shared meal.[54] Mary Steinmetz shows clearly that Rahner understood the human person 'as one who is created for the self-communication of God. This orientation toward Ultimate Mystery is the foundational characteristic of being human.'[55] Incarnational ministry is inductive, earthed and makes Christ's love visible in the midst of ordinary human life; its preoccupation is to incarnate life-giving Christian faith, making Christ visible through a commitment to service of our neighbour, of love and compassion, mercy beyond justice, wherever the need arises.

> Through compassion . . . we enter into the perceptual world of another person, to become sensitive to their fear or rage or tenderness or confusion. In that way we are able to travel with them into the deeper places of pain and struggle where healing needs to take place. This is the incarnational principle, indispensable for truly Christian ministry, which puts tender-heartedness at the centre of human relationships just as it is at the centre of the heart of God (Luke 6:36).[56]

Incarnational spirituality starts with an experience in ordinary life, a concrete personal experience of God, an experiential type of knowing. Rahner's approach to the mystery of the incarnation is rooted in the *Spiritual Exercises* of Ignatius, where a person is called upon to make a concrete choice for God. 'The incarnation encourages us to ask for knowledge of God from inside . . . any Christian truth

---

53. Karl Rahner, 'Christian Living Formerly and Today', in *Theological Investigations*, Volume VII, translated by David Burke (London: Darton, Longman and Todd, 1971), 15.
54. Margaret Lavin, *Theology for Ministry* (Ottawa: Novalis, 2004).
55. Mary Steinmetz, 'Thoughts on the Experience of God in the Theology of Karl Rahner: Gifts and Implications', in *Lumen et Vita* (2012), 2:2.
56. Margaret Whipp, *Pastoral Theology* (London: SCM Press, 2013), 134.

is also a truth of human experience.'[57] But this is not to denigrate theology or blur the distinction between subjective and objective. 'Rahner's account of experience is realist . . . truth is independent of human decision.'[58] Nevertheless, pastoral-practical theology is called upon to struggle to articulate the experience of the divine in ordinary life. An incarnational spirituality involves incarnating all our efforts and incarnating ourselves in the reality of ordinary life, with the pain, the joy and endless hope of the human condition in each and every context.

Margaret Whipp posits that an incarnational presence may be very different from the form of self-conscious detachment adopted by professional academics, counsellors, lawyers, medics and so forth.[59] Pastoral-practical theologians, write, teach and struggle to witness in our ordinary lives to the belief that we are invited by God into a personal, loving relationship. And that the practice of living and caring for our neighbour, beginning within the family, brings us closer to God in the incarnational mystery of Jesus Christ, who is at the heart of the divine-human encounter.

The Spirit cannot be confined by the walls of an institution or for that matter the boundaries of theology. An incarnational spirituality inspires the 'adventurous nature of a uniquely Christian ministry of "perilous paraklesis" to pick up the wind of the Spirit in whatever direction it may happen to blow'.[60] Edward Schillebeeckx affirms that Christ is the primordial sacrament of God and the church is the sacrament of Christ, and so God's self-gift to humanity, a reality that becomes concrete in human history through radical social, political and economic engagement. Schillebeeckx believes that human encounter proceeds through the visible obviousness of the body. 'The incarnation is an invitation to a personal encounter with God, the human encounter with Jesus is therefore the sacrament of the encounter with God, God's grace is bestowed in the encounter.'[61] An

---

57. Philip Endean, *Karl Rahner and Ignatian Spirituality* (Oxford; New York City: Oxford University Press, 2001), 239–246.
58. Endean, *Karl Rahner and Ignatian Spirituality*, 239–246.
59. Whipp, *Pastoral Theology*, 143.
60. Whipp, *Pastoral Theology*, 177.
61. Robert J Schreiter (editor) *The Schillebeeckx Reader* (New York City: Crossroad, 1984), 204–206.

incarnational theology articulates 'a renewed commitment to the human condition . . . a real theological engagement with the modern world.'[62] 'The wonder of the incarnation, [is] God drawing close to fragile humanity; the brokenness of the cross; the triumph of the risen life; the endless possibility of new beginnings', such insights are gleaned through an incarnational spirituality.[63]

Incarnational spirituality embodies faith in the risen Lord in all aspects of daily life; our human bodies become a source of wisdom, discernment and as we described above, a source of revelation. An Incarnational spirituality becomes concrete in living out the core values of the Gospel: 'authenticity, integrity, courage, love, forgiveness, hope, healing service and justice.' An incarnational spirituality involves an orientation towards serving Christ in the world, a conversion experience 'that awakens "a sense of being", "contemplates in action" for Christ.'[64] The *Spiritual Exercises* as an ecumenical paradigm of incarnational practice . . . The spiritual exercises are eminently practical while laden with potential to draw upon the mystical element of religion.

Synthesising academy with pastoral ministry, Elizabeth Conde-Frazier suggests that incarnational research provides tools for solving problems experienced by people in communities. 'Incarnational research focuses on improving the quality of people's lives. It uses a dialogical and hermeneutical approach that is more democratic, humanising, empowering, and life enhancing.'[65] Such research takes into account the concrete, local, national and global reality that affects all aspects of human activity; our actions are then informed by critical reflection. Such deliberation leads Conde-Frazier to maintain that we evaluate our pastoral-practical theological research by askingwhat

---

62. David McLoughlin and Gemma Simmons, 'Pastoral and Practical Theology in Britain and Ireland—A Catholic Perspective', in *Keeping Faith in Practice: Aspects of Catholic Pastoral Theology*, edited by James Sweeney, Gemma Simmonds and David Lonsdale (London: SCM Press, 2010), 27–30.
63. Whipp, *Pastoral Theology*, 184.
64. Ignatian Incarnational Spirituality, see: www.marquette.edu/faber/ignatianspirituality.
65. Elizabeth Conde-Frazier, 'Participatory Action Research', *Practical Theology* (Malden: Wiley-Blackwell, 2012), 241. See also Philip Sheldrake, *The Spiritual City: Theology, Spirituality, and the Urban*, (Chichester: Wiley-Blackwell, 2014).

impact it has on the daily lives of persons: 'when this type of inquiry is accompanied by theological reflection, it becomes praxis.'[66]

e. The primacy of pastoral praxis

The praxis model is, most simply, 'faith seeking intelligent action'.[67] Pastoral primacy requires an inductive theological method; it does not start with idealised words or concepts (deductive method) but rather, with the concrete lived reality. The difference between these two methods is very important. Thomas M Kelly contrasts the deductive and inductive approaches to reality; he argues that the former begins with something greater or whole which 'we can call a prototype or an ideal . . . while the latter will enter into an analysis of this world . . . it begins with what we know and builds a case.'[68] Kelly contends that to see the truth and understand it [is] 'to participate', to be active in seeking the truth. Bevans judges that a theology which is not rooted in praxis cannot be considered an adequate theology.[69] Leonardo Boff, drawing upon the praxis model and applying it to liberation theology, holds that the method consists of 'seeing *analytically*, judging *theologically*, and acting *pastorally* or *politically*, three phases in one commitment in faith'.[70]

A similar method is proposed by other 'practical' thinkers such as Bernard Lonergan, for example, whose 'transcendental precepts' guide us to be *attentive* to the 'national reality' (Ellacuría); *intelligent* in critique of that reality; *reasonable* in our discerning of reality; and *responsible* in our response. Following a process that assists in the recognition that something needs to be done, Sobrino asserts that the *primacy of praxis* is a much more comprehensive way of knowing than that of mere intellectual affirmation. A praxis model proposes

---

66. Conde-Frazier, 'Participatory Action Research', 241.
67. Bevans, *Models*, 73.
68. Thomas M Kelly, *When the Gospel Grows Feet* (Collegeville: Liturgical Press, 2013), 25–27.
69. Bevans, *Models*, 77.
70. Leonnardo Boff and Virgilio Elizondo (editors), *Theologies of the Third World: Convergences and Differences* (Edinburgh: T&T Clark, 1988), 12. See also Andrew Root, *Christopraxis: A Practical Theology of the Cross* (Minneapolis: Fortress Press, 2014).

a method of theological procedure, an imperative in recognising the need and identifying an appropriate pastoral response.

In presenting a number of seminal presuppositions for a praxis model, Bevans stresses that he continues to resist the temptation of linking the praxis model too closely with liberation theology. First, he argues, contextual theology does not 'necessarily have to take on liberation themes', and; second, 'the specificity of the model is not one of a particular theme but one of a particular method . . . its revolutionary impact has come more from its method as "critical reflection on action".'[71]

Claire Wolfteich outlines succinctly the recent history of the praxis method, drawing attention to Karl Rahner's turn to experience, Paul Tillich's correlation model, Bernard Lonergan's theological empirical method and David Tracy's revised correlation method.[72] A seminal contribution emanating from North America is the shared praxis in theological education of Thomas Groome, who describes praxis as purposeful, reflective action, based upon a five-step method that resonates with the pastoral-cycle methodology:

naming present experience
  critically reflecting on experience
    engaging scripture and tradition
      appropriating the faith through dialectical hermeneutics
        and deciding how to live [73]

Bevans draws our attention to an important caveat. He reminds us of the danger that *'praxis'* is becoming a 'trendy' concept, similar to Wesley Carr's concern with regard to the word 'pastoral' becoming 'broke-backed', due to overuse and misappropriation.[74] Bevans recalls that praxis is a technical term that has its contemporary roots in Marxism in the Frankfurt School and in the educational philosophy

---

71. Bevans, *Models*, 77.
72. Claire E Wolfteich. *An Invitation to Practical Theology* (New York City: Paulist Press, 2014), 37ff.
73. See Thomas Groome, 'A Proposed Pedagogical Approach', in Wolfteich, *An Invitation to Practical Theology*, 292–297.
74. Carr, *Handbook*, 9.

of Paulo Freire.⁷⁵ Bevans reaffirms that praxis 'is a method or model of thinking in general and a method or model of theology in particular'.⁷⁶

Most inspiring for Bevans is Jon Sobrino's critical cleave of modernity into two movements. The first characterised by the thought of Descartes and Kant, introducing the idea of rationality and subjective responsibility, the modern revolutionary 'turn to the subject', after which 'nothing is either true faith or right morality which is not our own'. In responding to this 'first' movement theology could no longer argue only from authority, thus speculative theology sought to probe the meaning of what could be believed as a way of meeting the challenge of rationality posed by the Enlightenment.⁷⁷

Sobrino is convinced modernity has a second movement, perhaps even more significant, one characterised by Karl Marx's 'discovery that rationality or intellectual knowledge was not enough to constitute genuine knowledge ... we know best Marx insisted, when our reason is coupled with and challenged by our action—when we are not just the objects of historical process but its subjects'.

> This is perhaps best summed up in the famous sentence in Marx's critique of Feuerbach: 'the philosophers have only interpreted the world in various ways; the point is to change it.'⁷⁸

Inspired by Sobrino, a Basque Jesuit theologian working at the University of Central America in El Salvador, Bevans believes that the praxis model calls on theology to provide not only relevant expressions of the Christian faith but also a commitment to the primacy of pastoral action. At its most profound level, drawing upon the thought of Sobrino, the praxis model consists of: 'the unity of knowledge as activity and knowledge as content.'⁷⁹ As Phillip

---

75. Paulo Freire, *Pedagogy of the Oppressed* (New York City: Herder and Herder, 1970).
76. Bevans, *Models*, 71.
77. Bevans, *Models*, 71–72.
78. Bevans, *Models*, 72 and Karl Marx, *Theses on Feuerbach*, 11, in *Writings of the Young Marx on Philosophy and Society*, edited and translated by LD Easton and KH Guddat (Garden City: Doubleday, 1967), 402.
79. Bevans, *Models*, 72 and Sobrino, '*El conocimiento*', 93.

Berryman explains, 'it works on the conviction that truth is at the level of history, not in the realm of ideas'.[80]

> Pastoral-practical theology seeks not only to understand scripture and tradition, but also to transform Christian life based upon the understanding of knowledge and truth as operative in the primacy of praxis.[81] Theology is challenged to delve into the messy business of ordinary life, to assist in the transformation of culture, particularly aspects of culture that condone, actively and passively, widespread suffering and oppression. Paulo Freire holds us to account, when he argues: 'Washing one's hands of the conflict between the powerful and the powerless means to side with the powerful, not to be neutral.'[82]

Since Vatican II, disciples of Rahner, such as JB Metz and Jon Sobrino, have extended Rahner's understanding of practical theology so that it becomes a theology of practice relating, for example, to basic Christian communities in Latin America and oppressed minorities of the global South. Practical theology through the application of a liberationist hermeneutic informs and inspires the primacy of Christian praxis, sounding a resolute and unapologetic call to engage with the political dynamic, stressing the Reign of God, and in the light of Pope Francis' most recent encyclical, the increasing global prayer, for the 'care' of planet earth.[83]

Conclusion

In sum, the five characteristics: (i) contextual theology as theological imperative; (ii) *ressourcement* for *aggiornament*; (iii) the integration

---

80. Bevans, *Models,* 72; and Phillip Berryman, *Liberation Theology* (New York City: Pantheon Books, 1987), 86.
81. Rebecca S Chopp, *The Praxis of Suffering: An Interpretation of Liberation and Political Theologies* (Eugene: Wipf and Stock, 2007).
82. Paulo Freire, *The Politics of Education* (Westport: Bergin and Garvey, 1985), 122.
83. Pope Francis has issued a major encyclical on the environment, called *Laudato Si'* (Praise Be), *On the Care of Our Common Home.* See also Gerald A Arbuckle, *The Francis Factor and the People of God* (Maryknol: Orbis Books, 2015), and Noel Connolly, *Pope Francis' Inspiring Vision* (Niddrie: St Columbans Mission Society, 2015).

of theological activity; (iv) an incarnational spirituality and (v) the primacy of pastoral praxis, taken together, embrace the breadth of the theological academy and present a theological *modus operandi* for pastoral-practical theology, *pace* Lonergan, nurturing theology to bear fruit in the context of the church in Oceania.

We saw above in Sobrino's 'first movement', that Descartes, Kant, *et al* awoke Western society from its dogmatic slumber. The 'second movement', arguably still to emerge, and dependent upon personal and institutional conversion, has the potential to awaken Western culture from the 'sleep of inhumanity', what Sobrino understands as 'structural sin', into which Western culture has sunk:

> It has not yet recognised or felt responsible for the denial of a just and decent life in the Third World. If it turns its eyes towards the Third World this awakening is possible. For there it will find a reserve of light, of hope and of love which can humanise it. I call this structural grace. The Third World offers the First World the possibility of conversion. If entire crucified continents do not have the strength to convert hearts of stone into hearts of flesh, we must ask ourselves, what can? And if nothing can, we must ask what kind of future awaits a First World built—consciously or unconsciously—upon the corpses of the human family.[84]

Evidently, the five characteristics have the potential to generate theological *strum und drang*, and perhaps even an existential-spiritual crisis. More simply, they represent an opportunity for personal, institutional and even cultural conversion.

Lonergan understood that conversion (intellectual, moral and religious) arises from the realisation of 'being grasped by ultimate concern'; moreover it is the religious conversion which he describes as an orientation to God.[85] Religious conversion is 'the fruit of

---

84. Jon Sobrino, 'Structural Sin and Structural Grace', The Pope Paul VI CAFOD memorial lecture, Salford Cathedral, England, March 1992, author's notes.
85. Bernard Lonergan, *Method In Theology* (London: Darton, Longman and Todd, 1975), 240. See also TJ Farrell and PA Soukup, *Communication and Lonergan: Common Ground for Forging The New Age* (Kansas City: Sheed and Ward, 1993), 316. See also William F Purcell, 'Converting Culture: Reading Chinua Achebe's *Marriage is a Private Affair* in Light of Bernard Lonergan's "Theology of Conversion"', in *Religion and Culture*, in 45/1 (Spring 2013): 81–95, especially

God's gift of his grace'.[86] For Lonergan, conversion is a life-long process. Conversion is the process of moving from inauthenticity to authenticity, which directly influences the human capacity for self-transcendence. 'It is total surrender to the human spirit: be attentive, be intelligent, be reasonable, be responsible, be in love.'[87] Lonergan maintains that when God's love enters the horizon of a human being, the entire horizon is transformed, for transcendent being has become the context for consideration of contingent being in the awareness. The self becomes a different self, because the horizon within which all reality is considered has been radically altered. Religious conversion is, 'the gift of God's love flooding our hearts, through the Holy Spirit given to us (Romans 5:5).'[88] This gift is properly itself not in an isolated individual, but only in a plurality of persons that disclose their love to one another. Lonergan is convinced that:

> God's gift of love (Romans 5:5) has a transcultural aspect. For it is a gift offered to all [people] . . . God's gift of love is free it is not conditioned by human knowledge . . . it is not restricted to any stage or section of human culture but rather it is the principle that introduces a dimension of other-worldliness into any culture.[89]

Sobrino calls for a radical re-thinking of the meaning of being Christian, a conversion of the heart to God understood in a pastoral-practical theological context as the 'care of souls'. Characteristically stated in simple terms by Sobrino, 'it is a question of beginning to see ourselves as a human family, "being grasped by ultimate concern", it is a question of being truly able to pray the "Our Father"'.[90]

92–95.
86. Lonergan, *Method In Theology*, 268.
87. Lonergan, *Method In Theology*, 268.
88. Lonergan, *Method In Theology*, 105.
89. Lonergan, *Method In Theology*, 283.
90. Jon Sobrino, 'Structural Sin and Structural Grace'.

2
'The Primacy of the Pastoral': Bridging the Divide Between Faith, Theology and Life in the Ecclesiology of Yves Congar

Anthony Maher

In relation to the lived life of faith, and mindful of the Roman Catholic Synod on the Family, summoned by Pope Francis, this chapter will briefly explore a seminal characteristic of Yves Congar's theological method, namely the *'primauté du pastoral'*.[1] Although the primacy of the pastoral became the acknowledged *raison d'être* of Vatican II, arguably this particular entreaty has struggled, since the Council, to find reception within the contemporary Catholic Church.[2] The chapter will illustrate that the primacy of the pastoral is an essential guide for true and false reform in the contemporary church and an essential conduit for pastoral ministry within the secular dynamic. Indeed, the primacy of the pastoral is an initiative capable of empowering the

---

1. Congar highlights liturgical renewal as a valid framework for a reform movement because it gives *'primauté du pastoral, non seulement il joint le recentrement christologique au retour aux sources originelles.'* Yves Congar, 'Retour au Principe', in *Vraie et fausse réforme dans l'Église* (Paris: Cerf, 1950), 338. For a detailed review of Congar's later work, that is most obviously pastoral in orientation, see Aidan Nichols, 'An Yves Congar Bibliography 1967–1987', in *Angelicum* 66 (1989): 422–66.
2. For example, see the first section of Congar's *'Déficit de la théologie'*. The expression 'primacy of the pastoral' became Congar's first principle of true reform; see Yves Congar, 'First Condition: The Primacy of Charity and of Pastoral Concern,' in *True and False Reform in the Church*, translated by Paul Philibert (Collegeville, Minnesota: Liturgical, 2011), 215–28. By 1950, with the publication of *Vraie et fausse réforme dans l'Église*, Congar had developed four primary principles for assessing true and false reform in the church: (1) the primacy of charity and pastoral concern, (2) remaining in communion with the whole church, (3) having patience with delays, (4) genuine renewal through a return to the principle of tradition (not through the forced introduction of some 'novelty').

church to fulfil its gospel mandate: 'Therefore go and make disciples of all nations, baptising them in the name of the Father and of the Son and of the Holy Spirit' (Matt 28:19) and 'I am with you always, to the very end of the age' (Matt 28:20).

The Congarian theological and ecclesial prognoses of 1935 looked rather bleak; Congar argued that faith had become 'disincarnate, empty of human blood . . . a false spirituality without warmth and without joy—like a voice without tone—betray[ed] a deficiency of incarnation.'[3] Arguably the division between faith, theology and life eventuated in the marginalisation of Christianity, particularly in Europe.[4] There was an ecclesial decline corresponding with the rise of a vitriolic atheism—what Congar might have called 'a mortal poison', again, particularly experienced in the European context.[5] Congar reminds the contemporary church that:

> Without incarnation and catholicity our Catholicism has the appearance of a particular grouping, something special that does not take up the values of life (but, on the contrary, diminishes and anathematises them). The church does not have the appearance of that ark in which all created things are saved, but of a party that assures the interest of a class or corporation.[6]

---

3. Congar, 'Une conclusion théologique', 244.
4. In the two essays Congar is more concerned with the internal ecclesial causes of the division, although the external realities inspired by the Enlightenment are significant. For an indispensable analysis in this regard, see Charles Taylor, *Sources of the Self: The Making of the Modern Identity* (Cambridge: Cambridge University Press, 1989) and Charles Taylor, *A Secular Age* (Cambridge: Belknap Press of Harvard University Press, 2007).
5. See Pope Benedict XVI, 'Faith, Reason and the University: Memories and Reflections', 'The Regensburg Address', University of Regensburg, 12 September 2006. Central to the pontificate of Benedict XVI is his attempt to re-evangelise Europe. The Pope argues that 'despite its origins . . . in the East, [Christianity] finally took on its decisive character in Europe.' In his address, Benedict strongly opposes all attempts at 'dehellenisation of Christianity . . . which first emerged with the Reformation in the sixteenth century.' Benedict believes Europe to be the epicentre of Christianity. If Christianity is undermined in its homeland the prognosis for world Christianity is bleak.
6. Congar, 'Une conclusion théologique', 245.

Congar argued that the church and theology had become detached from society and reality, which in part, facilitated the twentieth century growth of secularism and the subsequent rupture between faith and life. Congar insisted that faith is, of its nature, rooted in the deepest dynamism which dominates and unifies the totality of our existence. Faith, he goes on, demands the totality of the human; it is not an abstract question of speculation, but rather, as Congar noted, 'it is a question of ourselves and of the whole of ourselves; it is a question of the definitive realisation of the deepest depths of my personality'.[7]

A final objective of this chapter is to highlight the position articulated by Congar in his essays of 1935, that the church should not become a 'small, pure, "right-minded" sect or party'.[8] The documents of Vatican II reiterate the desire of Matthew 28:19–20: it is in being a church in the world, for the world, that 'we' go forth to 'baptise all nations'.[9] Today, within the church, the issues Congar raised remain largely unresolved; as a consequence, outside the church there exists a radical societal polarisation. The majority of folk appear apathetic to metaphysical or ontological questions, while an aggressive atheistic minority, aided by a sensationalist media, fires missiles at Christianity,[10] or rather more precisely, takes aim at the bleached bones of a nineteenth-century neo-scholastic caricature of Christianity.[11] That the atheist fails to recognise their own target, presumably contemporary religious faith, is in part a consequence of the separation of faith, life and theology; not even our most articulate

---

7. Congar, 'Une conclusion théologique', 218.
8. Congar, 'Une conclusion théologique', 249.
9. 'The followers of Christ are called by God, not because of their works, but according to His own purpose and grace. They are justified in the Lord Jesus, because in the baptism of faith they truly become sons of God and sharers in the divine nature.' *Lumen Gentium* 40. For the centrality of this calling, see further *Lumen Gentium* 7, 11, 14, 15, 24, 26, 28, 31, 32, 33 and 44.
10. Contemporary skirmishes appear in the work of Richard Dawkins, Stephen Hitchens and Lawrence Krauss. For a detailed analysis of the phenomenon, see Alister E McGrath, *Why God Won't Go Away: Is the New Atheism Running on Empty?* (Nashville: Thomas Nelson, 2011).
11. Walter Kasper emphatically claimed that 'There is no doubt that the outstanding event in Catholic theology of our century is the surmounting of neo-scholasticism.' Walter Kasper, *Theology and Church* (London: SCM, 1989), 1.

atheists—and how clever they are—know that which they fire arrows at.[12]

Revisiting Congar's two early essays of 1935 should encourage us to push further beyond a neo-scholastic time warp advocated by those who would champion a distortion in the continuum of space and time through a return to the pre–Vatican II Catholic Church. Revisiting the prophetic work of Congar allows the contemporary Catholic Church to understand better the significance of reform and unity, while studying theological history allows us to learn from our mistakes and chart a spiritually rewarding path between the Scylla of 'omnivorous immanentism' and the Charybdis of 'uncompromising transcendence'.[13]

Transcendence and Immanence

The Irish playwright Sean O'Casey was seen oft to stare puzzled at the heavens; he proclaimed in *Juno and the Paycock*: 'An as it blowed an' blowed, I often looked up at the sky, An' assed meself the question, What is the stars, What is the stars?'[14] In a not too dissimilar vein I can imagine the bishops at the Second Vatican Council starring at the heavens and asking a similar question: What is the Church, What is the Church?

Their initial focus upon the mystical and the transcendent nature of the (LG 1), allowed them also to articulate a resoundingly 'concrete' reality of Church.[15] We are a Church historically located, a Church desiring to focus upon the present, while courageously personifying the ancient practice of pilgrimage; we become the Church of the

---

12. Psalm 53:1: 'The fool has said in his heart there is no God', thereby asserting that which he denies.
13. For a more detailed development of the perils associated with this nautical dictum, see Anthony Maher, 'Tyrrell's Ecclesiology: Mysticism contra *Realpolitik*', in *George Tyrrell and Catholic Modernism,* edited by Oliver P Rafferty (Dublin: Four Courts, 2010), 76–93
14. Captain Jack Boyle, in Sean O'Casey's *Juno and the Paycock*, first staged at the Abbey Theatre, Dublin, 1924. See also, Gabriel Daly, *Transcendence and Immanence: A Study in Catholic Modernism and Integralism*. (Oxford: Clarendon Press, 1980).
15. For an insight into Congar's contribution to *Lumen Gentium*, see Yves Congar, *My Journal of the Council* (Adelaide: ATF Press, 2012), 919–21.

future, the pilgrim Church with great hope. One can still sense the excitement and expectation surrounding the council, allowing Pope John XXIII in 1959 to speak of the need for a 'New Pentecost' and, in 1962, in his opening address to the council, to challenge 'those prophets of gloom, who are always forecasting disaster, as though the end of the world were at hand.'[16]

Lumen Gentium understood that the Catholic Church is 'a people brought into unity' (LG 4); 'a gateway to Christ' (LG 6); quoting the Creed, it is 'one, holy, catholic and apostolic (LG 8); moreover, 'the Church is entrusted to Peter's pastoral care' (John 21:17; LG 8); the Church is 'raised up for all ages as the pillar and mainstay of the truth' (1 Tim 3:15; LG 8); and 'The Church . . . is always in need of purification, [and] follows constantly the path of penance and renewal' (LG 8). *Lumen Gentium* continues that: the Church is also 'the People of God' (LG 9); 'the Church is hierarchical . . . the holders of office . . . are dedicated to promoting the interests of their brethren' (LG 18); 'the Laity . . . are called to contribute to the sanctification of the whole world . . . so that through faith, hope and charity they may manifest Christ to others' (LG 31); 'all within the Church . . . are called to holiness' (LG 39); 'some within the Church are called to live a religious life, to consecrate themselves to the service of God' (LG 44); 'the Church is a pilgrim Church, it is carried forward in the sending of the Holy Spirit and through our faith we work out our salvation' (LG 48), supported by 'Our Lady . . . Who by the gift of sublime grace far surpasses all creatures, both in heaven and on earth . . . full of grace . . . Mary gave to the world the Life that renews all things' (LG 56).[17]

The supernatural, in truth, remains transcendent; it must not be humanised in the sense that the mystical body becomes identified with the visible realisation of Christendom; but, Congar argues, it must be humanised in the sense that it must be embodied in every human thing: wherever there is humanity, there must be the mystical

---

16. In his 1959 announcement of his intention to call a council, Pope John XXIII said that he hoped that the forthcoming council would open up a 'New Pentecost' in the church.
17. Citations from the documents of Vatican II are taken from *Vatican Council II: The Conciliar and Post Conciliar Documents,* edited by Austin Flannery (Dublin: Dominican, 1981).

body, the extension of the redemptive incarnation. Wherever there is growth of humanity there the church must be; to all extensions of the human in any one of the domains of creation, there too must correspond a growth in the church, an incorporation of faith.[18] This is the church, this is catholicity. The church is not a special little group, isolated, apart, remaining untouched amidst the changes of the world. The church is the world as believing in Christ, or—what comes to the same thing—it is Christ dwelling in and saving the world by our faith. The church is religious humanity; it is transfigured by grace into the image of God.

Following Vatican II ecclesiological discourse, loaded words became a particular stumbling block to fruitful ministry, allowing self-doubt to undermine the pastoral necessity of 'reading the signs of the times'.[19] Conceptual clarity is important and linguistic analysis is essential for theological discourse, for as JH Newman observes: 'Nothing is more common than for men [sic] to think that because they are familiar with words they understand the ideas they stand for.'[20] The Irish theologian Gabriel Daly writes of the necessity of contemporary Catholicism to recognise the importance of pre-conceptual experience and to venture beyond the neo-scholastic model of theology and Church: the Catholic magisterium, Daly argued, 'Continued to think and act primarily on the conceptual plane, whereas the crisis is occurring primarily on the plane of pre-conceptual experience'.[21]

---

18. Congar, 'Une conclusion théologique', 241–2.
19. For further insight, see, for example, Ormond Rush, *Still Interpreting Vatican II: Some Hermeneutical Principles* (New York City: Paulist, 2004); Gerard O'Collins, *Living Vatican II: The 21st Council for the 21st Century* (Mahwah: Paulist, 2006); John W O'Malley, Stephen Schloesser, Joseph A Komonchak and Neil J Ormerod, *Vatican II: Did Anything Happen?* (New York City/London: Continuum, 2008); John W O'Malley, *What Happened at Vatican II* (Cambridge: Harvard University Press, 2008).
20. John Henry Newman, Sermon 4, 'Secret Faults', in *Parochial and Plain Sermons*, Volume I (London: Longmans, Green and Co., 1907).
21. Gabriel Daly, 'Catholicism Contending with Modernity', in *Journal of the American Academy of Religion* 53/4 (1985): 788–9.

The Purpose of Theological Endeavour

The purpose of our theological endeavours, 'a moral obligation', is to engage in deeper theological reflection that pertains to human flourishing. Developing a pastoral *raison d' être* for theology, David Schultenover draws upon Teilhard de Chardin's noosphere, the web of human, personal relationship that stretches around the globe, binding soul to soul. (Similar perhaps to Newman's heart speaking to heart.) Congar often drew upon the thought of de Chardin, whose 'noosphere implies a moral interrelationship, a moral responsibility, particularly borne by the theologian who purports to tell us about God and about ourselves believing in God'.[22] Cognisant of Congar's theological vocation, Schultenover reminds us that when we write as theologians, we seek to serve the Church and the world; our aim is to clarify theological assumptions:

> not out of airy, abstract interest but out of pastoral concern, we seek to help people pray better, to know and love God better, to know and love one another better, and therefore image the Creator better, so that together we can engage in creative human community rather than in self-destructive rivalry.[23]

The notion of the common good dwells deep down in the heart of the Catholic community; it overflows in a plethora of pastoral activities from education and health care through to organisations, such as Caritas International, which give a profound witness to the Catholic faith. Making faith visible remained an extremely important aim for Congar. Divine grace, which flows from pastoral care, is dependent upon, at least in part, our motivation. We act out of pastoral concern, moved by *agape*; a consequence may be evangelisation, but evangelisation should not be our primary purpose. That surely would entail treating humanity as a means to an end. To act purely out of pastoral concern, spiritual and material, is the most intuitive and efficacious witness to catholicity that humanity can manifest. As a moral consequence, humanity experiences the love of God and reciprocates that love, deontologically building the kingdom of God by witness—particularly the witness of the saints.

---

22. David Schultenover, 'From the Editor's Desk', in *Theological Studies* 72 (2011): 1.
23. Schultenover, 'From the Editor's Desk', 2.

Articulating the Pastoral Imperative

Pastoral and practical theology, at least for the past fifty years, has evolved into a discipline that considers the relationship between faith and theological tradition, together with the practical issues and actions that are concerned with individual human wellbeing.[24] It should not be seen simply as an appendix to theology or clergy formation, but rather as a disciplined reflection on theology from the view of ordinary lived experience.

> More concisely, it is a critical dialogue between the Christian theological tradition and contemporary experience... pastoral and practical theology shades off into liberation theology wherever the 'ordinary lived experience' involved is seen as caught up in the process by which the large-scale distribution of power and opportunity in a society is arranged.[25]

Bernard Lonergan's thought affirms the significance of a pastoral hermeneutic. He conceives pastoral theology to be the final stage out of eight in theological method; indeed, pastoral ministry nurtures theology into maturity.[26] Karl Rahner taught that pastoral theology consists in theological reflection upon the entire process by which the Church as a whole brings her nature to its fullness in the light of the contemporary situation of the world. Thus Rahner believes 'everything is its subject-matter'.[27] In a definition which has particular

---

24. Terry Veling, *Practical Theology: On Earth as It Is in Heaven* (Maryknoll: Orbis Books, 2005); Terry A. Veling, 'Catholic Practical Theology: Reflections on an Emerging Field', in *Compass*, 45 (Winter 2011): 35–9. For an example of practical theology in action, see Ormond Rush, 'Parish on Mission: A Reflection on a Renewed Sense of Parish Leadership and Ministry in the Present Realties of the Church in Australia', in *Australian eJournal of Theology* 17 (December 2010): 95–103.
25. David F Ford, Mike Higton (editors), with Simeon Zahl, *The Modern Theologians Reader* (Malden: Wiley-Blackwell, 2012), 248.
26. See Bernard Lonergan, *Method in Theology* (London: Darton, Longman and Todd, 1972), 355.
27. Karl Rahner, *Theological Investigations*, Volume X, translated by David Burke (New York City: Herder and Herder, 1973), 350. Here Rahner considers '*caritas* as science', 369. For a systematic discussion of the term 'pastoral' in the context of *Gaudium et Spes*, see 293–8. See also Karl Rahner, 'Practical Theology within the Totality of Theological Disciplines', in *Theological Investigations*, Volume IX, translated by Graham Harrison (London: Darton, Longman and Todd, 1973),

resonance with the thought of Congar, Woodward and Stephen Pattison consider pastoral theology to be:

> A place where religious belief, tradition and practice meets contemporary experiences, questions and actions and conducts a dialogue that is mutually enriching, intellectually critical and practically (personally) transforming.[28]

Pastoral theology is not just the application of principles taken from other theological disciplines to practice; unlike other theological disciplines it is an operative or experience-focused theological discipline that contributes directly to the understanding of revelation and theology from the pastoral perspective.[29]

Congar's Primacy of The Pastoral

Congar's *'primacy of the pastoral'* reminds the Church of the reason why John XXIII called the council; it should also assist in keeping the Church on the pilgrim's path leading from the Pope's inspirational 'New Pentecost'. Congar's pastoral imperative came to fruition in his seminal work, *True and False Reform in the Church*, published in 1950. Indeed the 'primacy of the pastoral' is the *sine qua non* of Congar's prophetic ecclesiology. Experts on Congar consider *True and False Reform* in the Church to be 'Congar's most important and original contribution to Christian theology', his 'most powerful and most personal book'. Congar once remarked that 'if there is a theology of Congar, it is to be found there'.[30] It is also clear that Angelo Roncalli, later Pope John XXIII, was greatly influenced by Congar's prophetic pastoral work; indeed, John XXIII emphasised the primacy of the pastoral throughout his priestly life.[31]

104.
28. J Woodward and S Pattison, *The Blackwell Reader in Pastoral and Practical Theology* (Oxford: Blackwell, 2000), 9.
29. Woodward and Pattison, *Pastoral and Practical Theology*, 27.
30. Congar, *True and False Reform*, xi. Pope John XXIII continually highlighted the primacy of pastoral ministry throughout his priesthood; see Peter Hebblethwaite, *John XXIII: Pope of the Council* (London: Chapman, 1984), 240.
31. Giuseppe Alberigo and Joseph Komonchak, *History of Vatican II*, Volume I: *Announcing and Preparing Vatican II: Toward a New Era in Catholicism* (Maryknoll: Orbis Books, 1995), 37. When Roncalli assumed leadership of the

To aid the Church discern true and false reform, Congar searched for a 'phenomenology of behaviours for profound fidelity to the Church. The first of which is the 'primacy of the pastoral'.[32] Congar insists that 'a sense of Church keeps reforms within limits; to have a sense of Church is to never forget the family household, never to become a stranger to the Church'.[33] Congar understands reform as a renewal of life, which 'requires a commitment from a corresponding life if it is to achieve authenticity'.[34] This does not diminish the need for theological research; there would be nothing more dangerous than working to reform something in the life of the Church without being grounded upon a solid theology.

'Déficit De La Théologie'

In 1934 Congar set himself the task of assessing the health of theology. His article, published in January 1935, *'Déficit de la théologie'*, begins with his rationale for a pastoral departure as a foundation for doing theology. For Congar, measurement of theology, in the deficit sense, was evidenced by the expansion of secularism and exacerbated by the causal nexus, the increasing divide, as he saw it, between faith, theology and life.[35] The article amounts to a courageous undertaking

---

Archdiocese of Venice he placed over the door to his study the motto *Pastor et Pater*—Pastor and Father—to remind him of the nature of his new job. He liked to call himself Venice's parish priest. Hebblethwaite, *John XXIII*, 240.

32. Congar, *True and False Reform*, 217.
33. Congar, *True and False Reform*, 295.
34. Congar, *True and False Reform*, 295.
35. Congar understood secularism as a threat to Christianity; arguably today it acts as a bulwark for religious freedom within a context of plurality of beliefs and unbelief. Congar understood secularism in a negative, even polarised light, that is, religious faith and secularism at war; while today one may understand secularism as the protector of faith, all faiths and none. Catholicism is in the process of beginning to explore the concept of plurality in its own philosophical speculation and pastoral ministry. See, for example, the ground-breaking work of David Tracy: *Blessed Rage for Order: The New Pluralism in Theology* (New York: Seabury, 1975), *The Analogical Imagination: Christian Theology and the Culture of Pluralism* (New York: Crossroad, 1981), *Talking About God: Doing Theology in the Context of Modern Pluralism* (with John Cobb; New York: Seabury, 1983), *A Catholic Vision*, with Stephen Happel (Philadelphia: Fortress, 1984), *Plurality and Ambiguity: Hermeneutics, Religion, and Hope* (San Francisco: Harper and Row, 1987), *Dialogue with the Other: The Inter-Religious Dialogue* (Louvain: Peeters,

two decades after the *Oath against Modernism* (1910). He argued that theology became 'fixed' when the unity of the medieval world was dissolving and the new principles of the modern world were emerging, including those relating to the emergence of the secular state, the philosophies of immanence, and the *'ruptures de la Renaissance et de la Réforme'*. The consequence of all this movement, Congar maintained, was to cut the spiritual realm in two: the spiritual realm of the modern world, pursuing development, solving problems and building upon Christian tradition, in juxtaposition with 'the spiritual realm of the clerics', of those who, perhaps like Sean O'Casey, gazed in wonderment at the stars.[36]

I think it is fair to say that Congar was impatient with 'the heaven of the theologians'. Those he described as 'cut off from the world, going over and over their own problems in a different, dead language, problems that had been set once and for all, rendered eternal not so much by scholarly abstraction as by lack of scholarly faith and interest'.[37] Congar insisted that there was a growing chasm between the two spiritual realms (the realm of the modern world and the realm of the clerics), but the Church attempted to bridge the divide with apologetics and authoritarian criticism. In this sense, Congar argued that 'the theological balance sheet for 1934 was in deficit'. Although beyond the scope of the current article, it is arguably a pastoral imperative to reconsider Congar's questions and conclusions that we might begin to assess the health of theology today. In Congar's terms, is the theological balance sheet (2014) in credit or deficit? If we were to give contemporary theology a medical or to send the theologian to a developmental psychiatrist, what diagnosis would be forthcoming?

1990), *On Naming the Present: God, Hermeneutics, and Church* (Maryknoll: Orbis Books, 1994).

36. For a more contemporary discussion of secularisation, beyond the scope of the work, see Matthias Riedi, 'The Secular Sphere in Western Theology: A Historical Reconsideration', in Péter Losonczi, Mika Luoma-aho, and Aakash Singh (editors), *The Future of Political Theology* (Oxford: Ashgate 2012), 11–22. See also Peter L Berger, 'The Desecularisation of the World: A Global Overview', in *The Desecularisation of the World. Resurgent Religion and World Politics,* edited by Peter L Berger (Washington: Ethics and Public Policy Center; Grand Rapids: Eerdmans, 1999), 1–18.

37. Congar, *'Déficit de la théologie.'* For Section 2 of this article, I am indebted to the translation of Mettepenningen, *Nouvelle Théologie* (London; New York: T&T Clark, 2010) 43–6, 43.

Congar found theology in 1934 to be 'a technical discipline, a thing in itself, a professional or class activity, a corporate knowledge, a special, closed domain of interest to a select few'.[38] He insisted rather that theology 'should have a living connection to the rest of knowledge and human activity, which would give all the rest its direction, measure, complement and underlying fertility'.

Congar offers a 'fitness' regimen for contemporary theology; theology, he said, 'Should be open to all manifestations of knowledge or creation, welcoming them, adopting them all, and giving an "aim", a direction'. Theology 'should be the salt of the earth.' He argued that 'We must have the courage to recognise that too many questions that are the requests of life itself have not only gone unanswered, but have not even been considered by theologians'. Congar notes that he is not saying that the clerics have done nothing; he says: 'I know very well that a great number of them have worked and continue to work with a courage and fervor that give brilliance to the supernatural beauty of the Church in the twentieth century.' Congar ends his article—which has the feel of a manifesto, with his life's work ahead of him—with an appeal to theologians:

> There is an urgent need for us as clerics to turn our efforts and apply our vocation of 'salt of the earth' to theology itself, as a human *science* of the things of faith or that touch on faith. As long as we have not done the theology of all the great human realities that must be won back for Christ, we will not have done the first thing that is to be done. As long as we talk about Marxism and Bolshevism in Latin, as I've seen it done in classes and at conferences of theologians, Lenin can sleep in peace in his Moscow mausoleum. An enormous task of information, investigation, contacts and right-minded, ardent, living reflection lies before us. We must prepare, on the austere, laborious level of theological science, to reconquer the modern world. But the first condition for doing theology is believing in it.[39]

---

38. Congar, 'Déficit de la théologie', in Mettepenningen, *Nouvelle Théologie*, 43.
39. Congar, 'Déficit de la théologie', in Mettepenningen, *Nouvelle Théologie*, 44.

'Une Conclusion Théologique À L'Enquête Sur Les Raisons Actuelles De L'incroyance'

Six months after '*Déficit de la théologie*', in June 1935, Congar published a second inquiry, '*Une conclusion théologique* …'; the findings of this investigation also resonate with our time. In this article he moved his attention from theology in general to ecclesiology. Congar presents the history of the movement towards unbelief which we experience in our western culture today. In the seventeenth century the doctorate in medicine was given in the name of the Father and of the Son and of the Holy Ghost; the eighteenth century discovered philanthropy, the possibility of a love of humanity which is not charity. 'The abbé of Saint-Pierre (1743) uses the word beneficence for the first time and Voltaire praises him for it. The poor are no longer members of Christ, but citizens with a right to public assistance.' Thus Congar argues that little by little, all human activities, all human realties fashioned themselves outside the Church and withdrew from the faith. The clergy were relegated to the sacristy and religion declared a private affair.

Congar sought to discover the causes of contemporary unbelief and the future consequences for faith. He finds that unbelief has a social dimension: 'if one does not have faith it is because the environment removes it—society excludes faith, because progress has dispensed with it.' The attitude of the Church in opposing modern life has excluded faith, he insists; faith must be considered in its *totality*: 'it must have a concrete meaning beyond its theological sense as a virtue of the intelligence alone.'[40] Faith is made so difficult for many because of the environment of life. Congar clarifies: 'I mean by environment, all the mass of cosmic, institutional, psychological and social realities by which and in which we communicate with each other and lead our lives—this environment has become terrifyingly secularist. Faith should be the whole of human life.'[41] Neither the Church nor faith have any longer the totality of their visibility; of their expression of their radiation in life. We must again fill our world with signs of faith, or, just as truly, with the presence of faith. Faith must again become humanly present like Christ. 'A policy of presence, not a policy of

---

40. Congar, '*Une conclusion théologique*', 216.
41. Congar, '*Une conclusion théologique*', 248.

prestige of some sort of ecclesiastical imperialism, but a policy of the presence of faith in everything that is human ... to manifest the total value of faith with regard to human life.'[42]

Assuming that the Church was under attack, she adopted a disastrous state of defence. She became specialised and reduced to a particular group, 'and thus appeared in the face of a human totality that was sufficient for the development of life, as apart, as fenced off apart, something special and anti-progressive.'[43] The attitude of defence poignantly illustrated by the Oath against Modernism was foundational to the attitude of withdrawal from the world. Congar observed in his article of July 1935 that:

> the Church withdrew into herself, constituting a strictly conservative world apart, where the concern was to guard the deposit, and where men isolated from the movement of life repeated in language peculiar to themselves, cultivating the treasure of dogma almost uniquely in its abstract and 'scholastic' aspect. Consequently an immense section of human activity, a whole growth of humanity, of human flesh and blood—modern life with its science, its wretchedness, its greatness—has not had within it the incarnation of the world; the Church has not given her soul to this body which has developed and which should, like every human value receive the communication of the Spirit of Christ.[44]

Congar understood before many in the Church that 'We now live in a new universe—inspired by our modern mysticism of science as of our modern mysticism of humanity. Christian spirituality has been substituted for human spirituality or what Père Teilhard de Chardin called "the concealment of the revealed God by the world-God".' Henceforth, the world—that of France at least in 1934—was cut in two: on the one hand, the Christian world of the Church—of the clergy—attached to a form of life and thought received from tradition; on the other, the human spiritual universe entrusted to its single interior light, that of reason, freed from all the historical and dogmatic complex whole of Catholicism. Between these two

---

42. Congar, '*Une conclusion théologique*', 248.
43. Congar, '*Une conclusion théologique*', 224.
44. Congar, '*Une conclusion théologique*', 241.

there is an inexpiable opposition enveloping almost all the causes of contemporary unbelief. For the souls who are called to faith there is a tragic option between the two: 'To complete the universe intra or extra Christum.'[45]

Contrasting the Catholic position of defence, Congar concluded that, whilst Protestantism became liberal and the world of idealism and immanentism that was incorporated into secularism pursued its development, the Catholic Church closed in upon herself in a kind of isolation. The Church recoiled under the perceived triple attack of secularism, the Reformation and rationalism; she fell back upon her positions, put up barricades and assumed an attitude of defence. Congar summarised the position of the Church following the so-called Modernist Crisis:

> After a crisis police measures are imposed: so in the Church manifestations of thought were subjected to security measures: close inspection of writings, the anti-modernist oath... initiative, especially of lay leadership was curtailed. At the same time a narrow conformism dominated ecclesiastical teaching and the ecclesiastical sciences suffered from it. Newman deplored this and noted the freedom to think, to express oneself and sometimes even to deceive oneself is necessary for scientific life and the life of theological science.[46]

The consequence of the divide between faith and life led to the Church's falling back on herself and to contraction, resulting in Catholicism becoming a party, a specialty, a whole that is aloof, the affair of priests and their clientele, just as medicine is that of doctors and their clientele—that is, a part of life and not life itself in Christ. This is an eventuality, Congar laments, that allows dogma to become a particular opinion, the badge of a special group—of a world that is apart and closed, not interesting itself in human beings, in their needs, their aspirations; whereas there is also a catholicity of love and an incarnation of charity: '*quis infirmatur* et non infirmor quis scandalizatur *et ego non uror*'(2 Corinthians 11:29). Congar asks: how does one expect the universe to be completed in Christ unless by the Church, that is, by us?

---

45. Congar, '*Une conclusion théologique*', 238.
46. Congar, '*Une conclusion théologique*', 240.

Faith, for Congar, encapsulates the totality of our being. Congar continues that faith has credibility for the believer because we can see that it is for the absolute good of the human person. 'Credibility of belief stands or falls based upon the nature of faith being a characteristic of totality—totality being the condition of credibility.'[47]

Faith Became Disincarnate

Congar insisted that the divide between faith and life no longer provided for human persons that environment of total life in which faith has its adequate expression. For it is the nature of things that faith should not rest in the pure interiority of the spirit, but should invade whole persons and, quite literally, inspire them. Various circumstances have contributed to the divorce of religion from concrete life; while becoming more interior, faith has become, so to say, disincarnate, empty of human blood. Not only in art, it is in the spiritual life, in preaching, in teaching, in the catechism, in education, sometimes in worship itself that a false spirituality without warmth and without joy—like a voice without tone—betrays again a deficiency of incarnation. Congar insists that sensibility takes its revenge in sentimentalism; he argues that in many of its manifestations our Catholicism seems like a religion for women only, and the reality is more serious than it may appear. All this is not to be dismissed; all this is very important and directly concerns our question with regard to the reasons for unbelief in our time.

Congar's research leads him to the conclusion that faith no longer appears to the whole of humanity as the very light of life in Christ: it appears not so much as superhuman as inhuman. Faith no longer has visibility, which is, from the collective point of view, a condition favourable to belief. A person will not believe, said St Thomas, 'unless he sees that he must believe, either on account of the evidence of signs, or for other similar motives.' (cf John 20:25). And by signs St Thomas here understood miracles and prophecies. But miracles and prophecies are rare, and so for the ordinary person the visibility of faith in the ordinary world will suffice. This is the ordinary condition

---

47. Congar, '*Une conclusion théologique*', 224.

of the mass of humankind and of the motives that are favourable or unfavourable to a collective state of belief.[48]

Congar's message for today is clear: our signs of faith must both be dynamic and express a totality of life, one that is inclusive, open to the world, while true to its original message. Congar reminds the Church that Catholicism has to learn to be non-discriminatory in its outlook on life, and perhaps more than anything else in its morals, practice and theological formulation.[49]

Applying The 'Primacy Of The Pastoral' To The Contemporary Reality

To aid reflection upon the Synod on the Family, and drawing upon Congar's two articles, the following guiding principles come to light:

- Pastoral primacy ensures that Christianity draws upon the life of the community and everything that belongs to that life.
- While calling some elements of the Church into question, we can't call the Church herself into question; we can seek to purify the Church, but not to make an ideology out of purity.[50]
- Reform without charity fails to recognise the concrete reality of Church. Reforms that have succeeded in the Church have been made with a pastoral perspective, aiming for holiness. We must distinguish between reform aimed at holiness and reform aimed at criticism. Every true and lasting reform, wrote Pope Pius XI, had its departure in holiness inflamed by the love of God and neighbour.[51]
- Jacques Maritain taught that 'if instead of resting in the heart purity rises to the head, it creates sectarians and heretics.'[52]
- The Roman Church cannot be reformed through movements that are governed by rational-critical tendencies, such as the Enlightenment, Old Catholics and Reform Catholicism.

---

48. Congar, 'Une conclusion théologique', 246.
49. See John Henry Newman, 'Conscience', in *A Letter Addressed to the Duke of Norfolk on Occasion of Mr. Gladstone's Recent Expostulation* (London: BM Pickering, 1874), 246ff.
50. Congar, *True and False Reform*, 218.
51. Congar, *True and False Reform*, 219.
52. Congar, *True and False Reform*, 220, and Jacques Maritain, *Humanisme intégral* (Paris: Cerf, 1936), 265.

- Congar advises all priest-theologians to stay involved in pastoral ministry. He was reflecting on Loisy as one who had allowed his personal element to remain exterior to his thinking, which remained critical and cerebral.
- Pastoral concern puts us at the heart of the concrete Church . . . making thinking and planning fruitful in terms of practical measures that can avoid excesses, the unilateralism of personal enthusiasms, or fixation on one single issue.[53]
- Pastoral concern is manifest in realism, in points of view tending towards balance and equilibrium.
- Intellectualism devoid of concrete pastoral experience can easily be more daring, leading to a negation of pastoral responsibilities.
- One of the reasons scholasticism developed a greater and greater subtlety was that it became essentially the activity of religious and of university professors.
- The genuine prophetic spirit needs to be pastoral.
- Pastoral renewal aims at holiness.
- Pastoral ministry is a great teacher of what is true.[54]
- Congar draws upon the rule of Möhler: 'The Christian should not try to perfect Christianity, but rather desire to perfect himself in Christianity.'[55]
- The risk for theologians is that they may become cut off from the Christian family, neglecting to practice the faith in a concrete context.
- Vatican II was both a pastoral council and a council of (organic) reform.[56]
- Heresy is generally the tendency to explain Christianity in terms of ideas or systems without taking into account the concrete community. Heretics create systems; the spirit of a system turns a movement into a sect—a sect is the consequence of a proud intellectual game.[57]

---

53. Congar, *True and False Reform*, 221.
54. Congar, *True and False Reform*, 222.
55. Congar, *True and False Reform*, 223.
56. Congar, *True and False Reform*, 225.
57. Congar, *True and False Reform*, 216 and 227.

A great many difficulties in theology came from confusion with regard to Church structure and life. Congar insists 'that liturgical renewal offers an exceptionally favourable base or framework for a reform movement because it tends to give primacy to the pastoral and to link a re-centring on Christ to a return to the original sources'.[58]

The Church And The Future

A tripartite conversation between clergy, laity and secular culture remains the sine qua non of pastoral ministry; it requires ecclesial facilitation that is capable of building upon the philosophy of dialogue advocated by the bishops of Vatican II.[59] It is no bold claim to assert that the future existence of the Gospel in the world depends upon this tripartite discourse. Without distracting from their participation in the conversation, the laity are destined also to be the *mode* of that anticipated conversation.[60] Paradoxically it is a conversation in which words are secondary to the ordinary lived life of faith. In so much as the laity are the authentic witnesses to the Gospel, 'making disciples of all nations', and a *locus theologicus*,[61] they represent the future hope of the Church[62]—hope being 'the entrance of the soul into the joy of the Lord, into a sharing of the divine life so far as that life is made finite for our comprehension.' Congar believed theology has a central role in what I am calling the pastoral conversation.63 In 1935 he recognised that the conversation was breaking down, 'that the church and theology [had become] detached from society and reality, which

---

58. Congar, *True and False Reform*, 296.
59. See JG McEvoy, 'A Dialogue with Oliver O'Donovan about Church and Government', in *Heythrop Journal* 48/6 (2007): 952–71; JG McEvoy, 'Proclamation as Dialogue: Transition in the Church–World Relationship', in *Theological Studies* 70/4 (2009): 875–903.
60. Yves Congar, *Lay People in the Church*, translated by Donald Attwater (Westminster: Newman, 1965).
61. Stephen B Bevans, *Models of Contextual Theology* (Maryknoll: Orbis Books, 2005), 3–15.
62. George Tyrrell, 'Hope as a Factor of Religion', in *The Catholic World* 82 (November 1905): 193–8, at 194. See also Richard Lennan, 'Hope and the Church', in *Theological Studies* 72 (2011): 247–74.
63. Charles W Taylor, 'A New Pastoral Conversation Model', in *Pastoral Psychology* 40/2 (1991) : 105–12.

in part, made it easier for the twentieth century growth of secularism and the subsequent rupture between faith and life.'[64]

Congar insisted that the Church means salvation for the world, but the world means health for the Church; without the world there would be a danger of her becoming wrapped up in her own sacredness and uniqueness. Congar found that the Church was in need of continual reformation in its morals, practice and theological formulation to avoid the danger of a partial Catholicism—something that is removed from life and the world. Congar's Church would consist of an ark in which all created things are saved, and not a party that assures the interests of a class or a corporation. In 1935 Congar wrote that our environment has become 'terrifyingly secularist' and that we must 'fill our world with signs of faith'.[65]

The two early papers of Congar examined in this article show his concern that the Church should bridge the divide between faith, theology and life. This divide Congar believed was the reason for the growth of secularism in his day. Fifty years on from the Second Vatican Council, Congar's work continues to raise significant questions. For the contemporary theologian, Congar offers two roads: (1) the practical attitude that takes its point of departure from the reality of the Church and aims to serve its development in charity,[66] or (2) the adoption of an intellectual and critical attitude that takes its point of departure from a representation of ideas and develops a system that seeks to reform the existing reality under the influence of this system.[67]

In summation, and taking our lead from Congar's theological primacy, we see, perhaps more clearly, that Catholicism throughout the twentieth century struggled to morph into catholicity. Furthermore, we can begin to understand, again *pace* Congar, the enormous possibilities associated with the Synod on the Family. The Church stands and waits to be empowered to move away from

---

64. Congar, '*Une conclusion théologique*', 249.
65. Congar, '*Une conclusion théologique*', 248.
66. Congar, *True and False Reform*, 228. See also the pastoral (cycle) methodology: (1) concrete reality, (2) critical analysis, (3) theological reflection, (4) response/praxis. Paul Ballard and John Pritchard, 'The Pastoral Cycle', in *Practical Theology in Action: Christian Thinking in the Service of Church and Society* (London: SPCK, 1996), 73–150..
67. Congar, *True and False Reform*, 228.

idealised portraits, that frankly don't exist, and to begin to engage in constructive dialogue, regarding the reality of family life in the twenty-first century. Congar's first principle of reform remains to inspire the contemporary Church to hold its nerve and continue to embrace the primacy of the pastoral, as envisaged by John XXIII.[68] Congar advocated constructing a bridge to unite faith and life. Arguably today we need to construct a series of interconnected bridges, a plurality of theological bridges; beginning with the Synod on the Family, for it seems the divide between faith and life, as Congar described, is now too great for the span of a single bridge. Vatican II was one such bridge, in a sea of tumultuous cultural change. The bishops at the Council courageously reached out a hand across the secular landscape, recognising with Newman that 'in a higher world it is otherwise, but here below to live is to change, and to be perfect is to have changed often'.[69]

Finally, Congar's two articles of 1935 echo down the decades; they remind contemporary theologians to ensure that their work does not remain a 'technical discipline, a closed domain of interest to a select few'. Theology must strive 'to discover answers to the great questions of life'. Congar advises: where 'knowledge is concerned theology is wisdom itself'. Theology must have, 'a living connection with the rest of knowledge and human activity . . . (especially family life), and be open to all manifestations of knowledge ... welcoming them.' Theology 'should be the salt of the earth'.[70] But, more than anything else, Congar insists that 'the first condition for doing theology is to believe in it'.[71]

In 1935, Congar witnessed the Church 'put up the barricades' and portray a 'deficiency of Incarnation and Catholicity . . . a closing in upon herself in a kind of isolation... constituting a strictly conservative world apart.' Ultimately with regard to the Church's proclaiming the Gospel to the world (Matt 28:19–20), this will ever be a debilitating strategy. Nevertheless, Congar understood the Church to be 'religious

---

68. Hebblethwaite, *John XXIII*, 240, and Alberigo and Komonchak, *History of Vatican II*, Volume I, 6.
69. John Henry Newman, *An Essay on the Development of Christian Doctrine* (Notre Dame: University of Notre Dame Press, 1989 [first published 1845]), 40.
70. Congar, 'Déficit de la théologie', in Mettepenningen, *Nouvelle Théologie*, 44.
71. Congar, 'Déficit de la théologie', in Mettepenningen, *Nouvelle Théologie*, 45.

humanity; it is the universe as transfigured by grace into the image of God'.[72] When it is a question of collective belief or unbelief, there are favourable and unfavourable collective conditions on the plane of culture and sensibility. 'Faith, as we understand it, is the soul of a religion that is lived.'[73] Congar's two essays discussed in this chapter, remind the Church that we should rediscover 'a Catholic imagination and sensibility, to find again the joyful meaning of Christianity, the message of life'.[74]

---

72. Congar, '*Une conclusion théologique*', 241.
73. Congar, '*Une conclusion théologique*', 216.
74. Congar, '*Une conclusion théologique*', 249.

3
'I thank my God about you always' (1 Cor 1:4): Pauline Insights Toward Pastoral Theologies of Location for the Churches of Oceania Today

Catherine Playoust

The Catholic Diocese of Port Pirie encompasses most of South Australia and part of central Australia. Its area is 980,000 kilometres, more than the area of mainland France and Germany, but it is sparsely populated; indeed, its churches number only fifty-eight.[1] Its bishop, Greg O'Kelly SJ, explained in a 2012 interview that his pastoral visits around the diocese require a vast amount of travel: 'I drive about 55,000 miles [90,000 kilometres] a year in the car, and fly in a small plane to other Outback cattle stations and aboriginal communities'. He added that while the priests of the diocese do excellent work, there are few of them and some are quite elderly. The lay leadership within various facets of the Church's ministry is therefore particularly appreciated.[2] In a contribution to a 2013 eBook on the use of digital technology in the Australian Catholic Church to share the gospel, Bishop O'Kelly drew attention both to the benefits of the resources that reach him and the diocese electronically from the national and international Church and to how the scale and quality of communications within the diocese have been enhanced through various Internet and SMS tools, beyond the capacities of older technologies such as telephone voice calls or the postal service.[3]

---

1. The diocese includes Uluru in the Northern Territory but not Adelaide and environs in South Australia. See http://www.pp.catholic.org.au/about-our-diocese. Accessed 1 July 2015.
2. Jim McDermott SJ, 'To Be A Bishop Today: An Interview with Bishop Greg O'Kelly, SJ', in *The Jesuit Post* (18 October 2012), https://thejesuitpost.org/2012/10/to-be-a-bishop-today-an-interview-with-bishop-greg-okelly-sj. Accessed 1 July 2015.
3. Bishop Greg O'Kelly SJ, 'The Web and I', in Australian Catholic Bishops

From a pastoral theology perspective, the characteristics of the Diocese of Port Pirie raise the question of how to consider location as an aspect of church life.[4] We see the main strategies that are being adopted there in response to the wide range of locations in which the activities of the diocese occur; there are episcopal visitations, strong local leadership by clergy and lay people, and electronic communications both into and within the diocese. Negotiating the variety of places in which a community and its members are situated is a challenge that affects all church communities in some fashion, in Oceania and beyond. In some cases, as we have just seen, the church members or the smaller units of community are spread out over a considerable area; for Port Pirie, this holds true on both the diocesan and the parish level. On many groups of Pacific islands, the local churches are quite contained in physical scope but their extreme isolation from major landmasses brings its own hardships. Technology and travel can bridge such isolation, but the financial barriers are substantial.

My own experience as a Roman Catholic laywoman and an urban Australian leads me to think also of ways that Catholic parishes in Sydney and Melbourne operate—I consider some that are fragmented by age or cultural grouping into sub-communities that rarely meet together, others that have been clustered into large quasi-parishes because of the lack of priests, and still others whose members gather from all round the city because they find their official geographical parishes lacking in spiritual sustenance for them. Going further afield to my time in Boston, Massachusetts, I recall the pain of parish closures and the strong attachment that parishioners have to the site where they have been accustomed to worship. I note too the

---

Conference Communications Office, *Word Made Flesh and "Shared" Among Us*, 2013, eBook, https://www.catholic.org.au/word-made-flesh. Accessed as epub file on 1 July 2015.

4. An earlier version of this essay was presented at a keynote address for 'Practical Theology in Oceania: Explorations to Recover an Ecclesial Sense of Place and Purpose', Annual Conference of the Association of Practical Theology in Oceania (APTO), in Sydney on 28 November 2014 in Sydney, and again for a seminar at Catholic Theological College in Melbourne on 1 May 2015. My thanks to the organisers for these opportunities and to the participants for fruitful discussions. My thanks also to Elliott Gyger, Peter Golding, Denise Playoust and Sean Winter, who provided helpful feedback on written drafts.

tensions in Roman Catholicism over the last half-century in relation to the concept of subsidiarity, as the favour given at a high structural level to this ideal, whether for a diocese or for Oceania, has shifted repeatedly. And regarding Christian denominations whose polities are stronger on the congregational level or the national/regional level than is the case for Roman Catholicism, I contemplate how hard it is to foster and preserve the bonds of communion across geographical church groupings when their concepts of how to live the gospel today differ in some important ways because of their own experience in their local context. Doubtless these examples of how location plays a part in church life will have sparked your memories from your own ecclesial experience.

My academic formation is not as a pastoral theologian, however, but as a scholar of the New Testament and early Christianity. Consequently, my thoughts also turn to Christianity as it was emerging in the first century CE, and particularly to the churches founded by Paul. The Pauline communities were based in a wide range of cities in Greece and Asia Minor. Under Paul's leadership, in which he was absent more often than present, these communities needed to function well despite their customary physical separation from Paul and other churches. They developed strong local leadership and they maintained oral and written communication with Paul and his co-workers through travels and letters. Paul, his co-workers and the churches prayed for one another and reminded each other that they were doing so. In these ways they acknowledged their multiple physical locations and took practical steps to solve the problems rising from these. They also, however, discovered that physical separation was not the whole reality of their lives. Even in these earliest decades of what would become Christianity, they were developing ways to speak theologically about their ecclesiological unity, in a way that transcended physical separation, and to pray from the stance of that belief. As those who were in Christ, as members of Christ's body, they had what we might call the same ecclesial location by faith.

In this essay I will be developing these ideas by drawing upon 1 Thessalonians and, more briefly, several of the other undisputed letters of Paul, so as to elucidate what Paul was advocating and what the Pauline communities were doing. As you read, I invite you to keep in mind the challenges of location for the various kinds of churches in Oceania today. It would be unwise, however, to imagine that we could adopt the Pauline strategies wholesale and map them onto any particular modern context, or even to suppose that they simply constitute a repertoire of possible solutions from which we could choose. Rather, they can provide insights as we consider church structures and circumstances that, while in continuity with the Pauline tradition, differ from it in notable ways. If there are useful resources here, well and good, but what I encourage is that instead of remaining at the utilitarian level, we think and pray more broadly about the formation and flourishing of community in the light of the Scriptures and our own experience. In saying this, I have in mind some observations by Ellen Bradshaw Aitken:

> The various texts of the New Testament represent in diverse ways experiments in the formation of Christian community . . . The letters of Paul . . . represent experiments in new community, not by telling a story of Jesus [as the gospels do], but by revealing Paul's strategies to shape Christian communities along specific lines, to negotiate difference, and to link disparate groups within a network of mutual regard. Inasmuch as Paul's letters also allow some small access to the perspectives and voices of those to whom he wrote and with whom he negotiated, we also receive glimpses into those other experiments in Christian community, into ways other than Paul's of centering communal identity and practice around the memory of Jesus . . .
>
> If we regard New Testament texts as witnesses to various experiments in shaping or reshaping community, then it follows that in order to appreciate what a given text has to say about such issues as covenant, law, or communal identity (or anything else, for that matter), we should enter into the world and strategies of that particular text as fully as possible. We need to understand how that text 'works,' how it makes meaning, how it bears witness to an experience of God, how it remembers Jesus, how it attempts to persuade others of its point of view, and how it in itself constitutes its audience as 'the people of God.' This is a strikingly different approach to the biblical text from a more utilitarian approach that distills meaning for the present from a given passage, a story, or saying of Scripture. What I am advocating is not an approach that

lends itself easily to 'applying the Bible' to current problems; rather, it is an invitation to enter into other experiences of God, Jesus, and godly community in order to have our vision for the present and future refreshed, reinformed, and reinvigorated.[5]

Let us now look, then, at the Pauline letters, starting with 1 Thessalonians, as 'witnesses to various experiments in shaping or reshaping community', in the hope of refreshing our vision for the churches today and in the future.

Community and Location in 1 Thessalonians

The text known as 1 Thessalonians dates from around the year 50 CE and is probably the first letter we have from Paul.[6] Strictly speaking, though, it is not 'from Paul', for the letter has co-authors, as is normal for the Pauline correspondence—this letter is from Paul, Silvanus and Timothy, as we hear in its first verse. What is unusual in 1 Thessalonians is that the joint authorship is maintained quite strongly, whereas most of the undisputed Pauline letters are ostensibly by Paul and co-author(s) but shift to 'I' almost exclusively after their opening verse.[7] Only a few times does 1 Thessalonians exhibit first-person singular grammatical constructions and on these occasions the 'I' is always Paul; elsewhere, 'we' forms apply, to include at least Silvanus and generally Timothy as well.[8] Paul's dominance in the letter's composition is shown by his being the referent of these occasional

---

5. Ellen Bradshaw Aitken, 'The Ordering of Community: New Testament Perspectives', in *Anglican Theological Review*, 85/1 (2003): 19–34 (quotations from 20 and 22). See also her articles 'To Remember the Lord Jesus: Leadership and Memory in the New Testament', in *Anglican Theological Review* 91/1 (2009): 31–46 and 'Relentless Intimacy: The Peculiar Labor of an Anglican Biblical Scholar', in *Anglican Theological Review* 93/4 (2011): 563–580.
6. Gordon D Fee, *The First and Second Letters to the Thessalonians*, New International Commentary on the New Testament (Grand Rapids: Eerdmans, 2009), 4–5; Abraham J Malherbe, *The Letters to the Thessalonians*, Anchor Bible 32B (New York: Doubleday, 2000), 71–75.
7. The letter known as 2 Corinthians constitutes another notable exception.
8. The first-person singular constructions occur at 2:18, 3:5 and 5:27. In 1 Thessalonians 3:1, 'we' send Timothy while remaining in Athens; evidently 'we' at this point means Paul and Silvanus.

'I' forms, and thus it is all the more notable how carefully he includes his co-workers in the letter for the most part. Since Paul, Silvanus and Timothy were the ones who brought the good news to Thessalonica, this jointly-authored letter strengthens their existing bond with the Thessalonian believers.

The letter is written to a particular community, 'the church (*ekklēsia*) of the Thessalonians in God the Father and the Lord Jesus Christ' (1:1).[9] As often occurs in the undisputed Pauline writings, *ekklēsia* is being used here to mean a church or assembly in a specific location, rather than the church throughout the world, though it will soon become clear that the Thessalonian church has strong links to other local churches. The letter takes account of this local community and its history, while also bearing in mind the community's location relative to other sites of the Pauline mission.

A considerable portion of the first two chapters of this letter is taken up with recalling the first visit of Paul, Silvanus and Timothy to Thessalonica, when they founded this local church. I summarise here what they say, because it contributes to how the letter sets forth an understanding of location. (We should bear in mind that this is how the co-authors choose to remember and construct the history for the rhetorical purposes of this letter. In another context they might have told it differently, and the Thessalonians themselves would have had their own ways to shape the story.) Paul, Silvanus and Timothy say that their presence in the city allowed them to preach the good news and to demonstrate their good character (1:5). They laboured hard, day and night, to support their mission financially without burdening the Thessalonians (2:9). With pure motives and blameless conduct, free of the desire for human praise, they acted like a father in their encouragement and like a nursing mother in their nurturing (2:3–12). The affective dimension in all this was strong: 'So deeply do we care for you that we are determined to share with you not only the gospel of God but also our own selves, because you have become very dear to us' (2:8). As a consequence of all this, the Thessalonians 'turned to God from idols, to serve a living and true God, and to wait for his Son from heaven, whom he raised from the dead—Jesus, who rescues us from the wrath that is coming' (1:9–10). They changed their mode of

---

9. Biblical quotations in this essay are derived from the New Revised Standard Version, sometimes in adapted form.

life to become imitators of their founders and the Lord, even suffering persecution on account of the good news (1:6; cf 2:14).

While Paul, Silvanus and Timothy are careful to emphasise the humility and gentleness that they showed in their first visit, so as not to acquire a reputation for superficial impressiveness (cf 2 Cor 11:7–15), they are equally eager to recall the presence and action of God during that time. When they preached, their good news came to the Thessalonians 'not in word only, but also in power and in the Holy Spirit and with full conviction' (1:5). Reading this in the context of Paul's churches more broadly, this may mean that the Holy Spirit was active in a perceptible way during this initial visit, probably in the form of mighty works and/or spiritual gifts. Whatever happened, for the letter-writers it is evidence that the Thessalonians have been chosen, that is, chosen by God who loves them (1:4). The letter says also that the Thessalonians received the message as originating not merely with humans but with God, who is also working in these believers (2:13). The preaching and encouragement that the Thessalonians heard through human means have stemmed from God's own call to them (2:12).

The success of the missionaries' first visit to Thessalonica, through the will of God, has not only founded a new church in that city. It has also reshaped the network of churches by the addition of this new node and the forging of connections between them. The co-authors refer several times to churches in other cities and regions, which suggests that part of their goal is to foster such links. Paul, Silvanus and Timothy came to Thessalonica after they had 'already suffered and been shamefully mistreated in Philippi' (2:1), another city in Macedonia. More recently, while Paul and Silvanus remained in Athens, a city in the more southerly province of Achaia, Timothy has made a return visit to Thessalonica. When the Thessalonians are commended for their faith that withstands persecution, the letter says, 'you became . . . imitators of the churches of God in Christ Jesus that are in Judaea, for you suffered the same things from your own compatriots as they did from the Judaeans' (2:14).[10] These

---

10. It has sometimes been argued that 1 Thessalonians 2:13–16 (or part of this verse range) is a non-Pauline interpolation, given its sudden extreme hostility to the 'Jews' (*Ioudaioi*), but the majority opinion seems to be that the verses are authentic, though conceivably drawing upon pre-Pauline material. It

itineraries and comparisons give the context for the words of praise early in the letter: 'so that you became an example to all the believers in Macedonia and in Achaia. For the word of the Lord has sounded forth from you not only in Macedonia and Achaia, but in every place your faith in God has become known, so that we have no need to speak about it' (1:7–8). Even if they 'have no need to speak about it', evidently conversations have in fact been occurring, and this letter is continuing that process. Paul and his co-workers have brought into existence a network of local churches whose members take an interest in each other's faith and sufferings, with the understanding that this is part of loving one another (4:9–10, with particular reference to the brothers and sisters in Macedonia).

From what we have seen so far, Paul and his co-workers played a major role in the early stages of founding the church in Thessalonica. By writing in this way and by drawing attention in their letters to other churches they have founded, they continue to inscribe themselves deeply into the life of the Thessalonian community. This is an authoritarian move, to be sure, though the patriarchal tone is undercut by some of the language they employ. In retelling the community's history in 1 Thessalonians 2, they present themselves as a nursing mother as well as a father, as noted above, and they say they were temporarily orphaned by their physical absence from the Thessalonians (2:7, 11–12, 17). As Gaventa has commented, 'The frequently changing imagery may also subvert the popular notion that Paul takes a thoroughly hierarchical stance toward the churches. Particularly in a society with highly structured perceptions of maleness and femaleness, a man who speaks of himself as an infant or as a nurse-mother or as an orphan voluntarily hands over his place

---

helps to remember that in this period *Ioudaioi* primarily means 'Judaeans', a geographical/ethnic designation with religious import, and then to observe that the immediate context in the letter is geographical—they are Jews in Judaea not Jews across the Greco-Roman world. For further discussion of the authenticity and interpretation of the passage, see Fee, *The First and Second Letters to the Thessalonians*, 89–103; Beverly Roberts Gaventa, *First and Second Thessalonians*, Interpretation (Louisville: John Knox Press, 1998), 34–39; Malherbe, *The Letters to the Thessalonians*, 164–179; Ben Witherington III, *1 and 2 Thessalonians: A Socio-Rhetorical Commentary* (Grand Rapids: Eerdmans, 2006), 82–89.

in the conventional gender hierarchy, however fleetingly'.[11] That said, the ongoing role of these founding figures cannot be discounted.

What, then, happens when these leaders are absent? As we shall now see, several strategies are adopted to deal with the fact that most of the time Paul and his co-workers are in a different location or locations from the Thessalonian church, since they are ministering to other churches they have founded or spreading the gospel in a new city. Paul does the best he can to substitute for his presence through his co-workers, his fellow itinerant missionaries. The Thessalonian church members are encouraged to support one another, following leaders within their own city. Everyone engages in prayer for one another, and the knowledge that they are being prayed for is a source of encouragement for the Thessalonian church, Paul and his co-workers. And the letter itself mediates the presence of its authors to the Thessalonian church, bringing them to the community through its words.

Since the initial visit to Thessalonica, Paul in particular has wanted to return again and again but has been blocked by Satan (2:18). One of the ways he makes up for this is to send a co-worker as his mediator when he cannot go himself. Timothy's return visit relieves his concerns greatly:

> But Timothy has just now come to us from you, and has brought us the good news of your faith and love. He has told us also that you always remember us kindly and long to see us—just as we long to see you. For this reason, brothers and sisters, during all our distress and persecution we have been encouraged about you through your faith. For we now live, if you continue to stand firm in the Lord. (3:6–8)

This visit entails a two-way flow of information, but also of affection. The encouragement to 'stand firm' and Timothy's actual visit would also, and not very subtly, remind the Thessalonians that their life should continue to conform to the pattern that Paul and his co-workers have laid down. This is especially so in the wake of the praise

---

11. Gaventa, *First and Second Thessalonians*, 29–30. In her statement, 'infant' refers to 2:7; there is a text-critical issue in that verse about whether Paul and his colleagues call themselves 'infants' (*nēpioi*) or 'gentle' (*ēpioi*), but either way, Gaventa's point about gender performance stands.

given to them earlier for having been imitators of their founders and the Lord (1:6; 2:14). The Thessalonians should neither drift away through human frailty nor adopt a different set of priorities that a non-Pauline missionary of Jesus Christ might bring.

Another strategy for coping with Paul's absence is to develop strong mutual support at the local level. The members of the Thessalonian church should 'encourage one another and build up each other' (5:11), with particular attention to those who are idlers, faint-hearted, weak, or needing patience (5:14). They should 'always seek to do good to one another and to all' (5:15). Furthermore, the community has local leaders—we do not hear how they were appointed, but the letter's intended audience would have known the history. At any rate, paying attention to these leaders will also promote the strength of the community, and the letter says, 'we appeal to you, brothers and sisters, to respect those who labour among you, and have charge of you in the Lord and admonish you; esteem them very highly in love because of their work' (5:12–13). Here is an example of shared physical location operating to the advantage of the Thessalonian community: people living in the same area are supporting one another mutually and in leadership.

The most profound way in which Paul and his co-workers act at a distance for the benefit of the Thessalonian church is to pray for them. After the opening greeting, they write: 'We always give thanks to God for all of you and mention you in our prayers, constantly remembering before our God and Father your work of faith and labour of love and steadfastness of hope in our Lord Jesus Christ' (1:2–3). Indeed, the sense of thanksgiving is so strong that some scholars would see this initial prayer as extending into the next few verses or even beyond, as the letter describes the successes of the initial mission in Thessalonica.[12] The letter's closing lines include a

---

12. Gaventa (*First and Second Thessalonians*, 13) considers that the initial thanksgiving continues at least to the end of verse 5 and probably to the end of verse 10, while Fee (*The First and Second Letters to the Thessalonians*, 18–19) thinks it is 1:2–3 only. For Malherbe (*The Letters to the Thessalonians*, 78, 203–204), all of 1:2–3:10 is classed as thanksgiving and also autobiography, in order to take into account the additional explicit words of thanksgiving in 2:13 and 3:9; furthermore, it prepares for the paraenesis itself, beginning at 4:1. However, such a lengthy thanksgiving section would seem implausible, being too severe a distortion of the customs of the time; Witherington, for example, regards

prayer for them and a request for their prayers: 'May the God of peace himself sanctify you entirely; and may your spirit and soul and body be kept sound and blameless at the coming of our Lord Jesus Christ ... Beloved, pray for us' (5:23, 25). In the body of the letter, too, they mention their prayers at a number of points: thanking God that the Thessalonians received the good news from them as God's word (2:13) and for their joy about the Thessalonians (3:9); and asking God to strengthen the community's love and holiness (3:12–13) and to make it possible for the letter-writers to see them face-to-face and restore whatever is lacking in their faith (3:10). The deep trust that the writers have in the efficacy of these prayers is evident from the warmth and confidence of their declarations about them, and it would prepare the recipients to pray for them with the same intensity and trust.

Their declarations about the prayers are effective in another way too. By reporting that the prayers are occurring, Paul and his co-workers are assuring the Thessalonians that their church founders remember them and that God is active in all their lives. The joy and concern that Paul, Silvanus and Timothy feel for this local church flow over into a prayer-filled expression of love.[13] Even though the Thessalonian church cannot always have Paul and his co-workers physically present, it knows that it has not been forgotten by its human founders, neither spiritually nor emotionally, and that God's care for it is constant. The Thessalonians should thus imitate the prayer and thanksgiving that their founders are modelling: 'Rejoice always, pray without ceasing, give thanks in all circumstances; for this is the will of God in Christ Jesus for you' (5:16–18).

We should not neglect the role of the letter itself in bridging the physical gap between the Thessalonians and their founders. The care that Paul, Silvanus and Timothy have for this local church is manifested not only by their words but also by the fact that they wrote and sent this letter, entailing time and expense. The letter allows them to address some specific ethical and eschatological concerns,

---

1:2–3 as a thanksgiving/exordium and 1:4–3:10 as a *narratio*, within a work of epideictic rhetoric; see Witherington, *1 and 2 Thessalonians: A Socio-Rhetorical Commentary*, 21–29.

13. 'Paul writes a kind of love letter, one in which he pours out his own love for the Thessalonians, while sustaining himself with the knowledge that they love him as well. Most important, he acknowledges that their mutual love derives from God's own love for all.' Gaventa, *First and Second Thessalonians*, 9.

especially in chapters 4 and 5. It highlights and commends the good aspects of the local church's life, to encourage the Thessalonians to continue in the same direction but more fervently. It recalls their past and speaks of their good reputation among other local churches. It presents this church as one that has its own excellent resources but will also continue to benefit from its links with two networks: the geographically-fixed local Pauline churches and the small, flexible and geographically-mobile community of Paul and his co-workers. Working within a Pauline theological framework, it constructs an image of the Thessalonian church's past and present, setting forth the actuality and potentiality of the community and its relationships in such a way that the Thessalonian church may be 'blameless before our God and Father at the coming of our Lord Jesus with all his saints' (3:13). That is, the letter's rhetorical dimensions should not be forgotten—it aims to persuade and transform, despite the physical absence of its authors from its recipients.[14]

Concepts of Location in other Pauline Letters

We have seen that 1 Thessalonians does not disregard the restrictions and limitations imposed by one's physical location. What a human being or community can do is genuinely conditioned by where they are. Separation from other beloved people or communities causes practical difficulties and emotional pain. The letter also shows, however, that some of the limitations can be alleviated and that God's power and love transcend place. Similar strategies and insights are employed in the other letters of Paul to handle the multiple locations of the Pauline churches and the missionaries visiting them. I will draw attention to some additional ways of proceeding that are not strongly represented in 1 Thessalonians but can be found elsewhere in the undisputed Pauline correspondence. Ongoing two-way communications, both oral and written, are very important to the sustained health of the churches Paul and his co-workers have

---

14. Ancient Greek epistolary theory was well aware of the potential for a letter to convey the presence (*parousia*) of its writer to its recipient, despite the physical absence of the writer. See the classic study by Heikki Koskenniemi, *Studien zur Idee und Phraseologie des griechischen Briefes bis 400 n. Chr.* (Helsinki: Suomalainen Tiedeakatemia, 1956).

founded. Over time, Paul also faces the fact that he will not always be available to engage in such communications, and seeks ways to preserve the memory of what he has taught the communities. Paul also helps the communities to assess the teachings of other visiting missionaries, especially in cases where they conflict with his message or seem to do so. Furthermore, he draws each local church's attention to the existence of its counterparts in other cities, constructing a network of communications for them and teaching them to provide financial support. This is not merely a socio-financial network, but the expression of an ecclesiology whereby all the believers, wherever they may be, are one in Christ Jesus.

Strong communications are very important for the health of the Pauline communities. We have seen already the importance of letters by Paul and his co-workers. What has been handed down to us in the New Testament canon is probably only a fraction of the letter-writing that Paul undertook. For instance, there are certain indications within 1 and 2 Corinthians that Paul wrote more than two letters to the church in Corinth.[15] We have seen also that there are visits by co-workers who can then report back to Paul how the community is going. The local churches or subgroups within them can also instigate communications, both oral and written, as the Corinthian correspondence shows particularly well. Early in 1 Corinthians, Paul notes that reports have reached him from 'Chloe's people' that there are quarrels in the community (1 Cor 1:11). As the letter proceeds, Paul takes up at least one set of issues that has been raised in a letter they have written to him, namely, questions about marriage; the section starts, 'and concerning (*peri de*) the things about which you wrote' (7:1). His sudden changes of topic at some other parts of the letter, again with the *peri de* formula though not with explicit

---

15. In each of 1 Corinthians 5:9 and 2 Corinthians 2:3–9, Paul refers to some letter that he previously wrote to the Corinthians. In neither case does the letter concerned seem to be the other canonical letter. Additionally, some scholars argue that 2 Corinthians is composed of several letters of Paul to the Corinthians, edited together. On these issues, see Joseph A Fitzmyer, *First Corinthians: A New Translation with Introduction and Commentary*, Anchor Yale Bible 32 (New Haven: Yale University Press, 2008), 43–44; Ralph P Martin, *2 Corinthians*, Word Biblical Commentary 40 (Waco: Word Books, 1986), xxxviii–lii; and Thomas D Stegman SJ, *Second Corinthians*, Catholic Commentary on Sacred Scripture (Grand Rapids: Baker Academic, 2009), 17–24.

reference to a letter from the Corinthians, are also quite likely to be responses to oral or written communications from them.[16] Perhaps most remarkable is Paul's response to the situation in Corinth of the man living with his father's wife (1 Corinthians 5). Paul pronounces judgement on him, in the name of the Lord Jesus. He instructs that when the assembly acts to expel this man, Paul's own spirit will be present with the gathered church even though he is absent in body.[17] This is something of an exception, however; for the most part, Paul is clear that being physically absent from a community imposes limits on how he can act. His need of local leadership and travelling co-workers for communications and authority is therefore high, and we can see what a remarkable base he built when we read the catalogue of names in Romans 16, which greets many women and men (including the deacon Phoebe and the apostles Junia and Andronicus) with affection and admiration for their work.[18]

Coping with the long-term absence of a church's principal human founder, and finally with that person's death, is discussed in the letter to the Philippians. Paul, a prisoner by this stage, spends much of the first chapter musing whether he will be freed or killed, and considering what the consequences would be either way for himself and the Philippians. As we saw in relation to 1 Thessalonians, he knows that sending co-workers instead will be of some avail but not a full substitute for Paul's own presence in the local church (Phil 2:18–30).

---

16. The words *peri de* ('and concerning') occur at 1 Corinthians 7:1, 25; 8:1; 12:1; 16:1, 12. It has often been argued that each of them marks Paul's attention to a letter from the Corinthians, but the ancient use of the formula was more flexible than that: Margaret M. Mitchell, 'Concerning ΠΕΡΙ ΔΕ in 1 Corinthians', *Novum Testamentum* 31:3 (1989): 229–256.
17. My thanks to Christopher Monaghan CP for a timely conversation about this passage.
18. This is all the more remarkable when we recall that Romans was written to a community that Paul did not found. There is, however, a theory that Romans 16 was written not to the church in Rome but the church in Ephesus, and was added to the letter to the Romans later; the theory arose because the evidence of the early manuscripts regarding the presence of Romans 16:1–23 in the letter and the location of Romans 16:25–27 is complicated. Even if this were so, this would detract only slightly from the impressiveness of the catalogue. For a detailed defence of Romans 16 having a Roman destination, followed by an extensive examination of the names involved, see Peter Lampe, *Christians at Rome in the First Two Centuries: From Paul to Valentinus* (London: Continuum, 2003), 153–183.

He also insists strongly that the community members should humble their own preferences and opinions so as to be of one spirit and one mind (1:27; 2:1–5; 4:2). They are to have 'the same mind . . . that was in Christ Jesus' (2:5), including the humility that characterised his self-emptying and obedience (2:6–8). A more proximate model for their behaviour, however, is the way Paul has taught them to live and think; they are to continue 'just as you have always obeyed me, not only in my presence, but much more now in my absence' (2:12) and indeed to imitate Paul and to model their behaviour on him and his co-workers (3:17; see also 4:9).[19] Anticipating his death sooner or later, Paul is doing what he can to ensure that his notion of how to live is known by those he has brought to belief and will endure among them.[20]

Conflicts among missionaries come to the fore in several of the letters. Sometimes, according to Paul, these conflicts are only apparent and stem from excessive focus on the principal apostle over Christ himself. The early chapters of 1 Corinthians deal with this (1 Corinthians 1–4), though there is a tension in them as to how Paul sees his importance relative to that of other missionaries who have visited the Corinthians (contrast 1:10–17 and 3:4–7 with 4:14–21), which will not be surprising given my remarks just now about Philippians. There are also times in the letters when Paul considers that the other missionaries have such different teachings or different emphases that he should warn the communities against them in the strongest possible terms. Thus he calls anathema on those preaching a different gospel to the Galatians (Gal 1:9). He even goes so far as to wish that those who are preaching the need for circumcision to them would cut off more than their own foreskins (Gal 5:12; cf Phil 3:2).

---

19. In Philippians 3:17, having called for the Philippians to be co-imitators of him, Paul then advises the Philippians to observe those who live according to the example or pattern that they have in 'us'. He does not specify who is meant by 'us', but presumably in addition to Paul it would include Timothy (the co-author announced at the beginning of the letter) and the local and itinerant co-workers to whom he refers during the letter. See the discussion in John Reumann, *Philippians: A New Translation with Introduction and Commentary*, Anchor Yale Bible 33B (New Haven: Yale University Press, 2008), 568–569, 592.
20. On the aims of the letter to the Philippians, see Paul A Holloway, *Consolation in Philippians: Philosophical Sources and Rhetorical Strategy*, Society for New Testament Studies Monograph Series 112 (Cambridge: Cambridge University Press, 2001).

To the Corinthians, who find Paul impressive when he instructs them remotely by letter but think his bodily presence weak and his speech worthy of no account (2 Cor 10:10), he warns against the pseudo-apostles who are boastful of their successes, pointing out that 'Satan himself is transformed into an angel of light' (2 Cor 11:13–15).

Money is used by Paul both to foster the growth of the mission and to connect local churches to one another. He is cautious not to request money during an initial visit, though he considers himself entitled to do so as an apostle (1 Cor 9:3–18). He has two alternative strategies: working to support himself, as we saw above (1 Thess 2:9); and receiving donations from churches he has already founded (2 Cor 11:7–9). To the Philippians he recalls their outstanding help in supplying his needs in Thessalonica and even after he left Macedonia, as well as more recently (Phil 4:14–15, 18). However, he emphasises not the practical utility of their financial gifts—the context of this discussion is Paul's declaration of his self-sufficiency and ability to function well in any situation—but the virtue of them as an offering pleasing to God (4:18). As Paul's ministry goes on, he develops a substantial collection project among the Pauline churches for the saints in Jerusalem (1 Corinthians 16:1; 2 Corinthians 8–9; Rom 15:25–32). He puts this forth as a way to balance abundance and need (2 Corinthians 8:13–14; 9:12; cf. Gal 2:10) but also uses it as a way to encourage friendly competition among his churches—he tells the Corinthians he has boasted about them to the Macedonians that 'Achaia has been ready since last year' (2 Corinthians 9:2), as a way to ensure that the Corinthians will indeed give the money that they have promised (2 Corinthians 9:1–5). By raising awareness of the needs of churches in other locations, Paul strengthens the network of churches he has founded and connects them to Jerusalem as a symbolic centre for the whole church.

Undergirding all of these ways of handling a geographically-diverse network of churches is an emerging ecclesiology that has consequences for the idea of location itself. In Paul's time there is a developing sense of the unity of these churches as 'the' church (1 Cor 12:28; 15:9; Phil 3:6). Its members are 'in Christ' through their faith and baptism (Gal 3:25–28). Consequently, God's spirit dwells in them and they are adoptive children of God, heirs of the promise to Abraham (Rom 4:1–5:5; 8:9–17). There is therefore a strong pull to unity. This issues in the call to obedience and self-abnegation for the good of the community, as we saw in regard to Philippians, and also in the suppression of personal spiritual experiences for the sake of building up the assembly, as advocated in 1 Corinthians 12–14. That is, the church members are called to love one another (1 Cor 16:14; Gal 5:14), which in Pauline terms necessitates patience, humility and endurance (1 Cor 13:4–7). The unity should not be totally uniform, however, as Paul's deployment of the classic political 'body' *topos* indicates: diversity of needs and gifts within the community is to be respected and appreciated (1 Cor 12).[21] The church, the one body, demonstrates and strengthens its unity by partaking of the one bread of the Eucharist (1 Cor 10:16–17). While I would say that many of Paul's *ekklēsia* statements are, in the first instance, about a local community in a particular city, their emphasis on oneness and their declaration of what is true for all who are in Christ Jesus, irrespective of location (even if this is not one of the factors explicitly articulated in Gal 3:27–28), pushes theologically beyond the constraints of physical place. Paul's ecclesiology constructs a new kind of location, as it were, an ecclesial location in which all are gathered in the one place, by faith.

Location Today: Physical, Ecclesial, Technological

In this essay I have been examining the role of location in the Pauline communities, as shown in 1 Thessalonians and other undisputed Pauline letters. I have noted several factors: the urban setting of each of the Pauline churches; day-to-day leadership for these churches resourced from within the community; travels to these churches by Paul and his co-workers, providing the opportunity for oral communications; travels by local emissaries of the churches to these leaders, providing the same opportunity but perhaps more likely to be driven by the concerns of the local church; letters as written communications along the same routes; interest in the joys and sufferings of Pauline churches in other cities; financial support from

---

21. On the Greco-Roman *topos* of the body in discussions of political unity and its deployment by Paul in 1 Corinthians, see Margaret M Mitchell, *Paul and the Rhetoric of Reconciliation: An Exegetical Investigation of the Language and Composition of 1 Corinthians* (Tübingen: Mohr Siebeck, 1991), 157–164.

these churches for the mission and for the saints in Jerusalem; and an ecclesiology providing a way to conceptualise an emerging unity, a church of churches.[22] The strong emotional language in Paul's letters about his love and concern for these communities, combined with Paul's encouragement for them to use him as a model, would over time have developed churches that cared about each other's flourishing even though they were far away. All the individuals and communities in this network pray for one another, recall each other to mind and tell each other about these prayers and recollections. Paul's words near the beginning of 1 Corinthians, 'I thank my God about you always' (1 Cor 1:4), can stand here for several of the thanksgivings that he expresses in his letters and encourages the church members to reciprocate. I have argued that although the Pauline communities and their missionaries are aware of their separate locations in physical terms, their practices and their beliefs lead them to an ecclesiology such that they are unified by faith into a single 'ecclesial location'.

As I explained in the introduction, I have not undertaken this examination of location in Paul's letters in order to provide a blueprint for the church today. Anyone who wishes to serve today's churches of Oceania by discerning an ecclesial sense of place, or by engaging in a pastoral theology of location, must do so not only in the light of the Scriptures but out of the knowledge and love of the particular church that they serve. What Aitken advocates for approaching the biblical text—'to enter into other experiences of God, Jesus, and godly community'—is necessarily work that must be done by each person who is engaging in pastoral theology, in the awareness of their own experience of church and world. The work need not be done in isolation, and I would hope that by sharing my skills as a biblical scholar I have helped in the investigation, but every pastoral theologian, like any other reader, will bring their own lens to the reading.

By way of demonstration, though, I would like to offer some pastoral insights that have emerged for me through this enquiry in relation to the contemporary church context I know best, namely, Roman Catholicism in urban, Western-cultural settings in the early

---

22. I borrow this last expression from J-MR Tillard, *Church of Churches: The Ecclesiology of Communion* (Collegeville: Liturgical Press [Michael Glazier], 1992).

twenty-first century. Firstly, there are enough broad similarities between the Pauline situation and my own context that I recognise and affirm certain elements of wisdom easily; possibly you too will recognise these with respect to the churches that you serve. Just as the Pauline communities found, so today as well, both physical presence and physical absence of fellow believers are normal experiences. Engaging in communication and support can alleviate the disadvantages of absence and separation. Both the people and the ideas should keep flowing; some concepts and encouragements can be transmitted at a distance and some work best when the people concerned are in the same physical space. Beyond all this, the love bonding the churches and the prayers sustaining them will allow each local church to honour the reality of its location, yet also to transcend the limitations of place to realise its shared location with other churches in ecclesial terms.

Now for some points of distinction. The existence of these is only to be expected, for the church structures and circumstances most familiar to me differ from the Pauline churches in certain ways despite being in the Pauline tradition; this is chiefly because of the historical and cultural gap between them. The communities I know are composed of people whose cultures are more individualistic than Paul's.[23] There may, therefore, be churches today for which Paul's strictures about conformity and insistence on the community over the individual would be excessively harsh and ultimately unproductive. Perhaps the insight we might glean from the Scriptures for such churches is the viewpoint of certain members of the Pauline communities rather than that of Paul himself. This is not the way the Bible is most often used, but I would argue that the practices and beliefs of first-century churches, as gleaned from the New Testament, are part of our ecclesial heritage and thus worthy of our attention to see what they might offer us as we reflect upon them theologically and prayerfully. Recall that Aitken's notion of 'experiments in Christian community' includes the perspectives of all members of the community, not only its leaders.

My other points of distinction arise from the role of technology in today's world. Biblical scholars sometimes joke about how Paul would

---

23. Oceania does still contain some collectivist cultures, mostly of people who are marginalised by the dominant cultures, but even these collectivist cultures are now influenced by modern Western assumptions through globalism.

have loved the Internet. I fear that the combination would have been unhealthy, for he would never have stopped watching and checking on the churches he had founded. This observation is difficult to make in the current climate, and I do not wish to be misunderstood. We know that in our churches and other societal institutions, those who have been entrusted with the ministry of supervision, both bishops (*episkopoi*, 'over-seers') and others, have all too often chosen to overlook rather than to oversee, and so have failed to protect the vulnerable. It is right that we are taking steps to address this and we must never forget the horror of what has happened. However, going to the other extreme, of rigorous control over every action and utterance, would be unwise. We live in an age of electronic surveillance, from CCTV monitoring to 'helicopter parenting', and I would not like to see such modes of operation become normal within the churches at any level of authority. Those whom one is supervising need room to breathe and experiment, lest they fail to develop their gifts and to discover new ways to act in an ever-changing environment. By the principle of subsidiarity, local groups need some degree of autonomy, so that they do not constantly reach outside themselves for advice and so that decisions are not made for them centrally without due consideration of the needs of the specific place.[24] I speak here principally of electronic communications, but the same kinds of opportunities and dangers hold for travel between formerly remote places. Considering the way that the cost and speed of intercontinental travel have changed even in my lifetime, it can no longer be said that Australia is 'a long way from Rome', as used to be claimed by Roman Catholics in Australia.

In my discussion of the Pauline communities, I sketched two concepts of location: physical location (which separated them) and ecclesial location (which united them by faith). I would suggest that it is now possible, by means of the Internet and related technology,

---

24. Pope Francis has written: 'Nor do I believe that the papal magisterium should be expected to offer a definitive or complete word on every question which affects the Church and the world. It is not advisable for the Pope to take the place of local Bishops in the discernment of every issue which arises in their territory. In this sense, I am conscious of the need to promote a sound "decentralisation"'. Pope Francis, *Evangelii Gaudium*, Apostolic Exhortation (2013), n16, <http://w2.vatican.va/content/francesco/en/apost_exhortations/documents/papa-francesco_esortazione-ap_20131124_evangelii-gaudium.html>. Accessed 1 July 2015.

to conceive of a third sense of location.[25] The term 'cyberspace' is hopelessly dated now, but what it sought to express was the notion of a quasi-spatial realm of contact mediated through technology. Current technology allows for a group of people who might be physically located all over the world to share words and images with one another almost instantaneously, as if in the same room.[26] Human beings have had access to aspects of these capabilities for a long time, between the broadcast mass media of radio and television and point-to-point devices such as the telegraph, the telephone and the fax, but the newer technologies bring groups together better and share the data much faster. For world-spanning communications, whether email conversations or social media discussions, the obstacle now to seemingly-instant receipt of a message is no longer the delay in transmission but the difference in time zones—being embodied, we still need to sleep on occasion.

Such electronic communications should not be derided as trivial, as a mere shadow of face-to-face communications. The assumption needs to be questioned, especially given how much time and passion is devoted to email, texting and social media these days. The specialised computer terminology of 'real' and 'virtual' has at times been misleading in discussions of online communication, as if communications were not 'real' unless expressed in the same physical location. In our world, connections are made and strengthened electronically that cause behavioural changes reaching far beyond the screen. Whether for good or ill, electronic communications are neither insubstantial nor inconsequential. Yet they are often spoken of this way, in both religious and secular discussions. For example, Pope Francis' new encyclical, *Laudato Si'*, excellent though it is and so important for our world, slips for a moment into this way of categorising modes of communication:

> Real relationships with others, with all the challenges they entail, now tend to be replaced by a type of internet

---

25. My thanks to Elliott Gyger for a conversation that helped me crystallise my thoughts in this regard.
26. This presumes that the infrastructure is present and the individuals concerned have the technical and financial means to take advantage of it. In the church contexts about which I am speaking, the barriers are now quite low; I realise this is not the case everywhere.

communication which enables us to choose or eliminate relationships at whim, thus giving rise to a new type of contrived emotion which has more to do with devices and displays than with other people and with nature. Today's media do enable us to communicate and to share our knowledge and affections. Yet at times they also shield us from direct contact with the pain, the fears and the joys of others and the complexity of their personal experiences.[27]

His actual targets here appear to be the weak concept of 'friends' on Facebook and similar platforms and the more trivial end of social media communications, but the language runs the danger of ranking the quality of communication according to the technical means employed for it.[28] The passage acknowledges the capacity of new media for intellectual and emotional communication but then undercuts this by comparison with 'direct contact' with others' emotions and experiences. Of course, it is true that many electronic communications are trivial and ephemeral in their content—they do not attempt to be otherwise. The same could be said, however, for the face-to-face conversations at a barbecue in a backyard or at morning tea after a religious service. Their primary purpose is not to exchange information but to create and strengthen social bonds within an informal and leisurely context. In so doing, they may prepare the conditions for the provision of emotional support—and on occasion spiritual support too.

Some of the recent papal statements for World Communications Day are more sanguine about the communicative possibilities of the Internet. In his 2013 statement, Pope Benedict XVI wrote:

> Social networks, as well as being a means of evangelisation, can also be a factor in human development. As an example, in some geographical and cultural contexts where Christians feel isolated, social networks can reinforce their sense of real unity

---

27. Pope Francis, *Laudato Si'*, Encyclical Letter (2015), n47, <http://w2.vatican.va/content/francesco/en/encyclicals/documents/papa-francesco_20150524_enciclica-laudato-si.html>. Accessed 1 July 2015.
28. The large quantity of time that people spend on electronic communications these days has attracted various critiques, and this factor, along with 'information overload', is probably also of concern to Pope Francis in the paragraph from which I am quoting, but my focus here is the quality of the interaction.

> with the worldwide community of believers. The networks facilitate the sharing of spiritual and liturgical resources, helping people to pray with a greater sense of closeness to those who share the same faith.[29]

This would ring true with what I have observed over the last several years: the Internet is extremely effective at linking up people who are relatively isolated within their immediate geographical location, according to whatever the axis of their isolation is (for example, academic specialty, artistic taste, politics, ethnicity, occupation or religion). In the case of Internet connections to offset religious isolation, the effect is precisely to construct the kind of shared technological location of which I have been speaking. Many Christian churches and communities have started to recognise this, and are devoting substantial human and budgetary resources to mission and ministry in the sphere of digital technology.[30] Modern communications make it possible to form strongly bonded communities that are brought together online rather than in a physical space. The interaction is what counts, not its mode.

I would like to conclude by returning to the Scriptures and Pope Francis, though this time it is a different papal statement and the biblical text is the Gospel of Luke rather than the letters of Paul. The parable of the Good Samaritan emerges from the question, 'And who is my neighbour?' (Lk 10:29). This is, I suggest, a question about location: 'To whom am I adjacent? Who is near enough to me that I should care about them?' For the 2014 World Communications Day, Pope Francis wrote:

> Today we are living in a world which is growing ever 'smaller' and where, as a result, it would seem to be easier for all of us to be neighbours . . . The internet, in particular, offers immense possibilities for encounter and solidarity. This is something

---

29. Pope Benedict XVI, Message for the 47th World Communications Day, 'Social Networks: portals of truth and faith; new spaces for evangelisation' (2013), <http://w2.vatican.va/content/benedict-xvi/en/messages/communications/documents/hf_ben-xvi_mes_20130124_47th-world-communications-day.html>. Accessed 1 July 2015.
30. These major decisions have arisen in part from the success of the pioneering smaller-scale projects documented in works such as Australian Catholic Bishops Conference Communications Office, *'Word Made Flesh and "Shared" Among Us'*.

truly good, a gift from God . . . How can we be 'neighbourly' in our use of the communications media and in the new environment created by digital technology? I find an answer in the parable of the Good Samaritan, which is also a parable about communication. Those who communicate, in effect, become neighbours. The Good Samaritan not only draws nearer to the man he finds half dead on the side of the road; he takes responsibility for him. Jesus shifts our understanding: it is not just about seeing the other as someone like myself, but of the ability to make myself like the other. Communication is really about realising that we are all human beings, children of God. I like seeing this power of communication as 'neighbourliness' . . . It is not enough to be passersby on the digital highways, simply 'connected'; connections need to grow into true encounters. We cannot live apart, closed in on ourselves. We need to love and to be loved.[31]

Earlier in this essay, we saw that Paul's ecclesiology added to the normal concept of physical location another idea, which I termed ecclesial location, according to which all members of Christ's body are gathered as if in one place. In these closing pages, I have argued that within our modern, Western-cultural church contexts, we have access to a third kind of location, technological location, whereby people anywhere in the world can be together in the same discursive space. Given the importance of the Internet in the lives of so many people today, our churches and faith communities should make creative use of this new form of location to deepen their spiritual lives and spread the gospel. 'Those who communicate, in effect, become neighbours', as Pope Francis says. Loving communication calls into being the new location in which they are neighbours.

---

31. Pope Francis, Message for the 48th World Communications Day, 'Communication at the Service of an Authentic Culture of Encounter' (2014), <http://w2.vatican.va/content/francesco/en/messages/communications/documents/papa-francesco_20140124_messaggio-comunicazioni-sociali.html>. Accessed 1 July 2015.

Forum for Theology in the World Vol 2 No 2/2015

4
A Missional Church in Process and Willing to Learn

Neil Darragh

The investigation which I attempt here is carried out within the perspective of the APTO 2014 conference, 'Explorations to recover an ecclesial sense of place and purpose'. The place of Oceania and the purpose of the church are thus defining elements in the perspective adopted in this chapter.

This chapter is focused primarily on the resources a local church might draw upon in order to renew itself as a more authentically missional church. Such an investigation presupposes some starting points which are not in themselves obvious. These presuppositions are contestable, but I do not argue for their validity here. I simply list them as the premises from which the rest of the paper proceeds.

1. I presuppose here that the mission of the church is the wellbeing of all God's creation in that the church participates in God's mission.[1] 'Wellbeing' in its Christian sense is defined principally by the New Testament understanding of the reign of God. In brief, the church is *for* the reign of God.

2. Our understanding of the church's role in God's mission in the world should be a major determinant of church structure and ministry. That is to say, ideally missiology precedes and influences ecclesiology. This reverses a fairly common presupposition in theology where missiology is

---

1. The history of the concept of God's mission (*Missio Dei*) and its interpretations are summarised in Stanley H Skreslet, *Comprehending Mission: The Questions, Methods, Themes, Problems, and Prospects of Missiology* (Mayknoll: Orbis Books, 2012), especially 31–33.

an addition to or an application of an already established ecclesiology. My presupposition here is that ecclesiology is better derived from an already established missiology, not vice versa. The church's own internal organisation ought to derive to a significant degree from its missionary purpose, and should support rather than weaken or ignore that purpose.

3. In this paper, I normally use the term 'church' or 'Christian community' to refer to a group of people who commonly worship together or identify with a particular place of worship, that a local congregation or parish or particular ethnic Christian community. It is the missiology of this local community rather than that of a regional organisation such as a diocese or national or international denomination that is my focus here. The larger-scale church organisation is important to local churches but I presuppose here that it is the local church mission that needs more attention and support from theological reflection.

4. All members of the church are missionaries by the fact of being disciples of Christ.[2] Most missionaries in this sense are engaged in mission *in their own society*, i.e. most are not travellers to foreign countries or other cultures. Those who do travel to foreign countries need special consideration, but the major focus in missiology, as I understand it in this paper, is on the majority mission which takes place within the society in which a local church is itself embedded.

5. 'Witness' is a major component of mission. What we 'say' needs to match what we 'do' not only as individuals but also as Christian communities. The church's own internal relationships and corporate style need to be consonant with what that same church proposes as good for the wellbeing of society at large. The most debilitating criticism of a missional church is that it does not practice what it preaches.

---

2. Pope Francis, *Apostolic Exhortation Evangelii Gaudium* (Vatican City2013), nn 119–121.

Given these presuppositions, how might we develop an ecclesiology that is determined in a major degree by our missiology, and what resources may we draw upon to accomplish this?

My procedure in attempting an answer to this question is to (a) propose a perspective by which a missional church regards the wider society, (b) suggest some new, non-traditional dimensions of contemporary missiology, (c) draw some conclusions about church leadership, (d) look at the resources available to the church for its own renewal as missional, (e) focus more closely on secular organisations as an important type of resource for renewal in a missional church.

A Mission Perspective On Society

A secular society in the broad sense, where there is a separation of church and state, where religion normally has no privileged status in state institutions, and where nearly all the citizens like it this way, could be said to exist in Australia and New Zealand, but to a much lesser degree in most of the island nations of Oceania.

Discussions about the church's mission in countries like Australia and New Zealand, taking their lead from North Atlantic mission discussions, often adopt the perspective that contemporary mission is about outreach into a society becoming increasingly secular. In this case 'secularism' is the feature of society identified as important in mission policy.

It may be however that this misplaces the issue. I would suggest rather that the key features of 'society' that concern mission policy are those of de-privatised religion and pluralism.

The term '*de*-privatised religion' refers to the condition of contemporary society where religion is no longer regarded as just a private matter for individuals but can also be the common bond for associations or corporate bodies that make up civil society and need to be respected as such by state institutions. Modern pluralist societies are made up of many different groups, organisations and social forces, among which are Christian churches. Within this pluralist society, Christian churches have as much right to exist and play their part as any other organisation, but not in any more privileged way than others. Church communities are *within* that society, rather than *outside reaching towards*, and their membership overlaps with that of many other organisations within that society.[3]

The church's mission then is not simply *outreach into a secular society*, but rather an *engagement within a pluralist society*. The difference between these two points of view may be represented diagrammatically as follows:

Church Outreach Into Secular Society

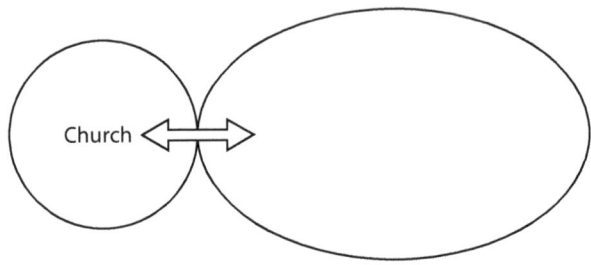

In this perspective, the church is regarded as having its own identity which resists absorption by society and repudiates its secularism. Nevertheless, the church has a mission outreach for the betterment of that society and for its conversion to Christianity. Intersection is two-way since missionaries go out into that society and members of society are invited into the church.

---

3. Cf Thomas Hughson, 'Missional Churches in Secular Societies: Theology Consults Sociology', in *Ecclesiology* 7 (2011): 173–94; also Roger Trigg, *Religion in Public Life: Must Faith Be Privatised?* (Oxford: Oxford University Press, 2007). For examples of engagement in the Australian context see Francis Sullivan and Sue Leppert (editors) *Church and Civil Society: A Theology of Engagement* (Adelaide: ATF Press, 2004).

Church Engagement Within A Pluralist Society

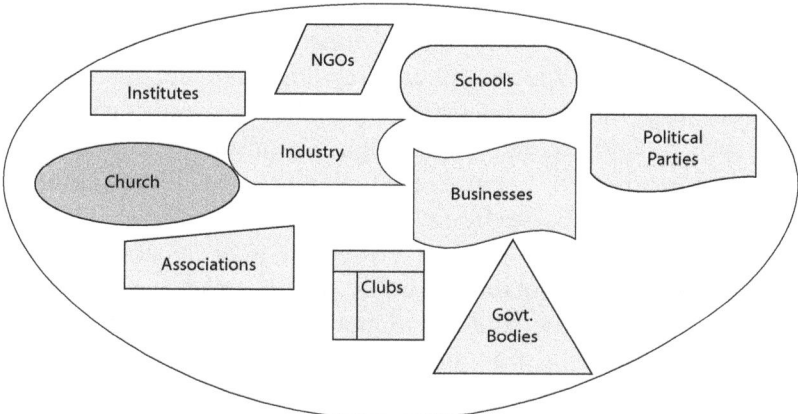

In this perspective, the church engages critically with the many other bodies that
> make up a pluralist society. Its purpose is to play a part in bringing about the reign of God in society.

New Dimensions

As we seek to clarify our missiology following upon the presuppositions I have listed above, there are a number of new dimensions, mainly positive from a missiological point of view, that were not part of traditional theologies of mission, but that may be important today:

(a) The amount of *information on the social, economic, and environmental conditions that affect wellbeing in society* has grown significantly over the last few decades. This information stimulates and complicates the church's involvement in society. A good deal of this information is publicly accessible through published reports and especially through the internet. In the area of social justice, for example, decisions about priorities (what will really make a difference) can now draw upon recent social, economic and ecological studies that were never previously available to church missionaries.

(b) Similarly, there is a great deal more information than before about the flow-on *effects of different kinds of human organisation and relationships*. Decisions about organisational structures that contribute to good community and mission need not rely just on traditional experience and personal insight but can now draw also on researched sociological and psychological conclusions as well as on recent historical research. I intend to look more closely at this kind of information in the final section of this paper.

(c) We have become used to 'evolutionary' or 'process' thinking which allows us to maintain continuity with our past as well as seek innovation without the confrontational discomfort of condemning the theologies of past generations.[4] The future evolves out of the past. This process thinking needs to be combined however with a *contextual*, rather than uniformly global, thinking—'an ecclesial sense of place and purpose'. A church in one contemporary context may evolve a leadership pattern somewhat different from a church in another context. It is now relatively common to think about church in a way that is both evolutionary and contextual, and this is an advantage in the current investigation. This investigation would be nearly impossible in the prevalence of a static and universally uniform view of church and mission.

Christian Community Leadership

The structures of leadership and ministry in a Christian church are commonly determined by that church's understanding of leadership in the New Testament and by its historically developed patterns of leadership. But what would church leadership look like if it were determined rather on the basis of the church's contemporary missiology? If, that is, the church's internal organisation were fitted

---

4. It does nevertheless require intelligent strategies. Gerard Mannion argues for the ecclesial virtue of 'creative fidelity' or 'loyal dissent' that steers between centralising and legalistic intransigence on the one hand, and at the opposite extreme, a drift toward total disregard for the rich traditions of the church in favour of an out-and-out relativism. Gerard Mannion, 'A Teaching Church That Learns?,' in *Church and Religious 'Other'*, edited by Gerard Mannion (Edinburgh: T&T Clark, 2008), 184.

more directly to its *contemporary purpose* rather than to its *historical origins*?[5]

It is unlikely that an existing contemporary church would want to abandon entirely its historical origins or scriptural justification, except perhaps in a time of crisis. Yet a clarification of missiological requirements for church leadership may at least alter, perhaps radically, our customary ways of recruiting, supporting, and reviewing our current church leadership. What qualities could we hope for in leaders of a contemporary church whose internal organisation is strongly influenced by its missionary purpose?

On the basis of the presuppositions and new dimensions noted above, leaders in a contemporary missional church could be expected to be:

(a) Able to read the signs of the times with a missionary attitude and demonstrated engagement in a pluralist society.

(b) Able to engage in society both at the level of compassion (issues of immediate survival such as food banks, emergency housing, women's refuges, and advocacy) and also at the level of structural transformation (such as healthy housing, unemployment, imprisonment, growing inequality, and accessible health care)

(c) Aware of available social and economic analysis of contemporary society.

(d) Attentive to local church members' experience and discernment as a source of knowledge and strategy for action—the lived experience of church members concerned with people's wellbeing is a source of information and mission strategy in addition to social scientific studies.

e) Committed to collaborative ministry within the church community—no single leader can have the knowledge or skills to initiate or oversee the wide range of interactions of church members in a pluralist society.

---

5. This paper is in agreement with and a partial response to Kenneth Wilson's observation that neither clergy nor laity are currently capable of responsible Christian conversation in the contemporary world; education for this conversation should be a focus of church action. Kenneth Wilson, 'Hoping to Learn: An Approach to Ecclesiology,' in Gerard Mannion *Church and Religious 'Other'*, 266–78.

f) Able to identify and facilitate the mission engagement of members of their own community—support and backup, capacity building, opportunities for learning, etc.

g) Skilled at the liturgical expression and empowering of mission attitudes and actions—the Sunday gathering, especially Eucharist, is the major foundation for mission empowerment.

We may need to ask ourselves here whether we find these qualifications in our own local church leadership. A local church with an outward focus into the wider society may need to adjust its traditional patterns of leadership to fit a contemporary missional focus.

Resources for Renewal in a Missional Church

Churches already have some available resources for carrying out such a re-adjustment. The most important of these, I suggest, are the New Testament, traditional patterns of church leadership, social justice traditions, other contemporary churches, recent discussion of collaborative ministry, and secular patterns of organisation.

These various sources need to be seen in interaction rather than in isolation. It distorts our use of contemporary secular patterns, for example, if we are not aware of how the New Testament sources provide criteria for accepting or rejecting some secular patterns or if we are not aware of how an adoption of collaborative ministry will affect our traditional patterns of leadership.

New Testament

The principle of *service* is central in New Testament ideas of ministry and leadership, but there are a variety of models of ministry and leadership.[6] Church denominations have traditionally cited some particular New Testament texts as justification for their own particular church structure. It is difficult to argue today that no church organisation other than one's own is legitimate. Many churches can

---

6. Let us be aware, though, of the lexical complexities of the New Testament Greek words relating to 'service' in the early Christian community. See John N Collins, 'Theology of Ministry in the Twentieth Century: Ongoing Problems or New Orientations?', in *Ecclesiology* 8 (2012): 11–32.

still claim however that their church organisation and its reputed origins in the New Testament is necessary for their own identity and heritage and are for that reason to be valued and maintained.

What is important for our focus here on mission, is that scripture still remains normative, not so much or not often for a particular style of church leadership, but for the values or implications of that leadership.[7] Gospel attitudes towards hypocrisy, for example, do not in themselves suggest or eliminate most styles of leadership, but do discredit any kind of leadership which allows hypocrisy to exist. Similarly, servant leadership (even though in a variety of forms) finds approval in the New Testament, while competitive and career leadership do not.

Social Justice Traditions

Principles of social justice or the social Gospel have been formulated in a variety of ways for different audiences or different situations. Let us accept the following as a reasonable formulation and communicable translation of these principles:[8]

- human dignity—all persons are made in God's image,
- solidarity—walking together,
- preferential option for the poor and vulnerable,
- common good—the good of each and all,
- subsidiarity—empowering communities,
- stewardship—being responsible guardians,
- participation—everyone with a part to play.

What is important for our focus here is that these principles of social justice have commonly been proposed for human relationships in society *outside* the church. They have not so often been applied *within* the church's own organisation. The church could reform its own patterns of leadership by applying these principles within the church.

---

7. In the matter of ministry and from out of the Anglican tradition, proposes a number of critical moves that are required in order for the church's ministry to remain firmly Christian and properly catholic yet move towards a more collaborative ecclesial ministry rooted in the Spirit. Stephen Pickard, 'A Christian Future for the Church's Ministry: Some Critical Moves,' ibid., no. 8: 33-53.
8. I use here the formulation adopted by Caritas NZ, <http://caritas.org.nz/resources/cst>. Accessed 21 March 2015.

The church could then become a 'witness' rather than just a teacher of these principles to the wider society. To these social justice principles, we might also want to add some other traditional 'virtues' such as transparency, truthfulness, a willingness to enter into dialogue, and humility as desirable in church leadership.[9]

Other Contemporary Churches

There now exist many 'experiments' of church organisation. Schisms and divisive heresies, however undesirable in themselves, have resulted in many experiments of different kinds of church ministry and leadership. We already know a good deal about the good and the bad of them. Most can find their foundations in the New Testament. We have existing examples of hierarchically organised churches alongside sixteenth-century Reformation churches who have made deliberate decisions *against* hierarchical structures and *for* congregational, constitutional, or collaborative structures of some sort. But now that we have more amicable relationships among churches we also know that each kind of structural arrangement has its own kind of missional or communitarian problems. It is important to note here too the intricate relationships between church structure and culture. Contemporary church structures often have culturally specific origins. And church structures that work well in one nation or culture may not work for churches in other nations with their own different cultural assumptions and practices.

What is important for our focus here is that we do not need to compare present reality with an idealised but untried version of leadership patterns. Often those patterns already exist in fact in other churches. From the point of view of our focus in this paper, churches other than our own can effectively function as concrete experiences of organisations different from our own. Nowadays, familiarity with other churches and their members means we are already aware of both the advantages and the defects in the organisational structures of other churches. Moreover, we are more aware now than we used to be of the value of diversity and the dangers of uniformity in both human society and in nature. What used to be called the 'scandal

---

9. For further discussion of such 'virtues', see Mannion, 'A Teaching Church That Learns?,' 177.

of division' loses much of its force and becomes simply 'diversity' provided we can be more open to one another and learn from one another in a critical and careful way.

Collaborative ministry

The idea of 'collaborative' ministry has been around for long enough now, with enough trial and error, success and failure, for it to be a contemporary resource, rather than just a bright idea, for rethinking ministry. Hierarchical or line-management forms of social organisation are vulnerable to authoritarian personalities, to the forces of control rather than empowerment and to incompetence in the person in charge. They are also wasteful of the diverse kinds of creative talent and commitment that is generated in more collaborative ways of decision-making. Collaborative ministry rather than line-management on the one hand or congregational decision-making on the other, can coordinate this variety of rights and gifts. There already exist models of collaborative structures in the church in a variety of church groups and communities.[10]

What is important for our focus here, is that (a) a collaborative model of ministry can successfully readjust a history of overly hierarchical as well as overly combative congregational models of ministry; (b) a collaborative model is about collaborative *decision-making* and is not the same as a *consultative* model which shares information but not decision-making; and (c) in a contemporary mission-oriented church, such collaboration among ministers, especially among community leaders, is necessary because of the complexity of the multiple engagements of the church in a pluralist society.

Secular Organisations

What models of leadership in contemporary secular organisations could provide models for leadership in a missional church?

---

10. See for example, Edward P Hahnenberg, *Ministries: A Relational Approach* (New York: Crossroad, 2003).

This question does not imply 'adapting' the church to the modern world. Rather it is looking for information about secular leadership in the contemporary world which it can then subject to theological discernment on its suitability for a Christian church.

Let me illustrate my intentions here by examining briefly an example of a contemporary model of institutional organisation. My example here is the International Association for Public Participation (IAP^2) which sets out in a succinct and accessible way its 'core values' for public participation in an organisation or project. The purpose of these core values is to help organisations make better decisions which reflect the interests and concerns of potentially affected people and entities (the 'public').[11]

Core Values for the Practice of Public Participation

1. Public participation is based on the belief that those who are affected by a decision have a right to be involved in the decision-making process.
2. Public participation includes the promise that the public's contribution will influence the decision.
3. Public participation promotes sustainable decisions by recognising and communicating the needs and interests of all participants, including decision makers.
4. Public participation seeks out and facilitates the involvement of those potentially affected by or interested in a decision.
5. Public participation seeks input from participants in designing how they participate.
6. Public participation provides participants with the information they need to participate in a meaningful way.
7. Public participation communicates to participants how their input affected the decision.

---

11. International Association for Public Participation, 'Core values', <http://www.iap2.org>. Accessed 21 March 2015.

How Do We Use This Example Ecclesiologically?

This model of public participation is not in any explicit way dependent on a traditional Christian leadership model. It is based on the principle that public participation is a right for those affected by a decision. Here the argument for public participation is an ethical one, a 'right'. Others would argue on a more practical basis that such participation makes for better or more effective decision-making. In any case, the IAP^2 provides a set of core values to effect such public participation.

The articulation of these core values provokes the question of participation in decision-making for those organisations that have so far ignored or belittled it. For churches it provokes the question of a) how much participation there is by church members in decision-making within the church itself (an ecclesiological issue), and the question of b) how much public participation does the church encourage or require in those social organisations in which the church takes part (a missiological issue).

The churches have been involved in debates about participation in decision-making for a very long time. These are debates about 'authority'. The arguments are important because fundamentally they are about the channels of divine communication—whether this occurs most decisively through elected representatives, charismatic leaders, apostolic succession, scholarly interpreters of scripture, or private inspiration. Fundamental to all this is the degree to which a church believes in the indwelling of the Holy Spirit in every baptised member of the church.

An association like IAP^2 works from the assumption that the organisations it addresses are not in the first place participatory or cooperative but are interested in becoming so or more so. That is, there is an initial division between the decision makers and the affected 'public'. The core values are intended to bring the 'public' into more participation in decision-making than has previously been the case.

Most contemporary churches are in a similar position (some more and some less) in that they have a leadership structure where some people make decisions for the membership as a whole. Such leadership structures have however changed over time as people's general understandings of political or corporate leadership have changed and as new members with different cultural understandings have entered the traditional churches. In this sense, most of the churches are not fundamentally different from secular organisations that traditionally followed 'line-management' or 'professional' styles of leadership and where that traditional leadership is not simply relinquishing its authority or responsibility but seeking to increase the amount of public participation in it.

I have used here the example of IAP^2 to illustrate how a secular model of organisation can stimulate our ecclesiology and our missiology from the point of view of 'participation'—an organisational concern both for the church as for secular organisation.

There are many kinds of leadership patterns however in secular organisations. What kind of models are we interested in from an ecclesiological viewpoint?[12]

---

12. I have used a number of secular organisations to test out the principles I list below to check their consistency and practicality. Besides the International Association for Public Participation, two other models have influenced me in particular. These are the model of the Public Promotion of Mental Health, (Theresa (Tess) Chow Wah Liew, 'Rising to the Challenge: Towards Enhancing the Wellbeing of an Urban Community in New Zealand' (PhD thesis, University of Auckland, 2011); and the model of Human Synergistics <http://www.hsnz.co.nz>. Accessed 21 March 2015.

5
'Re-placing the Church': Challenges and Prospects for Christianity Down-Under

Stephen Pickard

The Coming Church

In this chapter I want to address these three related concepts—place, pace and presence. My basic thesis is that if the coming Church is to be truly *present* in contemporary society two things are required (a) a church so *placed* that it can be found and (b) one that moves at a *pace* that is not easily missed in the busyness of life. Place, pace and presence are interwoven aspects relevant to the church's recovery of its place in the world. To speak of 're-placing' the church is not a matter of 'with what' but a question about 'where' and 'how' might a new ecclesial form of life contribute to the enrichment of wisdom in God's world.

If I have a text in the background it is that well known incarnational prologue to St John's Gospel: 'the Word became flesh and dwelt among us, and we have seen his glory....' (John 1:14). What does it mean to tabernacle, to pitch a tent in the midst of the world in such a manner that the glory can be seen? This is a great challenge for Christianity in Australia and more generally in the Western world. Tent-pitching has been difficult and the kinds of tents pitched have not always been appropriate for the conditions and cultures that make up this place. My own Anglican Church is a case in point. In the late 1950s, one commentator on the state of the Church of England in Australia stated that 'in no country to which the Church of England has been transplanted has she been less successful in evolving an organisation and outlook appropriate to the realities of her situation.'[1] But this

---

1. Leicester Webb, 'The Conciliar Element in the Anglican Tradition', *St Mark's Library Publications No. 2* (1957), 20.

problem may well be relevant to other churches, to some degree. My strong hunch is that the Christian churches generally, in spite of some gallant efforts, have struggled to find their place on Australian soil.

The Priority of Place

For Christianity to find its place is not simply a matter of geography, though I do wish to focus on this, if only because it has been largely ignored.[2] However it is as well to note that consideration of place will necessarily involve attention to the social, political, economic and communicative framework of the liberal democratic tradition of which this country is an heir. To make our place into a home, and becoming at home in a particular place is a complex and costly matter. The quest for an ecclesial sense of place in Australia is in its infancy.[3] More generally commentators remark on the loss of a sense of place in the Western intellectual and cultural traditions. This loss can be charted back beyond the Enlightenment to earlier periods of history. The reasons for this loss are complex and include an emerging scientific culture, which increasingly made sense of the world in terms of space and time rather than place. Edward Casey states: 'For an entire epoch, place has been regarded as an impoverished second cousin of Time and Space, those two colossal cosmic partners towering over modernity'.[4]

Why is a sense of place so critical to the life of Christianity? To what extent does the church of Jesus Christ need to be re-placed in order to manifest the wisdom of God in this land of Australia (Eph 3:10)? The process of adaptation and enculturation involves pitching the tent; dwelling in, rather than peering into the world beloved of God. So where do we begin? Often overlooked but actually quite central here is the fact that Antipodeans have their cultural and social identities shaped not by one fundamental reality that is land, but three—land, ocean and sky (with its infinite extension into space). Furthermore, since the majority who live 'down-under' occupy the costal fringes,

---

2. Tim Cresswell, *Place: A Short Introduction* (Oxford: Blackwell Publishing, 2004).
3. Stephen Pickard, *Theological Foundations for Collaborative Ministry* (Farnham, England; Burlington, Vermont: Ashgate Publishing Limited, 2009).
4. John Inge, *A Christian Theology of Place* (Aldershot, England; Burlington Vermont: Ashgate Publishing Limited, 2003), 11.

the fundamental experience for such a people is not one of living on the edge or at the margins. Rather, the fundamental experience is one of living at the point of intersection, the intersection of three great realities of our physical environment.[5] This constitutes one of the givens of our sense of place. The companion language to intersections is intervals and corridors. For example, the geography of the eastern seaboard of Australia (containing eighty per cent of the population) is an extensive land corridor from the tip of northern Australia to Melbourne in the South; a distance of over three thousand kilometres. This corridor is bounded by ocean to the east and the Great Dividing Range to the west, a distance usually no wider than one hundred kilometres. This is the matrix within which spiritual identity and life has to be crafted for the majority of Australians. It generates a 'coastal outlook' embodied architecturally in the veranda.[6]

When the focus of the church is on replication of the positive features of the former abode (that is, the mother country—wherever this is), albeit modified, the task of enculturation of Christianity is made more difficult. This difficulty was accentuated in Australia due to the harsh life of the penal colonies. As a result engagement with the place of habitation takes more energy and is costly. The reason is that it requires an exchange of a colonial preoccupation with the conquest of space, for a more relational approach to place.

The nature of antipodean geography has been highly significant for the identity and character of the Church I know best, the Anglican Church. Its history in Australia is an interesting example of the impact of place on the nature of a church. In Australia it has meant first, that the regionalism characteristic of the Anglican Church has been a major factor in the development of an independent diocesanism. This may be significantly influenced by place as much as any imported ecclesiastical party spirit. For example, the Church of England developed where the centres of population were established along the coast with access to resource rich hinterland and fresh water. Regionalism was a matter of survival. Second, the orientation of the coastal dwellers was outwards to the ocean, to home base, to England

---

5. Stephen Pickard, 'The View from the Verandah: Gospel and Spirituality in an Australian Setting', in *St Mark's Review*, Winter (1998): 4–10.
6. Phillip Drew, *The Coastal Dwellers: Australians Living on the Edge* (Ringwood: Penguin Books, 1994).

on another shore. Again, the strong links to the mother country were a matter of survival and comfort in a strange place. Significant links between these different regions were more difficult to sustain compared to perceived connections to origins abroad. Third, the continent was perceived as alien and strange by comparison with the place of origin. Under conditions of extreme isolation and alienated from home base 15,000 kilometres away, the most pressing need of the *quasi* 'established' Church of England, was to transplant as much as possible of that Church within the confines of the separated colonial settlements. Yet the process of transplanting is never simple; what results might be a 'highly distinctive variant' of the parent church.[7]

Nonetheless intentional creative adaptation was always going to be difficult, for the place itself was fundamentally alien and in need of charting, taming and ordering. Not only would this inevitably happen on a regional basis, it would also occur with as little disruption as possible to the inherited traditions of belief and worship. The fundamental need was reassurance and comfort in an alien environment. The Church was shaped by a sense of social, cultural and religious *dis-placement*. Its sense of place was construed negatively with a concomitant emphasis on creating a 'home away from home' to quell anxiety. By contrast in the different environment of Aotearoa New Zealand the emphasis was less one of response to an alien place, and more a question of relocation of home in a new place, minus the negative aspects of the mother country; in other words 'a better Britain'. However in both countries it is hard to overestimate the fact of dislocation of colonial life literally at the ends of the earth.

What the Church has been manifestly unable to do is develop an orientation and outlook more in keeping with the nature of the place. Whereas the inherited Georgian architecture had been modified by adding the veranda, this was not a significant feature of holy places of worship. Yet a 'church without walls'[8] resonates with the social geography of our place. The basic challenge for Anglicans in the antipodes is to become an outward looking and open community,

---

7. Pamela Welch, 'Constructing Colonial Christianities: With Particular Reference to Anglicanism in Australia c1850-1940', in *Journal of Religious History*, 32:2 (2008): 234.
8. Bruce Kaye, *A Church without Walls: Being Anglican in Australia* (North Blackburn: Dove Publications, 1995).

actively engaged with society and its concerns. This points suggestively to a veranda shaped church not only in architecture but in spirit and ethos.⁹ This picks up the Spanish meaning of '*varanda*' as 'rails to lean the breast on'; akin to a sympathetic spirit that inclines one towards the other. The veranda, like the place of our habitation, is a place of intersection between outer world and inner house. It is a corridor or interval, which catches the breeze; a safe and hospitable place, orientated outwards but mindful of the deeper recesses from within and from which it draws life. A church shaped in relation to this image feeds a notion of the church as an open sanctuary offering safety, nourishment and energy for work.

But the matter goes deeper. The recovery of a sense of place has implications for not only Anglicanism but Christianity more generally in relation to indigenous cultures in Australia. Indigenous peoples neither own, nor fill, nor colonise spaces. Rather they inhabit particular places. A Christian sensibility, fuelled by an incarnational theology, has resources to overcome the latent pressure of colonial conquest and recover a deeper sympathy with indigenous ways of community and gospel. Reconciliation will include a 'kenotic listening' by European diaspora (Anglo-Saxon and New Zealand pakeha) to the first inhabitants.[10] Indeed it is hard to conceive how we shall truly construct a 'home' church, without recovering something elemental about the body of Christ as a reality deeply rooted in the place of our habitation.

Amidst all the challenges for Christianity for those from the Antipodes, perhaps the critical issue is one of becoming dwellers in our own place; no longer merely creating a 'home away from home' but finding a different home with God in our part of the planet.[11] Reconciliation with the place of our habitation as a place loved by God is co-related to reconciliation with indigenous peoples. However, as I suggested at the beginning of this paper, 'place' is but one aspect of a renewed ecclesial presence and witness in this country. What

---

9. Stephen Pickard, 'Many Verandahs, Same House? Traditions and Challenges for Australian Anglicans', in *Journal of Anglican Studies*, 4/2 (2006): 177–200.
10. Matthew Brett, '*Canto ergo sum*: Indigenous Peoples and Postcolonial Theology', in *Pacifica*, 16 (2003): 247–256, 205.
11. John Martis, 'Living Away From Home—and Loving It: Tweaking a Christian Metaphor', in *Pacifica*, 15/2 (June 2002): 123–137.

about the *pace* of the place? The ecclesial complement to place is the dynamic concept of pace.

Recovering an Ecclesial Pace

It is a truism that 'nothing can be loved at speed'.[12] Nurturing good-quality friendships, suffering with another in trouble or pain, working patiently to see a dream or vision for a community realised, taking time to celebrate and laugh, attending to the welcomes and farewells of life, planting and watering seeds of new ideas, living with conflict while trying to harness it for good, working with others to effect change in church, society and politics, all requires perseverance, energy and time. We are called to enter into a 'longish moment', long enough for individuals and communities to listen to their souls, to feel the deeper impulses and questions, long enough 'for some of our demons to walk away'.[13] Good things do take time, but, however urgent we may feel the demands on our time, nonetheless 'hasten slowly', represents a greater wisdom than anxiety-driven church pragmatics. To my mind, what we need is to practice 'slow church' for an ancient land; we need a Christianity unfolding with the pace of the place.

With this in mind some years ago I was attracted to Carl Honoré's *In Praise of Slowness* (2005) which had the subtitle, 'Challenging the Cult of Speed'. Against a culture of 'everything faster', Honoré proposed 'slow is beautiful', the 'importance of being at rest', 'raising an unhurried child', 'the benefits of working less hard', 'doctors and patients' etc. The inside cover offered an apposite word from Gandhi, 'There is more to life than increasing its speed'. Not surprisingly the book is full of anecdotes about the consequences of living life at speed without developing the capacity to slow down. Honoré quotes from the 1996 novel *Slowness* by Milan Kundera, 'When things happen too fast, nobody can be certain about anything, about anything at all, not even about himself.'[14]

---

12. Michael Leunig, 'Another Way of Being' in *The Prayer Tree* (North Blackburn: Dove Collins, 1991).
13. Rowan Williams, *Writing in the Dust: Reflections on the 11 September and its Aftermath* (London: Hodder & Stoughton 2002), 81.
14. Carl Honoré, *In Praise of Slowness* (New York City: Harper Collins, 2005), 9.

For Honoré, fast and slow 'are shorthand for ways of being or philosophies of life. Fast is busy, controlling, aggressive, hurried, analytical, stressed, superficial, impatient, active, quantity-over-quality. Slow is the opposite: calm, careful, receptive, still, intuitive, unhurried, patient, reflective, quality–over–quantity.'[15] Slow was about connections real and meaningful with everyone and everything. The author noted the paradox that 'Slow does not always mean slow'. For example, doing a task in a slow manner can often yield faster results; a 'slow frame of mind' may be perfectly congruent with doing things quickly or dealing with significant stress. In short, the 'slow movement' is not a recipe for living at a snail's pace nor an attempt to turn the clock back with respect to technology to some imagined utopian past. For Honoré, the key word is *balance*. This includes learning to live at a speed appropriate for the occasion, and this in turn required a 'slow frame of mind'. Honoré's proposals point to the importance of developing a certain habit and character that gives strength and resilience; those necessary virtues that breed freedom to find an appropriate pace and presence in the world. Slow church, like the slow food movement, is local, fresh and organic. What would it look like for Christianity in Australia to recover an ecclesial life that was truly local, fresh and organic? A well placed and well-paced body on the journey.

Such a pace is extremely difficult to achieve given the considerable forces that thwart such endeavours. There are two basic defaults for the church which are hard to avoid in the prevailing competitive environment of late Western capitalism. On the one hand there is the church that has dropped out of the race, so to speak. It has become moribund with its feet firmly nailed to the floor boards of the house while the water rises. Such a church is no longer reading the signs of the times and remains locked in a steady-state condition. This occurs when the church recycles the habits and ways of the past without attention to the changing contexts. Such a church is dying or in a comatose state. It lacks resilience, determination and joy. For the most part, we inhabit a church culture, which appears at times wilfully blind to the precariousness of its situation and apparently content to remain on the well-worn paths of yesterday. Permanence, fixity and constancy are prized above all else.

---

15. Honoré, *Slowness*, 14.

One response to this-not-untypical situation is to react in the opposite direction. In this scenario, the church and especially its leaders, furtively begin the search for the program or action plan that will arrest decline, turn the ship around and rebuild the church. They slip into over-functioning and become exhausted or exhaust others. The diagnosis of the presenting ills of the church may be quite accurate. The problem arises in the recommended course of treatment. Unfortunately, the response to a dying church is anxiety and an overreaction that easily succumbs to the values of the host culture. The consumer, fast lane management approach, results and outcomes driven strategic plans operating within a competitive market driven culture, is the environment in which we live and move and have our being. It infiltrates the church's often admirable attempts to recover the energy and vitality of the gospel, engage people and be involved in mission for the sake of the kingdom.

The future church will have to find an alternative pace which is neither dead slow nor frenetic. This third way is the 'coming slow church', and it has echoes from an earlier period in the Christian tradition.[16] It can be found in the monastic slow which exemplified in its chequered history an 'extraordinary resilience and recuperative power' of Christian monasticism.[17] Bosch quotes from an earlier writer, Christopher Dawson, who stated that even if ninety-nine out of one hundred monasteries were burnt down and the monks killed or driven out, nonetheless,

> [t]he whole tradition could be reconstituted from the one survivor, and the desolate sites could be re-peopled by fresh supplies of monks who would take up again the broken tradition, following the same rule, singing the same liturgy, reading the same books and thinking the same thoughts as their predecessors.[18]

Bosch's comments are apposite. The monks knew that things took time, that instant gratification and a quick-fix mentality were an

---

16. Stephen Pickard, *Seeking the Church: An Introduction to Ecclesiology* (London: SCM Press, 2012), 210-39.
17. David Bosch, *Transforming Mission: Paradigm Shifts in Theology of Mission* (Maryknoll: Orbis Books, 1991), 230-36.
18. Bosch, *Transforming Mission*, 232.

illusion, and that an effort begun in one generation had to be carried on by generations yet to come, for theirs was a 'spirituality of the long haul' and not of instant success. Coupled with this was their refusal to write off the world as a lost cause or to propose neat, no-loose-ends answers to the problems of life, but rather to rebuild promptly, patiently and cheerfully, 'as if it were by some law of nature that the restoration came'.[19]

If slow church was the order of the day in an earlier era, is it relevant any longer? George Steiner, in his remarkable *tour de force* of Western culture in the twentieth century, gives the theme of slowness a much broader canvas.[20] In a celebrated final few paragraphs, Steiner speaks about the 'transitional circumstances' of our times. He proposes that we are a culture and a people who are in-between the old and the new, we are waiting in between. It is a place that is full of pain and the occasional glimmer of hope. Such a context requires, above all, patience and perseverance and a reticence for quick-fix solutions. At the end of his work, Steiner searches for a symbol to situate our times and the form of life it requires. He finishes his book thus:

> There is one particular day in Western history about which neither historical record nor myth nor Scripture make report. It is a Saturday. And it has become the longest of days. We know of that Good Friday which Christianity holds to have been that of the Cross. But the non-Christian, the atheist, knows of it as well. This is to say that he knows of the injustice, of the interminable suffering, of the waste, of the brute enigma of ending, which so largely make up not only the historical dimension of the human condition, but the everyday fabric of our personal lives. We know, ineluctably, of the pain, of the failure of love, of the solitude which are our history and private fate. We know also about Sunday. To the Christian that day signifies an intimation, both assured and precarious, both evident and beyond comprehension, of resurrection, of justice and a love that has conquered death. If we are non-Christians or non-believers, we know of Sunday in precisely analogous terms. We conceive of it as the day of liberation from inhumanity and servitude. We look to resolutions, be

---

19. Bosch, *Transforming Mission*, 232.
20. George Steiner, *Real Presences* (Chicago: University of Chicago Press, 1989), 231f.

> they therapeutic or political, be they social or messianic. The lineaments of that Sunday carry the name of hope (there is no word less de-constructible). But ours is the long day's journey of the Saturday. Between suffering and, aloneness, unutterable waste on the one hand and the dream of liberation, of rebirth on the other. In the face of the torture of a child, of the death of love which is Friday, even the greatest art and poetry are almost helpless. In the Utopia of the Sunday, the aesthetic will, presumably, no longer have logic or necessity. The apprehensions and figurations in the play of metaphysical imagining, in the poem and the music, which tell of pain and of hope, of the flesh which is said to taste of ash and of the spirit which is said to have the savour of fire, are always Sabbatarian. They have risen out of an immensity of waiting which is that of man [*sic*]. Without them, how could we be patient?

The waiting that Steiner speaks of is not passive. It is a cultivated waiting that brims full of vigour, life and resilience. It is a waiting, which does not glory in triumphalist claims nor ultimately does one get the sense of an infinite emptiness and uselessness. He recommends a hopeful waiting that breeds holy patience as the new life emerges from the old. But it is not an easy, comfortable waiting, how can it be amidst the endless round of pain and violence in this world? Thus he concludes: 'But ours is the long day's journey of the Saturday'. The slow of Holy Saturday becomes a paradigm for a culture in need of recovering its own humanity in the midst of our inhumanity to one another and the earth.

And to speak of Holy Saturday slow opens up into a consideration of the slow God. A slow God may appear at first sight a challenge. Indeed, a reading of the Gospels suggests a Jesus always on the move from one village to the next; up to Jerusalem, down by Galilee; on the borderlands between Judea and Samaria; at table, at parties, constant engagements, disputes, controversies, teaching, healing. Mark's Gospel is instructive in this respect, for here there is a note of urgency and movement in Jesus' ministry. It could be compressed into a few months. In this Gospel, Jesus is a man on a mission, and slow is not a word one would readily associate with his ministry at least according to Mark.

Yet, the gospels as a whole including Mark's gospel also record a Jesus who sought solitude, knew how to relax and refused to rush but appeared purposeful even as he moved about. We might say he inhabited the 'slow frame of mind', even in his active ministry. More particularly Jesus walked. His was a peripatetic ministry; quite normal for the time and hardly worth commenting on, except for the fact that this mode of travel all over the land provided the space and rhythm for his ministry of saving presence. The significance of Jesus walking is beautifully captured in the Emmaus road story of Luke's Gospel. The scene of companions on the road in conversation; gathering at the table, touched so deeply by Christ's presence that the only response they can imagine is to set off again on a return journey to Jerusalem to share the story. From the seedbed of such journeys with companions, Christian pilgrimage has gone to the ends of the earth.

The deeper significance of Jesus walking impressed itself upon the theologian Daniel Hardy:

> I woke one night with a strong sense of the power of Jesus walking. It wasn't theory; it wasn't theology or doctrine. He was walking, step by step through the land, and after every set of steps he met someone, stood by someone, one to one, and in some way touched and healed each one . . . God's presence is out-working among us in a low-key way [a code for slowness?], and we may not have been looking for so modest a way; as simple as the quality of Jesus' walking, the way people respond to him, the way he is present to them and the way they are deeply healed.[21]

Moreover, the healing that emerged in this pattern and pace of ministry constituted 'a powerful presence, which goes down to the depths, *surfaces slowly* and attracts a kind of healing'.[22] 'Jesus slow' indicates a particular kind of pace and presence that enables healing and transformation. It is embedded in his walking on the land in the company of others. In like fashion, the 'pilgrim who finds him-

---

21. Daniel W Hardy with Deborah Hardy Ford, Peter Ochs and David F Ford, *Wording a Radiance: Parting Conversations on God and the Church* (London: SCM Press, 2010), 80.
22. Hardy, *Wording a Radiance*, 81, my italics.

or herself walking–healing is not walking alone but together with the church.[23] It gives rise to the idea of a 'moving ecclesiology'; *'the wandering* ecclesia: *measured by Jesus' steps'*.

The slow of Jesus is remembered and celebrated in the Eucharist. Here is displayed and enacted through word and sacrament, the way of Jesus slow. Eucharist 'names the element of church practice that most clearly typifies the whole: the name *per se* of God's redemptive presence in the life of the Church ... [the Lord's Supper] ... is the pure primal event by which righteousness was constituted in Jesus' time, and it is fully recalled each time it is re-enacted'.[24] Participating in the risen life of the walking and healing, Jesus generates a thanksgiving on the part of the pilgrim. In terms of our reflections on slowness, the Eucharist may be understood as slow release energy giving rise to gratitude and praise. This is sufficient to carry the pilgrim through 'the long day's journey of the Saturday' in faith and hope and love.

Place and Pace in the Service of Presence

I have suggested that it is incumbent upon the church to recover its place and pace in the world. 'Slow church' is in fact a code for the recovery of an appropriate pace and rhythm. Place and pace are the twin co-ordinates for ecclesial presence. The church seeking its place has to operate at a pace that facilitates maximal ecclesial presence. When Christianity operates in the fast lane there is little prospect of the church taking root and developing a genuine inculturated presence. On the other hand, the church that is trapped within its own walls, sealed from the contemporary host culture becomes an irrelevant presence. In this latter case, the church is out of step with the times, most probably dead slow and certainly unable to mediate a genuine ecclesial presence.

The anxiety that attends the question of ecclesial presence interestingly presents itself through the rise of the quest for community. The language of community has become the default for those of the church who are desirous of recovering an ecclesial presence, which is authentic and faithful to the gospel of Jesus. Ecclesial presence has become a question of authentic Christian community. It might

---

23. Hardy, *Wording a Radiance*, 85.
24. Hardy, *Wording a Radiance*, 65.

even be possible to speak of an obsession with community or at least an obsessive fixation on creating community, often with little understanding of how this occurs and endures. Perhaps we need to slow the rush to community.

Church: Companions on the Way

My concern with the emphasis upon community as the mode through which we now make judgements regarding ecclesial presence is that community itself is easily colonised by host cultures and can quickly become the habitations of the 'like-minded' or as Peter Berger once called it, 'lifestyle enclaves'.[25] Community can function as rhetorical language that unintentionally masks a hermetically sealed, non-porous sociality, which trades on dualisms between the church and the world, an us-and-them notion, which has little if anything to do with the good news of the kingdom of God. Maybe, things are worse than we have thought and even the ideal of community is vacuous. The slow church coming may have to come from a quite particular place in a particular form, which is not antithetical to notions of community and presence but more foundational.

The idea of community may be made to bear too much weight for the being of the church, or rather there may be more originative modes of life, which provide the seedbed for the slow church coming. Prior to communitarian emphases, there is companionship as the form through which ecclesial presence is ignited and expands into full-orbed ecclesial practices. If you like, companionship is a bedrock condition without which the church cannot be the church. The key features of companionship– acknowledgement of otherness; capacity for self-reliance as a counter conformity; appreciation of other selves and our humanness; recognising and welcoming difference; the joy of the bonds of affection—are only what they are as time goes by, as we learn patience as persons, as we bump up against the imponderables, disappointments and failed expectations in relation to self and other selves. Companionship crafted in such dynamics of human life in the world can't be rushed; rather it has an emergent gift-like character that continually surprises and lures us towards each

---

25. Robert Belah, *Habits of the Heart: Individualism and Commitment in American Life* (Berkeley: University of California Press, 1985), 71–75.

other and God. Perhaps the slow church coming will be the kind of church which is formed and nurtured through intricate and complex webs of companionship. It will be a church which lives with a certain restraint and reserve regarding its own claims and temptations to self-promotion. This opens up possibilities for a deeper resonance with the muted colours, vastness of this continent and understatedness of our life in *Terra Australis*. The richness and potential of this place requires patient listening and sympathy for and a willingness to give up any claim to the place.

In my view the paradigm for a future Christianity in Australia is beautifully unfolded in the Emmaus Road story of Luke 24. Here place, pace and presence are woven together and what emerges are companions on the way from Jerusalem to Emmaus; from Emmaus back to Jerusalem; from Jerusalem to the ends of the earth. Companionship with the risen Lord, listening to the Word, breaking bread at table, sharing on the way the joy of the Lord; such are the ingredients of a travelling caravansary nurturing companionship, collecting pilgrims on the journey, sharing food, attentive to God and discovering the secrets of a life of praise. This is the coming church of the kingdom and it involves a radical re-placement of the church.

Forum for Theology in the World Vol 2 No 2/2015

6
Challenges and Prospects for Christianinity Down-Under—A Response to Stephen Pickard
Gerard Kelly

Stephen Pickard has offered a stimulating paper, which I am sure will raise questions for those who read and ponder it. It is not my intention to comment on everything in the paper, but rather to identify a few points that may focus a study of the paper. I will begin by commenting on the notion of place, then refer briefly to pace and finally say something about place and the Eucharist.

Place

As I was reflecting on the priority and importance of place, I found myself thinking about some of the earliest European artists in Australia. If you go to any of the major art galleries in Australia you can see early depictions of the landscape, but you know almost instinctively that something is wrong with them. While the flora and fauna look reasonably accurate the light is wrong. Apparently, it took a couple of generations before they could get the light right, and thereby show us what our land was really like. In other words, it took time for their senses to adjust to the world around them, but once they did, they captured this place extremely well.

Our Australian poets also have a heightened sense of place. If you think of some of the ballads of the early twentieth century you find stories of people learning to live with the land, to live in a particular place. There is even a good body of religious poetry that does this.[1]

---

1. See, for example, *Anthology of Australian Religious Poetry,* edited by Les A Murray (Melbourne: Collins Dove, 1986).

Of course, I am speaking of a generation that read poetry and learnt it by heart. Often it was easy to remember and it told the stories of their world. I think, for example, of someone like John O'Brien whose poems have a religious backdrop as they present life on the land. Surely, 'Said Hanrahan' is one of the best known poems from this era.[2] It is as though 'we'll all be rooned' is a phrase that has entered into our national lexicon. This was the way we came to terms with our place.

The point of mentioning art and poetry is to suggest that a way to become more alert to our place might be through the arts. Yet, we seem to have less of it now, especially since our society and churches have become more multicultural. Perhaps a single expression of this place and our relationship to it is no longer possible.

Stephen Pickard points out that the settlement of the Australian population predominantly around the coast shapes the national outlook. He uses this fact to suggest that we need an ecclesiology shaped by this geography—what he calls a veranda ecclesiology. This is an attractive proposition because it suggests a church that is a place of intersection between an outer world and an inner house. Perhaps another way of expressing this is to say that the church is to be a place of intersection between the geographical location and an inner, spiritual realm that has been nourished by the word of God and enlivened by the Spirit.

Theologically, this raises questions about a local church. I wish to identify two sets of issues. The first concerns the meaning of 'local' in our current situation. If we look at the earliest Christian witness we discover that churches grew up in different locations. So, Paul, for example, can refer to the church of God at Corinth or the church of God at Colossae, etc. Our situation is very different. Pickard rightly spoke of how the Anglican Church took shape in Australia and developed a local identity or identities. The same could be said for any of our churches. I referred earlier to the poetry of John O'Brien; it reflects an Irish Catholic Church taking shape in the interior of Australia. If I stay with my own Roman Catholic Church for a moment, the thing that characterises it here and now is that it is less and less an Irish Catholic Church, and has people from many other parts of the world. This takes particular shape for Maronite or

---

2. John O'Brien, *Around the Boree Log and Other Verses* (Sydney: Angus & Robertson, 1973), 80–83.

Melkite Catholics. These are true local churches, but they are very different from the Catholic Church of which I am a member. These people bring traditions and experiences of other places to this place. They have not brought a European expression of Christianity with them, but rather a Middle Eastern expression. How will they develop as they take root in this soil?

This is a question about the intersection of this place, Australia, with another place that has shaped them, Lebanon, Syria or elsewhere. It suggests that place is never simply the place where I am here and now; there are other places that shape our identity. So the bigger question is: how might there be an Australian Church? How might all of our Christian traditions from elsewhere become a church for this place? Our theologians and pastoral theologians have not yet thought this through with sufficient seriousness. Some might be hoping for one big Christian church that is uniquely Australian. For me the challenge will be whether or how the one Christian church will find a variety of expressions precisely because of the intersection with other places.

The second issue concerns the problem of isolationism and nationalism. Expressed in more careful theological language, it is the question of the relationship between a local church and the church spread throughout the world. There are examples of churches in recent times that became so caught up in their national identity (and we could think here of Nazi Germany or Apartheid South Africa) that they effectively ceased to be Christian. This suggests that the place or location of the church, which is central to the nature of the Christian church, is always in dialogue with something beyond itself. A strong sense of the local should not cut us off from the church in other places. In fact, it should contribute to the life of these other local churches.

Pace

Let me turn now to the second major issue raised by Pickard, namely pace. We can hear him making a plea that we dip into our Christian traditions. The monastic tradition seems particularly relevant here, because it can teach us something about the rhythm of life. It is important to consider rhythm quite broadly, so that we take account of annual, weekly and daily rhythms. The liturgy offers us these sorts of rhythms. The problem, of course, is that even if we follow a liturgical calendar we do not necessarily slow down. Here, I believe, we are called on to listen more carefully to those who are living the monastic life today. This, indeed, might be the specific gift they have for our times.

Eucharist and Place

A final point in this brief response concerns Pickard's concern that communities may become 'lifestyle enclaves'. His point is well made that companionship is a bedrock condition for the church to be church. However, I would also like to link this to the question of the Eucharist, which he addresses in a different context. In my own ecclesial tradition there has emerged in recent decades a close connection between Eucharist, communion and local church. In fact, it is common place today to speak of communion ecclesiology. This is both a Eucharistic ecclesiology and a baptismal ecclesiology. To speak of community here is really to speak of the church as a community of salvation.[3] This suggests that the community exists because the Saviour has gathered those who are scattered—to use the imagery of the early centuries in describing the Eucharistic assembly. They have not gathered because they are friends, although they may become friends. The Eucharistic community is not a self-selecting group, rather it is a group gathered by God. The very point of calling it a community of salvation is that it is the community of the baptised who have been drawn into life with God. It is a community where reconciliation is visible. The Spirit of the living God gathers together people marked by all the diversity of humanity—rich and poor, young and old, male and female, saint and sinner.[4] This diversity truly manifests the kingdom of God. If our gatherings for the Eucharist are self-selecting then we may not be much different to the Corinthians that Paul scolded for being riven by factions. The body of Christ is not discerned in such gatherings. The point of the Eucharistic

---

3. Gerard Kelly, 'Vatican II's Theology of *Communio*', *Proceedings of the Canon Law Society of Australia and New Zealand* (2014): 3–15.
4. Jean-Marie R Tillard, *L'Église locale: Ecclésiologie de communion et catholicité* (Paris: Édition du Cerf, 1995), 148–151.

gathering is that it is *not* a gathering of people who have a natural affinity. This is where we see the importance of place. The Eucharistic community is the place where the gospel of God—this gospel of reconciliation—is made real and visible. Perhaps we are losing the idea that the gathering for the Eucharist is a gathering in a particular place. Think of the many people these days who choose to abandon their own place for the sake of gathering with those with whom they feel more comfortable. This, in fact, may make the church invisible in that particular place.

7
Hunger Games: Addressing the Young Catholic Slide to the Periphery

Chris Duthie-Jung

Introduction

A truly fascinating episode in modern Catholic history has been unfolding ever since Jorge Mario Bergoglio first shunned the papal Prada shoes and stepped out onto the balcony at St Peter's as Pope Francis. Catholics and Christians of all denominations have watched in amazement as Francis has gone about his business showing, at times, near disregard for ingrained Church modes that were until recently beyond question. As a pastoral theologian with a particular concern for the plight of young Catholics, I share keenly in the prevailing optimism that we may just be witnessing the Spirit being given that long-awaited freedom to move in structure, pastoral application and even in doctrinal formulation.

And yet it is sobering to ponder how so much appreciation can attach to such minor steps forward, while, simultaneously, the Catholic Church in the developed world becomes all but bereft of its young people of European descent. Even as Catholic parishes all over Australia and New Zealand fail to function as spiritual homes for new generations, we find ourselves excited that some remarried divorcee Catholics may soon be permitted to re-join the communion line. While we as a Church community struggle to provide a Catholic education that results in active Christian discipleship, we find seemingly immense reassurance in the fact that the recent (2014) Synod on the Family could nearly (but not quite) say that there might be some goodness to be found in same-sex unions.

Without doubt, these movements are significant for they illustrate an ecclesial openness to dialogue that has, for many, seemed lacking in recent decades. But in terms of pastoral perspective are we striking a balance? Perhaps we can ask, for the average nineteen-year-old Catholic European Australian or New Zealander, does incremental ecclesial progress on communion eligibility and acknowledgement of same-sex commitment offer almost anything at all in terms of contemporary relevance to the world in which they live? Clearly such questions are not exclusive to Oceania and, equally clearly, they almost certainly carry more weight in Australia and New Zealand than among the Pacific Island inhabitants of Oceania. And yet if it is an ecclesial sense of purpose we seek here in this place, then the issue of today's young Catholics cannot be ignored. The recent book and film series, *The Hunger Games,* treated an enslaved and hungry humanity eventually led to freedom by a courageous young woman. The hunger addressed in this paper is of a different nature—the spiritual hunger faced by contemporary generations who are missing out on the Good News of Jesus Christ.

The context is in fact very broad for these are the children of the Catholic disappeared—the children of the children of Vatican II. Not only their parents but also their peers of other Christian mainstream denominations face a similar situation, that is steadily declining connection to the faith community we call church. In this paper I narrow the focus to a quite particular context—that of the young Pakeha[1] Catholic in New Zealand. How is faith to be experienced—transmitted to and lived by them in a very secular era? And yet this is anything but a micro issue today! It can be well argued that the present unrest in the Middle East and North Africa has to do with reaction to the excesses of western secularism. For this reason alone what follows has, I believe, implications for the macro discussion that is unfolding before us.

Faith Amid Secularity—*The New Zealand Study*

Four years ago I completed a study of the Catholic identity of a sample of young adult Pakeha Catholics in New Zealand.[2] All of the young

---

1. Used here to describe New Zealanders of European descent.
2. This paper draws heavily from my doctoral study and thesis. See Christopher Duthie-Jung, 'Faith Amid Secularity: A Critical Exploration of Catholic Religious Identity among Young Adult Pakeha Catholics in Aotearoa New Zealand.' DMin diss, Sydney College of Divinity, 2011, 69.

participants in my qualitative study opted to describe themselves as Catholic. Along with this nominal affiliation almost all demonstrated a strong sense of the presence of God, of the value and richness of symbol and image, and of the importance of issues of social justice.[3] In this regard they exhibited something of what can be called a Catholic religious world-view, although beyond these elements, everyday engagement in Catholic religious practice was noticeably missing. Most of the young participants exhibited embarrassment at their own inability to articulate an understanding of what they did recognise to be the central themes of Catholic faith.[4] For the great majority, their Catholic religious experience was characterised by uncertainty and a discomfort born of a sense of disconnection with the institutional Church. They had, it would seem, adapted their Catholic religious world-view to suit their own individual personal circumstances, a response which illustrates the individualism that has been found to characterise Gen Y.[5]

It may be helpful to distinguish at this point between (i) Catholic faith as a *personal belief system*, and (ii) the Catholic Church as an *institution*.[6] All of the young adults self-identified as Catholic and almost all willingly claimed and were proud of their Catholic faith. All readily accepted key beliefs although their interview responses indicated only a relatively superficial level of understanding.

The young adults were clearly less attached to institutional elements of Catholicism (that is, ritual participation, following of Catholic moral teaching, etc) than they were to the more familial/cultural aspects of being Catholic (that is, the belief that I am Catholic because I was raised and educated Catholic).[7] This was illustrated in their lack of regular church involvement and also in their desire to think and make moral decisions for themselves rather than automatically obeying Catholic Church teaching.[8] The

---

3. Duthie-Jung, 'Faith Amid Secularity', 72–5, 80.
4. Duthie-Jung, 'Faith Amid Secularity', 86–8.
5. Duthie-Jung, 'Faith Amid Secularity', 26 and 84–5.
6. The two are admittedly inseparable theologically but the point here is to address a difference that appears to exist between the young adults' personal perspective on Catholic faith and their relationship with the institutional Church in which that faith has traditionally been expressed.
7. Duthie-Jung, 'Faith Amid Secularity', 82–4.
8. Duthie-Jung, 'Faith Amid Secularity', 80–1.

nature of the Catholic identity observed was more akin to cultural affiliation than religious conviction and its strength varied from the almost completely disconnected majority through to those whose engagement was in fact quite comprehensive.[9] For the bulk of the sample in this study Catholic identity was largely superficial—apart from denominational terminology, it was a Catholic identity that was almost indistinguishable from what would be the expected Christian identity of their Protestant peers.[10] In fact, religious terminology aside, the evidence suggests that there was little difference from what one would realistically expect from any non-religious young adult 'person of good will.'[11]

In summary—while these young adult Pakeha Catholics generally did hold a Catholic religious world-view, it was a customised version and their sense of Catholic identity appeared, for the large part, quite weak.

A Failure of Religious Language

Roger Lenaers suggests that the *language* of the Church, so familiar and acceptable to Christians for over a thousand years, has steadily become a foreign language to the contemporary Western Christian. By 'language' Lenaers means the words and their combinations used and understood by a community as well as the systematic means of communicating ideas or feelings using signs, symbols, sounds, gestures, etc. with commonly understood meanings.[12] Language belongs to cultural groupings, some ethnically defined, but some also institutionally bounded including the different religions.

---

9. Duthie-Jung, 'Faith Amid Secularity', 58.
10. Duthie-Jung, 'Faith Amid Secularity', 89 and, for comparison with the international literature, Duthie-Jung, 'Faith Amid Secularity', 38–9.
11. This observation finds an interesting resonance with Charles Taylor's description of the Enlightenment shift toward Providential Deism. Taylor asserts that during the sixteenth and seventeenth centuries human flourishing became the key purpose of humanity's existence. With the fading of a sense of grace, of mystery and of a God-desired human transformation, God became a distant benefactor and it was but a short step from there to a position of exclusive humanism without need of God at all. See Charles Taylor, *A Secular Age* (Cambridge: Belknap Press, 2007), 221–34.
12. Roger Lenaers, *Nebuchadnezzar's Dream or the End of a Medieval Catholic Church* (Piscataway: Gorgias Press LLC, 2007), 6.

The Christian cultural group in its Western form has over the ages developed various means of expressing its collective thoughts and feelings: its own language in the narrow and broad sense of the word. It has formulated laws and creeds, shaped rituals and enforced them, built churches and monasteries, and decorated them. It has given expression to its conscious and unconscious ideas, expectations, fears, joys, certainties and doubts, in words and in images, in colours and in sounds.[13]

Grounded initially in the experiences and ideas of the early church, the language in which the gospel message was expressed evolved only slowly, reflective always, in Lenaers's opinion, of the surrounding dominant culture. With the advent of exclusive humanism in the sixteenth century and the subsequent rise of the modern sciences, the language that had served the church so well began to lose ground. Words and images began over time to shift in meaning while rituals, practices and rules gradually became obsolete.[14]

For the majority of people today, asserts Lenaers, religious language from bygone eras has become a dead language system understood only by those who are especially devoted to it. Although the Second Vatican Council did much to 'update' ecclesial belief and practice,[15] the institutional Catholic Church continues to struggle to confront the deeper acceptance of a changed world-view that must precede language and articulation. For Lenaers, the Church continues to express a medieval vision of the world, a world-view that has ceased to speak to contemporary generations.[16] While it can be reassuring to point to emerging expressions of religion and spirituality within (and without) Catholicism, Lenaers sees a more fundamental update as critically necessary before there can be any chance of truly addressing the cause of religious decline in the West.[17]

---

13. Lenaers, *Nebuchadnezzar's Dream*, 6.
14. One only has to reflect on the many examples that accompanied the Vatican II liturgical shift from Tridentine (Latin) to New Rites (vernacular).
15. See for example the Second Vatican Council Constitutions, *Lumen Gentium* and *Sacrosanctum Concilium*, in *The Documents of Vatican II*, edited by Walter M Abbott (London: Geoffrey Chapman, 1966).
16. Lenaers, *Nebuchadnezzar's Dream*, 9.
17. Lenaers is not alone in identifying ossifying religious structures, traditions and language as key to understanding religious decline. Variations on this idea are

It is not a prognosis that is easily accepted nor applied, as it necessarily entails a courageous modernisation that goes well beyond the reforms of Vatican II and will inevitably impact upon every aspect of Church life. Beginning with credal notions of who and what God is, so many beliefs and practices with origins in a now untenable medieval theological world-view face critique.[18] Theological issues such as atonement (sacrifice), worship (liturgy) and even trinitarian belief will need reviewing in light of a contemporary cosmological world-view. Kevin Treston proposes just such a critique outlining why, in his estimation, the current expression of the doctrine of original sin needs to be reviewed and at least reformulated.[19] For reasons of pastoral concern, accepted ecclesial practices such as a strictly hierarchical Church structure, exclusive gender roles and sacramental exclusion will subsequently require re-examination. Without doubt, a paradigm shift is occurring in (Western) society and to ignore the 'signs of the times' risks a gospel proclamation that is incomprehensible to contemporary generations.

In my doctoral thesis[20] I propose a pastoral ministry response with young Catholics that specifically aims to:
- facilitate an encounter with God;[21]
- emphasise relational incarnation;[22]
- recover the theology of sacrament;[23]

---

also developed in the following works: Gabriel Daly, 'Catholicism and Modernity', in *Journal of the American Academy of Religion,* 53/4 (1985), Robert A Ludwig, *Reconstructing Catholicism for a New Generation,* 2nd edition (Eugene: Wipf and Stock Publishers, 2000), and Gilles Routhier, 'From a Project of Adaptation to Re-founding: Working out a Guided Image of Mission in Secularised Societies', in *Secularity and the Gospel: Being Missionaries to Our Children,* edited by Ronald Rolheiser (New York: Crossroad, 2006), 151–67.

18. For treatment of these and related themes see: Richard Lennan, *Risking the Church* (Oxford: Oxford University Press, 2005). Pierre Hegy, *Wake Up, Lazarus!* (Bloomington: iUniverse, 2011).
19. Kevin Treston, 'Why the doctrine of Original Sin needs to be reviewed, or reformulated, or even discarded in its current form of expression', 2014, <http://www.catholica.com.au/gc1/kt/002_kt_print.php>. Accessed 2 November 2014.
20. Duthie-Jung, 'Faith Amid Secularity', 140-6.
21. The NZ Catholic Bishops' Conference, *The Catholic Education of School Age Children,* 2014, <http://tinyurl.com/nzcbc-cesac>. Accessed 3 November 2014.
22. Karl Rahner, *The Practice of Faith: A Handbook of Contemporary Spirituality* (London: SCM Press, 1985), 114–20.
23. Lieven Boeve, *God Interrupts History: Theology in a Time of Upheaval* (New York:

- locate the Church as a companion on the journey of life;[24]
- be optimistic toward secularity;[25]
- offer constructive critique of contemporary secularity.[26]

Each of these aims warrants significant development in its own right. In the remainder of this paper, however, I wish instead to explore some critically important underlying issues relating to the situation of the young adult Pakeha Catholic exodus.

The Call for Deeper Contextualisation

As the Western Church moves into the third millennium with fewer active young members, the need for a far-reaching response is increasingly being acknowledged. The apparent disconnect between young adult Catholics and their faith tradition may be symptomatic of a more extensive rupture between the Church and the contemporary Western population. The suggestion here is that the contextualisation of Catholic theology that is now needed is of such a magnitude that it may require a broadening of our understanding of the concept of 'contextualisation' itself in order to adequately encompass the extent of the changes needed in the very structure and language of the Church.[27] As Stephen Bevans notes,

> I think we can paraphrase Bouillard by saying that a theology that is not somehow reflective of our times, our culture, and our current concerns—and so contextual—is also false theology. Charles Kraft says practically the same thing when

---

Continuum, 2007), 96.
24. At the 1995 World Youth Day in the Philippines, Pope John Paul II called for the Church to become the travelling companion of the young as Jesus was with the disciples of Emmaus. The analogy is a good one in so far as the relationship takes place in the context of the young peoples' lived experience. Cf Luke 24:13–35.
25. See Ronald Rolheiser, *Secularity and the Gospel: Being Missionaries to Our Children* (New York: Crossroad, 2006), 41–3. Secularity is not to be confused with secularism—the former is a state in which religious and nonreligious views are permissible but none is considered pre-eminent. Secularism, on the other hand, finds it necessary to attempt to eliminate religion. See Pope Paul VI, *Evangelii Nuntiandi*, No 55.
26. Rolheiser, *Secularity and the Gospel*.
27. Lenaers, *Nebuchadnezzar's Dream*.

he says that theology, when it is perceived as irrelevant, is in fact irrelevant.[28]

Re-Imagining Ecclesial Structures

One such contextualisation is captured in Gilles Routhier's call for a 'paradigm shift' from adaptation to re-founding.[29] At a time when the Catholic Church faces a reduction in the financial and ministry resources it has at its disposal in Western countries, the Church faces the double danger of the risk of retreat into a reduced parish ministry base while, simultaneously, avoiding the necessity of mission to modern secular culture. Neither of these developments is an acceptable prospect for Christians who take seriously the mission call of the gospel.

> The pastoral situation we find ourselves in encourages the use of creativity and imagination to restructure our whole pastoral system and undertake total reform, something beyond a simple facelift or a replastering of a façade. It is time for rebuilding.[30]

Current Western parochial structures were established for the pastoral care of the faithful and today they find themselves burdened with the role of mission for which they are unsuitable. Mission came first and parish was established to nurture those who were evangelised. While adaptation of existing structures and approaches

---

28. Stephen Bevans, *Models of Contextual Theology* (Maryknoll: Orbis Books, 2005), 5.
29. Routhier, 'From a Project of Adaptation to Re-founding: Working out a Guided Image of Mission in Secularised Societies', 151–67. For more on this notion of re-founding see Gerald Arbuckle's extensive bibliography including: *Re-founding the Church: Dissent for Leadership* (Sydney: St Paul's Publications, 1993); *Culture, Inculturation and Theologians: A Postmodern Critique* (Collegeville: Liturgical Press, 2010); *Catholic Identity or Identities?: Re-founding Ministries in Chaotic Times* (Collegeville: Liturgical Press, 2013); and *The 'Francis Factor' and the People of God* (Maryknoll: Orbis Books, 2015). Arbuckle's more recent works look closely at culture and inculturation and call for a freeing-up of central control in Catholicism in order to begin to bridge the gap between gospel and culture. In the Church led by Pope Francis he sees this beginning to happen.
30. Routhier, 'From a Project of Adaptation to Re-founding: Working out a Guided Image of Mission in Secularised Societies', 160.

is encouraged to a certain degree in the Vatican II documents and more recently by Pope Francis, what is in fact now needed is a 're-founding' of the Christian experience—a move from restructuration to reinvention.[31] For Routhier, Vatican II did not go far enough in dispensing with outdated forms of Church practice. The renewal that began at the Council has slowed in the decades since and what is now urgently needed is a greater willingness to relinquish what it is in our structures and ministry that holds the Church back in the contemporary era.[32] As Routhier puts it, 'we are entering into a new stage in the history of Christianity in the West; we live in a new world, one in which the Church cannot simply dream of re-establishment, reconquest, or restoration.'[33] A focus on mission aligns well with Pope Francis' recent call for a 'whole Church missionary transformation.'[34] For Routhier however, it is creativity in mission that matters most—the envisioning and development of new modes of Catholic Christian activity in the community coupled with a move away from reliance on the parish as the basic model.[35]

---

31. Routhier analyses the Vatican II texts for occurrences of the notion of adaptation (sixty three in all) and notes that, just as the Church was revising its understanding of universality, two profoundly impacting historical phenomena were beginning to unfold—the decolonisation of the South and enveloping cultural change in the West. These two elements render the Council's encouragement of 'adaptation' as just a beginning—a recommendation to 'patch up' our old clothes. But, Routhier claims, the bishops could not have known how soon new clothes would become necessary. Routhier, 'From a Project of Adaptation to Re-founding: Working out a Guided Image of Mission in Secularised Societies', 153–6.
32. The debate over the continuity/discontinuity of Vatican II is crucial and will continue to shape theological reflection in the years ahead. For a recent treatment of this issue see Neil Ormerod, 'Vatican II: Continuity or Discontinuity? Toward an Ontology of Meaning', in *Theological Studies*, 71 (2010): 609–36.
33. Routhier, 'From a Project of Adaptation to Re-founding: Working out a Guided Image of Mission in Secularised Societies', 156.
34. Pope Francis, *Evangelii Gaudium*, 2013, <http://tinyurl.com/FrancisAEEG> Accessed 20 June 2015.
35. For more on this notion of re-founding see Gerard A. Arbuckle, *Re-founding the Church: Dissent for Leadership* (Sydney: St Paul's Publications, 1993). Arbuckle's most recent work looks more closely at culture and inculturation and calls strongly for a freeing up of central control in Catholicism in order to begin to bridge the gap between gospel and culture. See Gerard A Arbuckle, *Culture, Inculturation and Theologians: A Postmodern Critique* (Collegeville: Liturgical Press, 2010).

Experiential Renewal of Catholicism

In a similar vein, but going well beyond traditional ecclesial structures, Robert Ludwig makes a plea for the retrieval of the experiential base of all religion and especially Catholicism.[36] For Ludwig Catholicism needs reconstructing for a new era that is utterly different from that of preceding centuries. Today the context in which Catholicism must situate itself is the reality of global pluralism, democracy and individual self-determination.[37] Ludwig names four essential building blocks for the reconstructive process each centring on a different but related personal experience: the experience of Jesus, of grace, of sacramental community and of liberation. It is this 'experiential' element that is key, so much so, that Catholicism is described by Ludwig as being essentially an experience.

> It is the human experience informed and understood metaphorically by the experiences of others, stretching back two thousand years and beyond, and by the rich and diverse pattern of stories and symbols, practices and ideas, that interpret and hand on those experiences. It is *the experience of God*, the immense mystery that is both source and continuing context of everything that exists, informed and interpreted through the historical event and symbolic understandings of Jesus of Nazareth.[38]

This experiential base is of critical importance for younger generations for whom the passing on of faith by cultural means alone is no longer effective. The need to experience religion, to feel it resonate strongly with one's own life is essential for a new contextualisation of Catholic identity. A focus on the essentials of Catholicism is needed such that what is simply superstructure (the inculturations of previous cultures) can be let go of and what is infrastructure (essential meanings and belief) can be reframed and redescribed for new generations in terms they understand and can themselves own.[39]

---

36. Ludwig, *Reconstructing Catholicism*.
37. Ludwig, *Reconstructing Catholicism*, 60.
38. Ludwig, *Reconstructing Catholicism*, 59.
39. The debate over the role and significance of experience in Christian faith remains strong. Boeve calls the described process of reframing, 'recontextualisation' and it is this which he proposes must replace the method of 'correlation' in theology.

Catholicism and Modernity

Distinguished Augustinian theologian Gabriel Daly confronts the challenge of the relationship between Catholicism and modernity by contending that a vital way forward for Catholicism is the reappropriation of a reality that is usually subsumed under the imprecise label of the 'mystical'.[40] The reality he identifies is a perspective on the world that readily finds God mysteriously present in the cosmos rather than apart from and over against it. Catholic Christianity has focussed from its earliest centuries on the importance of defined theoretical explanation, but what is needed today is a new recognition of the importance of the pre-conceptual experience. As Daly puts it:

> I am merely observing that to conduct the engagement (with modernity) exclusively on the conceptual plane is to by-pass the primary interface between faith and culture. Secularisation is an undifferentiated experience before it is a conceptual threat to doctrinal tradition . . . The Catholic magisterium continues to think and act primarily on the conceptual plane, whereas the crisis is occurring primarily on the plane of the pre-conceptual experience.[41]

The crisis to which he refers is precisely the dilemma that has been uncovered in the *Faith Amid Secularity* study—a far-reaching disconnection between the contemporary Westerner and Christian faith practice. For Daly what is missing is the imaginative, the affective, and the intuitional, elements that need to be brought to the fore to operate alongside the discursive, the logical and the scientific. Even as Catholicism gradually abandons an innate defensiveness toward the explanatory power of modern science,[42] it must acknowledge the extent to which it has dealt with faith in recent centuries as if it were itself scientific. It is apparent in the research reported here that Western young adult Catholics find doctrinal formulas incomprehensible and their underlying images less and less

---

For a full discussion of his ideas see Boeve, *God Interrupts History: Theology in a Time of Upheaval*, 37–41.
40. Daly, 'Catholicism and Modernity.'
41. Daly, 'Catholicism and Modernity', 788–9.
42. Daly points to the 1907 condemnation of modernism as a basis for this claim.

convincing. What we are seeing is what Daly calls a 'linguistic collapse' within Catholicism, a growing inability to adequately name God coupled with a stubborn determination to maintain the definitions developed by our theological predecessors in a quite different age.[43] Speaking of an earlier era of unquestioned self-assurance, Daly says:

> They named not only with confidence but with abandon, and they have left us a heritage which both enriches us and embarrasses us. They have left us a game to be played as they played it, but we are no longer sure that we are playing on the same field, with the same ball, or under the same rules.[44]

It is not that doctrinal formulas have no cognitive role in the Church. Today, however, it has become critical to acknowledge the inadequacy of our doctrinal formulation to capture all that is important in the Christian faith. The spiritual hunger addressed in this chapter is largely the result of a failure to acknowledge this critical point and it is now vital that the Church more and more actively encourages the creative exploration of faith experience. Behind doctrine and formula lie experiences which, Daly notes, take precedence over them, experiences that are accessible in ways that go beyond the speculative intellect. 'The institutional Church may seek to control the formulas, but it has absolutely no control over the experiences from which they derive.'[45]

The experiences to which Daly refers are surely witness to the ongoing work of the Spirit. Daly's notion of the variety of experience of God's presence corresponds well with Charles Taylor's conviction that the currently recognised ways of being Catholic Christian are only the beginning of what is possible and what will inevitably unfold.[46] By limiting the legitimate expression of Catholic faith to past modes the Church risks failing to recognise new and creative possibilities of faith experience that resonate with contemporary generations.[47] To insist on a form of authoritarian heteronomy at a time when

---

43. Daly, 'Catholicism and Modernity', 792.
44. Daly, 'Catholicism and Modernity', 792.
45. Daly, 'Catholicism and Modernity', 788.
46. Taylor, *A Secular Age*, 504. See also Duthie-Jung, 'Faith Amid Secularity', 101.
47. The recent changes in the English liturgical texts illustrate this well. While liturgical creativity is tightly controlled, English-speaking Catholics now find the language they are required to pray with is cumbersome and outdated.

the limitations of its usefulness are unquestionably evident is to succumb, in Daly's words, to a 'Catholic form of fundamentalism.'[48] The cost of such a rear-guard defence of ecclesiastical magisterium is increasingly obvious in the disconnection the Church finds with modern generations, the large majority of whom cannot relate to the world-view and modes of operation and expression that continue to be required of Catholics.

The 'turn to the subject' that began with Descartes and became normative in the West with the Enlightenment started an inescapable process that can now be seen to require a rethinking of modern religion and, within it, Catholic Christianity. One hundred years ago George Tyrrell was already recognising the disconnect that has been highlighted in this study. Dismissed from the Jesuits and excommunicated as a Modernist, Tyrrell's observations are increasingly recognised as relevant to today's questions of meaning and modernity.[49] Somewhat prophetically he warns of the consequences if contemporary human experience of God is disregarded:

> [Our forefathers] knew nothing of that fatal discord which arises when religion is derived from outside and civilisation from inside. To their belief we must return in a better form, and derive both one and the other from God, but from God immanent in the spirit of man [sic]. Else we must expect to witness a steady advance of that alienation of the laity from the Church, of which there are manifest signs all round us.[50]

For Tyrrell the root of the problem was the steady closing off of the magisterium in his own time to the legitimate influence of the *sensus fidelium*, the people of God. It would seem that the call for deep-seated change is hardest to hear from within the relatively isolated confines of the institutional Church.[51] And yet the call today is increasingly

---

48. Daly, 'Catholicism and Modernity', 794. Heteronomy here refers to a world-view that holds our created world as subject to another world (heaven) where God lives.
49. For a recent collection of essays about Tyrrell and his thought see, *George Tyrrell and Catholic Modernism*, edited by Oliver P Rafferty (Dublin: Four Courts Press, 2010).
50. George Tyrrell, *Through Scylla and Charybdis: or The Old Theology and the New* (London: Longmans, Green, 1907), 383.
51. Speaking of the difficulty many Church leaders have in finding the positive in

difficult to avoid even though its demands are intensely challenging. It is not capitulation to religion-less secularity that is needed, but acknowledgement that the transcendent is to be encountered in secular as well as explicitly religious forms.[52] The Church is not to be equated to the kingdom of God in its entirety. Rather, it is the herald of a kingdom that is visible wherever people of good will treat each other and love and respect.

Concluding Comments

> The problem of secularisation is not the same as the problem of enlightenment. Enlightenment was of the few. Secularisation is of the many.[53]

With these words, historian Owen Chadwick pinpoints the immensity and swiftness of the current secularisation of Western society when compared with the much more gradual impact of the Enlightenment. The evidence suggests that the Catholic Church in New Zealand and Australia is experiencing the gradual detachment of its young people from active ecclesial involvement. Simultaneously, a general religious illiteracy has taken hold among young Catholics; unfamiliarity with the tradition that makes only the more remarkable their continuing desire to be called 'Catholic' at all. How long this will be maintained is impossible to estimate with any certainty.

---

the contemporary, Pope John XXIII's words as he opened the Second Vatican Council remain apt: 'In the daily exercise of our pastoral office, we sometimes have to listen, much to our regret, to voices of persons who, though burning with zeal, are not endowed with too much sense of discretion or measure. In these modern times they can see nothing but prevarication and ruin. They say that our era, in comparison with past eras, is getting worse, and they behave as though they had learned nothing from history, which is, none the less, the teacher of life. They behave as though at the time of former Councils everything was a full triumph for the Christian idea and life and for proper religious liberty. We feel we must disagree with those prophets of gloom, who are always forecasting disaster, as though the end of the world were at hand.'

52. Daly, 'Catholicism and Modernity', 794.
53. Owen Chadwick, *The Secularisation of the European Mind in the Nineteenth Century* (Cambridge: Cambridge University Press, 1975), 9.

A fundamental change has taken place running in parallel to post-Vatican II efforts to modernise Catholicism. My own and other research indicates that fear for the fate of one's soul can no longer be restored by the Church as a key method of motivation for faith practice.[54] The significant societal shift that has occurred has seen an embracing of the autonomy and subjectivity of the individual such that modern young adults in Western society are largely immune to the multifaceted aspects of coercion to which previous generations were susceptible. Moreover, their world is immense—a universe now acknowledged to be of unfathomable magnitude. The contemporary young person's search for God within that world renders them incapable of relating deeply and personally to limited monarchical images formed in, what is to them, the ancient past.

Whenever Catholics gather to ponder the situation of declining participation, there is inevitably a repeated call for the Church to 'listen to young people.' But is the Church really ready to listen? Reflecting on the proceedings of a relatively recent Fordham University conference entitled 'Twenty-Somethings and the Church: Lost?' Tom Beaudoin insightfully notes the following in his blog response.

> . . . deep listening is predicated on a willingness to be changed by the encounter, to have one's conceptions, even basic conceptions, revised by the other (as well as a trust that the other brings this same fundamental openness). This openness, as much literature on interreligious dialogue shows, is not a weakness or a bracketing of real difference, but rather the (litmus-test) for whether the truth of, in, and through the other can be acknowledged, and thus whether real hearing can happen.[55]

---

54. Duthie-Jung, 'Faith Amid Secularity', 88; John Fulton *et al*, *Young Catholics at the New Millennium: The Religion and Morality of Young Adults in Western Countries* (Dublin: University College Press, 2000); Dean Hoge *et al*, *Young Adult Catholics: Religion in the Culture of Choice* (Notre Dame: University of Notre Dame Press, 2001).
55. Tom Beaudoin, 'Twenty-Somethings and Catholicism: Reflections on the Fordham Conference', *America – The National Catholic Weekly*, In All Things group blog, 31 January 2011, <http://www.americamagazine.org/blog/entry.cfm?entry_id=3852>. Accessed 16 February 2011.

Beaudoin's point is that it is no longer of any use to describe as dialogue a situation in which one partner has no intention or ability to be open to change at a significant level. Meeting young adults 'where they are' is of little use if it is only to try to convince them why the Church is right about God, faith, church organisation, sex, justice, etc.[56] What is needed may in fact be beyond what is possible for the contemporary Catholic Church. In the leadership of Pope Francis we are witnessing signs of hope on an unprecedented scale. But the task remains formidable with so many key ecclesial leaders seemingly dead-set against it.

The contemporary Church must learn to acknowledge its own weaknesses and failings if it is to speak 'with' rather than 'at' today's younger generations. Courage is needed to admit that the Church does not understand everything and in fact has much to learn in a new era in human history. This humbling reality is what we must learn from the lesson of a disconnecting young adult membership. To engage the coming generation of adult Catholics requires of the Church a willingness to join them on their search for authenticity—a commitment that can only lead to a rediscovery of the Church's own authenticity as it seeks to announce the kingdom of God in a new epoch.[57]

> At that time the disciples came to Jesus and asked, 'Who is the greatest in the kingdom of heaven?' He called a child, whom he put among them, and said, 'Truly I tell you, unless you change and become like children, you will never enter the kingdom of heaven. Whoever becomes humble like this child is the greatest in the kingdom of heaven. Whoever welcomes one such child in my name welcomes me. If any of you put a stumbling block before one of these little ones who believe in me, it would be better for you if a great millstone were fastened around your neck and you were drowned in the depth of the sea' (Matthew 18:1-6).

---

56. Beaudoin, 'Twenty-Somethings and Catholicism.'
57. Cf Taylor, 'An Age of Authenticity,' in *A Secular Age*, 473–504.

Forum for Theology in the World Vol 2 No 2/2015

8
Creating Spaces between: Women and Mission in Oceania

Katharine Massam

Historians are fundamentally storytellers,[1] and this chapter offers two stories, one from the Pacific in recent times and one from Western Australia in the late nineteenth century. Each story deals bears on the question of women in mission, and the power of the space 'between' conventional categories. The discussion begins in the Pacific, moves through discussion by historians and others about the significance of place and space, picks up the nineteenth-century example from Western Australia, and then reflects briefly on the intersections in the material, or to put it another way, on the significance of the disrupted categories. In all there are four short sections in what follows.

The Visit of the Presbyterian Women's Missionary Union of Vanuatu

In November 2011, thirty-four members of the Presbyterian Women's Missionary Union of Vanuatu (PWMU) travelled to Melbourne to visit sites that were sacred to them. The trip had been a focus of fundraising concerts in Vila for three years, before the PWMU President Anne Kare proposed it to a Uniting Church in Australia

---

1. This view undercuts some assumptions about history as concerned with 'material facts' in relation to theology, but is mainstream in the discipline itself where interpretation of evidence ('facts') has always been a governing concern. See for example, Inga Clendinnen, *The History Question: Who Owns the Past?* (Melbourne: Black Inc, 2006); WK Hancock, *Professing History* (Sydney: Sydney University Press, 1976); Robert A Orsi, *Between Heaven and Earth: The Religious Worlds People Make and the Scholars Who Study Them* (Princeton: Princeton University Press, 2005).

(UCA) network of former missionaries to Vanuatu. The Australians were surprised and a bit perplexed. The practicalities of the visit were daunting and the aims unclear, but bound into this community by traditions of hospitality and also deep affection, they rallied their own network to host an extraordinary fortnight.

At the welcome in the auditorium of the UCA Centre for Theology and Ministry in Melbourne, a large portrait of Reverend John G Paton filled a section of the wall. In dark frock coat and carrying his top hat, the nineteenth-century dress of the famous 1840s missionary to the New Hebrides presided over the gathering. In stunning contrast, the women had given Island shirts and dresses to the local organisers, and they were themselves wearing their choir uniforms. This 'Island Dress' had been adopted in Paton's day, modelled on the pattern for children's rompers. The pattern proved practical however, and the now 'traditional' choir uniforms were claimed proudly by the women as a symbol of Presbyterian identity.

Also in contrast to the Tom Roberts painting, the next day the women unveiled a banner they had made. It shows two turtles approaching the island of Ambryn carrying traditional lamps. In this banner the women said, a traditional creation story was re-told in relation to the foundation of the Presbyterian Women's Missionary Union in the New Hebrides, and the two turtles represented the Presbyterian deaconesses from Victoria Miss Amy Skinner and Miss Catherine Ritchie who had made a crucial journey to the New Hebrides in 1944. It was to honour these two as their 'founding mothers', to hear their stories and to mark their graves that the Ni-Vanuatu women had come to Australia.

The banner named the enterprise as 'Returning Mission'.

In the opening ceremonies the following day, the visitors re-enacted the story of the Australian deaconesses. In 1944 after nearly a century of mission work in the New Hebrides, the Presbyterian Church in Australia resolved to send two deaconesses to explore ways to connect with the Pacific women. The metaphor was that in the same way as you need to fix an outrigger to a canoe to be able to steer it and make it stable, so the church needed the women if it was going to go anywhere. So Amy Skinner and Catherine Ritchie, who had both previously worked in Korea, travelled through the Pacific war zone, to visit and report. As a result in March 1945, Amy Skinner returned to Vila and began to network women already connected to the Uniting Church. As she reported to the *Missionary Chronicle*, the magazine for mission work within the Presbyterian Church:

> We really wanted to see whether or not the women would like some form of women's meeting. Seventeen women turned up when we rang the bell in the afternoon, and we initiated what I believe to be the first PWMU in the Islands.[2]

From that gathering the local structure of the PWMU went from strength to strength. And women set out in teams of three to visit villages across the whole network of islands, investing their time and energy generously. This was not always appreciated by the men who found there was plenty of other work to do also. A message sent to one party of missionary women on a village visit, said simply: 'Tell our wives to come home. We are tired.'[3]

The heavy work and low status of the Island women, and the Christian challenge to the idea that the wife came last in the family after the pig was often repeated in the missionaries' stories.

It is an example of what the intersectionality feminist and post-colonialist scholars have remarked on now for a decade.[4] the way in which religion can work within a set of mutually constituted categories of analysis so that belief intersects with gender, class, and race to open up discussion of 'identity', or make neat categories unstable. The power is in the 'between'. But the Returning Mission group did not comment directly on the impact of gender in their lives, or comment explicitly on the reasons the memory of Miss Skinner and Miss Ritchie drew them so strongly. Through the fortnight they gave concerts, talked about church structures, networked in Melbourne, avoided when they could the staggering escalators and other unfamiliar even frightening trappings of the industrial city, and marked the graves of Amy Skinner and Cath Ritchie in simple and moving ceremonies.

---

2. *The Missionary Chronicle*, 9 August 1945. Copy held at the Archives of the Uniting Church in Australia, Synod of Victoria and Tasmania.
3. Sheila Jamieson, Talk on Furlough, c1950. Papers of Sheila Jamieson.
4. Devon W Carbado, Kimberlé Williams Crenshaw, Vickie M Mays, and Barbara Tomlinson, 'Intersctionality: Mapping the Movements of a Theory', *Du Bois Review: Social Science Research on Race*, 10 (2013): 303–312.

On the last day of the visit, a copy of a newspaper article circulated quietly through the group. It concerned findings of combined task group from the United States and Australia that had heard shocking details of the level of violence against women in Pacific countries; including Vanuatu.[5] Our visitors were weighing luggage, piling into the bus, and promising to keep in touch. There was also talk about a wider conversation back in Vila about Women and Leadership. In the intersections, in the co-incidence, some of us thought that perhaps at last, we understood, why the memory of Amy Skinner and Cath Ritchie mattered so much.

We had also seen that there were places in Melbourne that were sacred for these women. Powerfully so, and sacred in a way that connects to wider discussion of sacred place more generally, as the second part of this paper will show.

Sacred Space and Place

Belden Lane is an American historian and theologian who has been working on sacred place since the 1990s.[6] He suggests there are four axioms that Christians and others might use in discussion of sacred place. In an overall context of sacred space as 'storied', as carrying memory, he offers the touchstones that such places are firstly not chosen, but instead choose us so that we notice or remember them. Second, they are ordinary sites, somehow made extraordinary perhaps by being approached in silence, or with a ritual sense; third, our awareness of their sacredness is not automatic, it cannot be predicted or guaranteed, it might vary from individual to individual or from day to day. Finally, sacred places do not just draw us in, but they also, perhaps after a time, send us out; they do not absorb us permanently, but refresh and reinvigorate us. Most of the stories of sacred place Lane offers are relatively simple: an awareness of being drawn in to a

---

5. *Sydney Morning Herald*, 21 November 2011.
6. Belden Lane, *Spirituality in Time and Place* (London: The Way, 1992); Belden Lane, *Landscapes of the Sacred: Geography and Narrative in American Spirituality* (Baltimore: Johns Hopkins University Press, 2002); Belden Lane, *The Solace of Fierce Landscapes Exploring Desert and Mountain Spirituality* (Oxford: Oxford University Press, 2007). <http://public.eblib.com/choice/publicfullrecord.aspx?p=716685>.

place that is sometimes quite familiar, certainly ordinary, somehow made distinct, and of being drawn in not to stay there, but to be changed, refreshed, restored, affirmed, sent out.[7]

The idea that Australia has such sacred places for non-Aboriginal Australians is one we have trouble with. Other papers in this collection describe our strong assumptions about being alien, and point to the unresolved history of invasion that means we have a 'tenuous psychic hold on the land'.[8] How do we belong? The reality is that for many Australians our heritage, or at least part of it, was 'brought here' transported like plants in a flower-pot, to form a complex mix.

Among several writers who urge us gently to explore this, David Malouf has argued for accepting this reality as a foundation for an authentic relationship with place. Both his novels and his social commentary show a strong interest in place and space. When he gave the Boyer Lectures for the Australian Broadcasting Corporation in 1998 he talked about the immigrant experience, shared by all non-Aboriginal Australians, and the complex mix of what was brought meeting what was already here. He offers an encouragement to acknowledge the reality that there is no alternative to the mix. He urges immigrant Australians to claim the local place, and to move from assumptions about transportation to assumptions about translation, moving between, claiming both.

> The belief we must make a choice [between heritages] is an illusion, and so, I would suggest, if we are to be whole, is the possibility of choosing.

It is our complex fate to be children of two worlds, to have two sources of being, two sides to our head. The desire for something simpler is a desire to be less than we are. Our answer on every occasion when we are offered the false choice between this and that, should be, 'Thank you, I'll take both.'[9]

---

7. His paradigmatic example at the beginning of *Landscapes of the Sacred*, 13–15, for example, is of an unexpected encounter with a deer in a familiar clearing.
8. James Paull, *An Ambivalent Ground: Re-Placing Australian Literature*, PhD thesis, University of New South Wales. English, Media, and Performing Arts, 2007.
9. David Malouf, *A Spirit of Play: The Making of Australian Consciousness* (Sydney: ABC Books, 1998). See also his more recent trilogy on related themes: *A First Place* (North Sydney: Random House, 2014); *The Writing Life* (North Sydney:

So rather than assuming faith is only 'transported' brought in pots, this is an invitation to consider how the heritage of faith can be read in the context around us, drawing on what we brought, and on what we find. It is not possible for the place not to make a difference. European stained glass lit up by the Australian sun is not the same thing as it was in the completely different light of Birmingham or Dublin.

This encouragement to claim the reality of connection to place also comes through the work of Peter Read. Read is perhaps best known in Australian history circles as the man that coined the phrase 'stolen generations', one of the founders of Link-Up, and the biographer of Charles Perkins,[10] so he is certainly not someone who would down play the importance of Aboriginality. But he is also vitally interested in questions of belonging for non-Aboriginal people here.[11] He warns Europeans in settler societies not to downplay the power of environment just because we are not Indigenous. We inherit a disrupted sense of place, one that is provisional and uncertain, perhaps, but nevertheless a sense of place. Read is opposed to Stanner's contention that 'white man got no dreaming' and insists instead that all Australians need to pay attention to the spirituality of place and our own response to that located sense of the sacred.[12]

It is in his 2003 book *Haunted Earth* that Read explores the question of inspirited place in non-Aboriginal Australia most intensively.[13] In one of a number of 'site visits' described in this work, he travelled to the former mission town of New Norcia in Western Australia, and canvassed the views of the monks who live in the place that has been the site of Christian liturgy in constant repetition since 1846.

Random House, 2014); and *Being There* (North Sydney: Random House 2015).

10. Peter Read and New South Wales Ministry of Aboriginal Affairs and Aboriginal Children's Research Project, *The Stolen Generations: The Removal of Aboriginal Children in New South Wales 1883 to 1969* (Sydney: Government Printer, 1982); Peter Read, *Charles Perkins: A Biography* (Ringwood: Penguin, 2001); also Peter Read, *Tripping Over Feathers: Scenes in the Life of Joy Janaka Wiradjuri Williams, a Narrative of the Stolen Generations* (Nedlands: University of Western Australia Press, 2009).
11. See his discussion especially in *Returning to Nothing: The Meaning of Lost Places* (Melbourne: Cambridge University Press, 1996).
12. Peter Read, *Belonging: Australians, Place and Aboriginal Ownership* (Cambridge: Cambridge University Press, 2000).
13. Peter Read, *Haunted earth* (Sydney: University of New South Wales Press, 2003).

Read was rather disappointed to find the Benedictines were generally unmoved and unromantic about place. But in his interview with Dom Placid Spearrit, the sixth abbot of the community, he finds both a detachment from place and a respect for the interconnectedness of the created order of God's world against the vast eschatological horizon.

On a short excursion to the dry creek bed that it a favoured place for prayer and meditation, the abbot succinctly re-framed the historian's questions.

> The country does not know I'm here, and conceptually that's important to me.
>
> Nor does the country change. Rather it changes me and changes itself at the same time. It's not bothered by me, nor are those galahs over there. Those trees just receive what they've been given, they don't try to change themselves... It's not the site, it's the view I get from there. I can stop just as well as look at the road trains going through the town. Let things be what they are. [14]

Does the phrase 'let the road train be the road train' have potential as a worthy catch-cry for the meditation movement, and perhaps Australian spirituality more generally?

The Aboriginal Telegraphists of New Norcia

New Norcia is a very particular place. If my first story was a relatively unproblematic mission story, the second one is more complex and also concerns intersections.

The broad outline of New Norcia's history as a mission settlement is relatively well known. In brief, the founder Rosendo Salvado established a Benedictine town in the 1840s with the hope that the Spanish monks and Aboriginal families would work the land together.[15] The mission enjoyed a reputation for success and local

---

14. *Haunted Earth*, 181, 183.
15. For example David Hutchison, *A town like no other: the living tradition of New Norcia* (South Fremantle: Fremantle Arts Centre Press, 1996).

Yued families remember Salvado as a friend of the Aboriginal people.[16] However, the twentieth-century story is more mute. To explore this, I will sketch to related two examples of Aboriginal women's work.

First, from the 1870s, and arguably at the high point of the mission's enterprise, the skilled work of Aboriginal women as telegraphists astonished colonial authorities. Mary Ellen Pangerian Cuper, Sarah Caruingo Ninak and Carmine Gnarbak, all managed the complex task of postmistress well. We know their names (and in the case of Mary Ellen and Sarah we have their photographs) because the postal authorities, and the government, and other missionaries, thought they were exceptional and requested their images.[17]

Salvado was proud of their achievements but resisted any celebration of these women as remarkable. He noted that Aboriginal Australians were often gifted; their capacity for intellectual work was, he said, simply like the capacity of fire to heat and to burn.[18]

Fifty years later, in a new century, under a different Benedictine leader, Aboriginal achievement at New Norcia continued to surprise the wider culture but in a much more conventional arena. As New Norcia's women and girls won local prizes for their embroidery and saw the work featured in national and international exhibitions, newspapers reported their 'almost unbelievable aptitude' for fancywork that would be 'the envy of cultured ladies'.[19] The tone was as astonished as the reports of amazing feats with Morse code, but expectations had narrowed considerably; the field of work was domestic and generally unpaid.

So, if we ask again what changed in this mission town from the later-nineteenth century to the mid-twentieth century, there are several things to notice, and once again it seems a matter of intersections and interconnections, not single causes and simple effects.

---

16. For example, the Aboriginal Corporation of New Norcia, Preface, in John H Smith, *Salvado 1814-2014* (New Norcia: Benedictine Community of New Norcia, 2014).
17. See Katharine Massam, 'The Spiritual and the Material: women and work in the Benedictine mission of New Norcia, 1860-1910', in *New Norcia Studies*, 22 (2015), forthcoming.
18. Rosendo Salvado, *1883 Report to Propaganda Fide*, translated by Stefano Girola, forthcoming 2015, working draft, mss 99.
19. For example, *West Australian,* 29 April 1885: 3; *Freeman's Journal,* 7 November 1891: 15, *Daily News,* 28 September 1891: 3.

Aboriginal agency is crucial: in essence the women withdrew their labour. Mary Ellen fell sick, and moved away for her health but died after a strange wasting illness. When Sarah also fell ill, Aboriginal opinion was against the role, and she and Carmine resigned.[20]

Second, the Aboriginal community was under greater pressure as European population increased dramatically with the gold-rush of the 1890s and pastoralism and agriculture stretched out.[21] A measles epidemic in the 1880s decimated New Norcia in particular, and after legislation in 1905 the proportion of children in town and being sent to the mission from elsewhere made institutional care a stronger focus. The separate world of New Norcia was much harder to maintain.

Third, Salvado's successors brought a more clerical mindset, perhaps a racialised one, to the mission.[22] They failed to see the work of the Aboriginal lay people at New Norcia. While they held to the Rule of Benedict that valued all work as equal, they did not take account of Benedict's insistence to pay close attention to the gifts and capacities of the all the people. There were no longer Aboriginal matrons at the girls' hostel as the local women were replaced by Spanish nuns, the Aboriginal choir director was replaced by a monk.[23]

As the theologian Timothy Gorringe says at the outset of his *Theology of the Built Environment*, 'to be human is to be placed',[24] bodies must be somewhere. The people of New Norcia found they were effectively displaced. They were not seen for who they were, the relationships that had been at the heart of creating the particular

---

20. *1883 Report to Propaganda Fide*, trans. Stefano Girola. Working draft. On avoidance of a place of death, see South West Aboriginal Land and Sea Council, John Host with Chris Owen, *'It's Still in My Heart, This is My Country: The Single Noongar Claim History* (Crawley: University of Western Australia Press, 2009).
21. Ian Esmond, 'Bush to building: the first Aboriginal cottages of New Norcia', in *New Norcia Studies*, 15 (2007): 14–33; Penelope Hetherington, *Settlers, Servants and Slaves: Aboriginal and European Children in Nineteenth-Century Western Australia* (Nedlands: University of Western Australia Press, 2002).
22. For more on the changes under New Norcia's second abbot see Katharine Massam, 'Cloistering the Mission: Abbot Torres and Changes at New Norcia, 1900–1910', in *Australasian Catholic Record*, 89 (2012):13–25.
23. Massam, 'Cloistering the Mission.'
24. Timothy Gorringe, *A Theology of the Built Environment: Justice, Empowerment, Redemption* (Cambridge: Cambridge University Press, 2002), 1.

sense of place dissolved. Aboriginal families protested that the town was no longer their home.[25]

The shift from Aboriginal workers in positions of responsibility being replaced by monks fostered a very different style of missionary work—less collaborative, and reflecting clerical and probably racial hierarchies. We can trace that change spatially—in the development of the cloister, in the definition of zones within the town, divided by neat new walls.[26] There was already an east-west axis that linked the first camp site to the monastery buildings across the river, running through the church and up to the cemetery. Whereas in the time of Salvado the women had had free access to the work areas of the monks—the butcher and the baker shops especially, now a north-south axis developed, broadly gendered, with women on the south, men on the north, the shop was moved to the edge of town and access to the monastery restricted. Both the permeable boundaries of Salvado's town and the walls of the later cloister speak metaphorically.

Themes of Intersection and the Power of 'Between'

Returning to the idea of 'between' and the significance of 'intersection', it is important to note there is a tension in Christianity between a sense of place and of placelessness; between God's place as 'here' or 'local' on the one hand, and 'beyond' or 'universal' on the other.[27] We have traditions of pilgrimage in which faithful people are both moving towards a future place, holy ground promised by God, and holding firmly to the presence of God-with-us in the particular circumstances of the journey, of being already on holy ground.

Part of this paradox, or intersection and even interconnectedness of opposites, is that just as we distinguish between *chronos* and *kairos* in terms of time, so there are two ways of understanding place in relation to God. The steady measured time of *chronos* and the elastic, clock stopping moments of revelation that are *karios* correspond to

---

25. George Shawto, the Chief Protector, 12 December 1910 and 28 April 1911, State Record Office of WA, 1911/ 0474; Jackamarra to the Chief Protector, 27 April 1911, State Record Office of WA, 1911/ 0474.
26. See Massam, 'Cloistering the Mission'.
27. Philip Sheldrake, *Spaces for the Sacred: Place, Memory and Identity* (London: SCM Press, 2001), 1–4.

the Greek concepts of place as *topos* and *khora*. *Topos* on the one hand about the map, the topography, and *chora* about the site of encounter, the space for being, the 'interval' between musical notes. The interval between two firmer points is where the new insight often appears. In the Vanuatu visit we sensed the creative edge of hope for a new way of addressing the questions of gender that might emerge through reclaiming memory.

In the New Norcia story we saw the collapse of the creative space occupied by the telegraphists as boundaries became ordered, conventional and tight; at the same time as the memory of their achievement and their own resistance to being categorised is inspiring. Awareness of the dichotomous thinking that limited the prospects for Aboriginal women, for other women defined as 'other', also invites us to consider the potential for dynamic interaction between other paired categories. Reflecting on these stories perhaps we can see more in the in-between of 'secular' and 'sacred', 'innovation' and 'tradition', 'world' and 'church' than we find in a firm dividing boundary. In the play between categories we might expect to find space for the unexpected.

9
The Dreaming and a Spirit of Place: Ancient Origins and Twenty-first Century Relevance

Kathleen Butler-McIlwrath

The Dreaming is widely acknowledged as the fundamental concept that underpins Aboriginal societies. It is therefore essential that any discussion claiming to be representative of Aboriginal perspectives include spirituality.[1] An open-minded appraisal reveals the continuity of The Dreaming in contemporary practices such as connection to place that is masked by a stubborn refusal by many academics to render the binary between traditional and contemporary thereby continuing the process through which 'Indigenous rights to country have been transformed into something called something called Aboriginal heritage—a past oriented discourse'.[2] In showing the continued relevance of the Dreaming and connection to place as an explanatory mechanism in Aboriginal cultures this chapter discusses the ways the term has been defined and identifies examples that reveal its contemporary relevance.

From the outset it is important to acknowledge that the term, 'Dreaming', is not of Aboriginal derivation *per se*, but an attempt by WEH Stanner to describe Aboriginal cosmologies. For some Aboriginal peoples this is problematic and they prefer to use the

---

1. C Baskin, 'Re-Generating Knowledge: Inclusive Education and Research', *Paper presented at the Annual Conference of the Canadian Indigenous and Native Studies Association*, 2002, 6, <http://www.eric.ed.gov/ERICWebPortal/custom/portlets/recordDetails/detailmini.jsp?_nfpb=true&_&ERICExtSearch_SearchValue_0=ED476849&ERICExtSearch_SearchType_0=no&accno=ED476849>. Accessed 26 June 2003.
2. S Hemming, *Managing cultures into the past*, 2005 p.5, viewed on 13 June 2014. <http://ehlt.flinders.edu.au/humanities/exchange/asri/ucl_symp_pdf/2005_UCL_SH.pdf>. Accessed 13 June 2014.

specific localised terms.³ Although I do use the localised terms where possible, the huge diversity among Aboriginal cultures necessitates recognition of this plurality.⁴ I am not opposed to using the Dreaming as a concept in my work, particularly where I am referring to general trends rather than specific examples.

Like many of the world's religions, Indigenous spiritual expressions in the Dreaming provide an understanding of the creation of the world. Within all Indigenous Australian cultures, there is some form of conscious creative action, by an entity which may be in the form of spirit, animal or human-like figure or interplay of a number of these.⁵ The Dreaming explains the formation of the landscape; the interconnected creation of animals and humans;⁶ the initial reasoning behind Indigenous law and the ramifications for transgressors; the complexities of the kinship system including the regulation of marriage; and affiliation to country and totem.

Broadly, it is now commonly acknowledged that Aboriginal people have significant links to land and alternative understandings of creation and beliefs in tabooed behaviours which, if compromised, can lead to physical and spiritual peril.⁷ Consistently absent from discussion however is the development of discourses, which recognise the subtleties, and specificity of Aboriginal beliefs.⁸ In presenting a homogenised pan-Aboriginal position, stories such as the Rainbow Serpent (a favourite resource of the infants and primary school system)

---

3. P Tripcony, 'Too Obvious to See: Aboriginal Spirituality and Cosmology', paper presented at the National Conference of the Australian Association of Religious Education, 1996, <http://www.oodgeroo.qut.edu.au/academic_resources/academicpape/tooobviousto.jsp>. Accessed 29 April 2013.
4. G Phillips, 'Relationships, Respect and Responsibility: Cultural Safety and Ensuring Quality Curriculum for Indigenous Health in Medical Education', *AUQF Engaging Communities*, 2005, <http://www.auqa.edu.au/auqf/2005/program/papers/session_a2.pdf>. Accessed 3 May 2014.
5. DB Rose, *Nourishing Terrains: Australian Aboriginal Views of Landscape and Wilderness* (Canberra: Australian Heritage Commission, 1996).
6. L Leonard, 'Designing a Virtual Reality: Nyungar Dreamtime Landscape Narrative', in *Fourth International Seminar of New Technologies of the International Master Program in Landscape Architecture*, 2003, 5-6, <http://www.masterla.de/conf/pdf/conf2003/63leonar.pdf>. Accessed 31 May 2011.
7. H Groome, *Teaching Aboriginal Studies Effectively* (Wentworth: Social Science Press 1994), 96–7.
8. G Partington, '"In Those Days it was Rough": Aboriginal and Torres Strait Islander History and Education', in G Partington, editor, *Perspectives on Aboriginal and Torres Strait Islander Education* (Katoomba: Social Science Press, 1998), 28.

are often presented as being the beliefs of the Aboriginal population as a whole.[9] This does not reflect the diversity of Aboriginal positions and tends to replicate models of Western monotheism, rather than Indigenous complexity.[10]

The Dreaming is a concept constructed as fluid in a temporal sense that is manifestly different to the hegemonic Judeo-Christian linear time that most people are familiar with. In contrast, the Dreaming refers to past, present and future. WEH Stanner's work is illuminative:

> The Dreaming, as an activity, is represented as a continuing highway between ancestral superman and living man, between life-givers and the life, the countries, the totems and totem-places they gave to living men, between subliminal reality and immediate reality, and between the There-and-Then of the beginnings of all things and relevances and the Here-and-Now of their continuations.[11]

This is a very important distinction as common sense wisdoms and many academic discourses confine Aboriginal spiritualities to static and primordial status as 'the archetype of a closed society'.[12] The many effects of this paradigm include a consistent judicial rejection of contemporary expressions of Aboriginal spirituality, particularly where 'traditions' have been modified due to contact with other cultures. The resultant denial of a number of Land Rights and Native Title claims has ensued from this.[13] Yet, from within an Aboriginal cosmology, additions and contestations over the telling and interpretation of the Dreaming are entirely consistent. The judicial error relies on yet another limiting binary that for the mainstream change is inevitable and desirable, while for Aboriginal people it reflects a diminished cultural authority.[14] Additionally,

---

9. L Leonard, 'Designing a Virtual Reality: Nyungar Dreamtime Landscape Narrative', in *Fourth International Seminar of New Technologies of the International Master Program in Landscape Architecture*, 2003, 4, <http://www.masterla.de/conf/pdf/conf2003/63leonar.pdf>. Accessed 31 May 2011.
10. K Butler, 'Overcoming Terra Nullius: Aboriginal Perspectives in Schools as a Site of Philosophical Struggle', in *Educational Philosophy and Theory*, 32/1 (2000).
11. WEH Stanner, *After the Dreaming* (Sydney: ABC Books, 1969), 6.
12. Partington, 'In Those Days', 28.
13. Partington, 'In Those Days', 28.
14. Hemming, *Managing Cultures*.

the Aboriginal perspective that actions and events rather than time inform knowledge needs to be understood with regard to a number of highly publicised Aboriginal struggles and helps to address the difficulties in understanding the ways in which the Dreaming has contemporary relevance.

Seen through an Aboriginal lens, The Dreaming is, as Wallaga Lake Elder Merv Penrith asserts,

> our identity as people. The cultural teaching and everything, that's part of our lives here . . . it's the understanding of what we have around us.[15]

Hughes claims:

> To understand the Dreaming you must live it. It is not possible to explain The Dreaming in a conference paper. But Indigenous people insist that The Dreaming is the centre and wellspring of their culture and social organisation.[16]

Herein lies a dilemma. How can Aboriginal and non-Aboriginal people have a dialogue about a concept that relates to everything but needs to be lived to be understood? From my experience, this can only be achieved if all participants are challenged to become *involved* in the Dreaming, to attempt to position themselves as actors, audience and interpreters as part of its continuity. As such, the understanding of Dreaming stories, related to physical manifestations of landscape and implications for Indigenous socio-cultural factors are crucial.

It is worth encouraging non-Aboriginal people to familiarise themselves with the Dreaming of their own areas and to prioritise this as an initial means of understanding the Indigenous cosmology of the areas in which they work. For example, it may therefore be more relevant for an early childhood teacher to know the creation story behind a river, mountain or plant that their students can physically interact with, as this is an integral part of the oral transmission.[17] I

---

15. Rose, *Nourishing Terrains*.
16. I Hughes, 'Ganma: Indigenous Knowledge for Reconciliation and Community Action', in *Action Research Report*, 2000, <http://www2.fhs.usyd.edu.au/arow/arer/pdf%20e-Report%20version/014.pdf>. Accessed 12 November 2010.
17. Leonard, 'Designing a Virtual Reality'.

am not suggesting that it is invalid for the stories of other areas to be told, nor that one must be physically located in country to participate in an oral culture. Non-Aboriginal people should be aware that the Aboriginal peoples with whom they interact could be from other areas, relating their spiritualities to those places not their immediate residential country. In contrast, peoples from other areas may adopt local custom or take on the role of 'custodial' participant in their place of residence.[18] Those involved in areas such as welfare and health should also be aware that disassociation from country or perceived damage to country can act as indicators of depression and ill health.[19]

Beyond this is the understanding that as non-Indigenous people engage with Aboriginal people they are also part of the ongoing Dreaming where their place may be construed as cultural participants or cultural impediments. This means listening to Dreaming stories and considering their historical, cultural and structural implications. In their performative aspect, Dreaming stories may take the form of what the West regards as the creative arts such as story, art, dance and song. There may also be a complex interplay between these, for example, a painting may be the result of group action under the direction of a senior lore person attempting to pass on a story where there is then a requirement to 'dance it into life'. As such creative artistic representations of the Dreaming and place occupy a central place in many representations.

This is not to say that the Dreaming cannot provide a narrative for the introduction of new material, but this is based on actual events not fantasy. Dreaming stories are still being created.[20] While Dreaming stories were once primarily localised cultural histories their multi-level functionality may now encompass a pan-Indigenous relevance as well. Stories of ancestors, of political struggle, sporting triumph, natural disaster, moving from past to present may all be part of the

---

18. A Vanderwyk, *Western Epistemology Versus Indigenous Knowing: Valuing Aboriginal Experience*, unpublished thesis, 2004, 60.
19. D Vicary and T Westerman, '"That's just the way he is": Some implications of Aboriginal mental health beliefs', in *Australian E-journal for the Advancement of Mental Health*, 3:3, 2004, <http://www.auseinet.com/journal/vol3iss3/vicarywesterman.pdf>. Accessed 27 October 2011.
20. ER Knudsen. *The Circle and the Spiral: A Study of Australian Aboriginal and New Zealand Maori Literature* (Amsterdam: Rodopi, 2004).

> 'Dreaming Narrative . . . employing the tenets, structure, and style of the ancient Dreamtime stories, [where] authors narrate personal experience, inverting and undermining the dominant, Anglo-Australian discourse while simultaneously rescuing a threatened Aboriginal heritage and constructing a modern definition of Aboriginal culture.[21]

Consider as an example, a short piece written by Oodgeroo Noonuccal. There is a story of a woman who wanted to find the stories of her people. Baiame told her to gather the burnt sticks from the campfires and the bark from the paperbark. With these she would make markings that would return the stories to the people.

> And when next the paperbark-trees filled the air with the scent of their sweet, honey smelling flowers, they took her into their tribe as one of their own, so that she would never again be without the paperbark she needed for her work. They called her Oodgeroo. And this is the story of how Oodgeroo found her way back into the old Dreamtime. Now she is happy, because she can always talk with the trees whenever she wants to. Time has lost his power over her because Baiame has made it so.[22]

As Oodgeroo herself commented many people assumed this was a recording of an ancient Dreaming story, but in fact it was an autobiographical vignette, describing the process by which Oodgeroo took on her name and identity as storyteller for her people, those of Stradbroke Island and beyond. It is her Dreaming, that she terms 'the new Dreamtime'.[23] People are often surprised to discover this is 'modern'. This alerts them to the potential that they unconsciously categorise narrative according to designations of past/present and truth/fiction, where Aboriginal narrative is automatically assigned the place of past and fiction.

---

21. K Crocker, 'The Dreamtime Narrative: Australian Aboriginal Women Writers, Oral Tradition and Personal Experience', in J Gifford and G Zezulka-Mailloux (editors), *Culture and the State: Disability Studies and Indigenous Studies*, 2003, 4 <http://www.arts.ualberta.ca/cms/>. Accessed 4 February 2009.
22. O Noonuccal, 'Recording the Cries of the People': Interview with Gerry Turcotte', in A Rutherford (editor) *Aboriginal Culture Today* (Sydney: Dangaroo Press-Kunapipi, 1988), 32.
23. Noonuccal, 'Recording the Cries', 31.

If I were going to tell the story in a way more consistent with a Western narrative I would say this:

Kath Walker was an Aboriginal woman of the Noonuccal people of what is now called Stradbroke Island. She became a national advocate of Aboriginal rights in the 1960's, travelling Australia raising awareness on behalf of organisations such as FACATSI and OPAL (One People of Australia League). Her key means of communicating was through her writing in which she used poetry as a particularly effective tool for making the mainstream aware of Indigenous issues and the racism that continued to impede the achievement of equity for Indigenous people. In 1988, Kath Walker, along with author Colin Johnson, decided to adopt Indigenous names that reflected their place of origin as part of their protest against the celebration of the Bicentennial of the landing of the First Fleet. At the suggestion of Pastor Don Brady that she call herself Paperbark as a designation of her position as an author, Kath Walker chose to become Oodgeroo Noonuccal—literally Paperbark of the Noonuccal people.[24] While her work was of national relevance it cannot be over emphasised that this name anchored her back spiritually to a specific place and people.

Among the 'common-sense wisdoms' that many non-Aboriginal people are able to recite with regard to Aboriginal culture, the position that 'Aboriginal people do not own the land it owns them' and 'the land is their mother' are commonly expressed. The full import of this does not seem to be comprehended and extends to a positioning of connection to country as a static tradition. As such Aboriginal people who move away from country become objects of pity or derision, as through either lens they become defined as having 'lost' their culture.[25] My position differs markedly from this. As Indigenous peoples have moved away from country through state coercion, economic deprivation and choice, they share with many diasporic populations the ability to conceive of a 'homeland' that exists in both temporal and sacred domains.

---

24. Noonuccal, 'Recording the Cries', 33.
25. Y Walker, 'Aboriginal Family Issues', *Family Matters*, 35, 1993, <http://www.aifs.gov.au/institute/pubs/fm1/fm35yw.html>. Accessed 19 August 2012.

Contextualised within the field of diaspora studies, Aboriginal continued beliefs despite physical dispersal should be recognised as a trait of cultural continuity not lessened authenticity. Just as it would not be correct to suggest to those of Semitic or Islamic faiths that their global dispersal negates their spirituality, the argument cannot be sustained against Indigenous peoples either. While the work by Indigenous academics encompassing diasporic spiritualities is growing it is still relatively small there is a larger body of resources in auto/biography[26], surveys for National Parks and Wildlife[27], children's books,[28] and multimedia that can be used.

Jackie Huggins, Rita Huggins and Jane Jacobs'[29] earlier discussed work that details a trip to Carnarvon Gorge shows an example. For Rita, it is a pilgrimage, a return to the country from which her family originates, which is as she poetically puts it, her 'born place'. The removal of her people, the Bidjara-Pitjara, during the hated Protection period placed her in decades' long physical separation from her country but did not sever her connectedness to the country. Rita says:

> I was a small child when we were taken from my born country. I only remember little of those times there but my memories are very precious to me. Most of my life has been spent away from my country . . . but I remember about the land I come from. It will always be home, the place I belong to.[30]

For Rita's daughter Jackie, the visit to Carnarvon Gorge is a first opportunity to walk her land, sharing the experience with her mother. It shows connectivity not gained by being born there, but by a multi-generational matrilineal belonging.

---

26. R Langford Ginibi, *My Bundjalung People* (St Lucia: University of Queensland Press, 1999). J Huggins, R Huggins, and J Jacobs, 'Kooramindanjie: Place and the Post-colonial', in *History Workshop Journal*, 39/1 (1995).
27. J Kijas, *Revival, Renewal and Return: Ray Kelly and the NSW Sites of Significance Survey* (Hurstville: Department of Environment and Conservation, 2005).
28. M Stone, 'Colonial and Post-Colonial Children's Literature: Australia', in P Hunt (editor), *Children's Literature: An Illustrated History* (Oxford: Oxford University Press, 1995), 332.
29. Huggins, Huggins, and Jacobs, 'Kooramindanjie.'
30. Huggins, Huggins, and Jacobs, 'Kooramindanjie', 232.

This was our place, my sense of becoming. The land of my mother and my maternal grandmother is my land too. It will be passed down to my children and successive generations, spiritually, in the manner that has been carried out for thousands of years.[31]

As another example, in *My Bundjalung People* Ruby Langford Ginibi[32] provides a story that combines belonging to country, creation Dreaming, diasporic transmission via orality and reconnection through kinship. The ability to retain a Bundjalung Dreaming within a distanced urban context is striking, with Ruby's descriptions of her son Nobby and her affirmation '[Bundjalung land] was his country but he'd never been here before'.[33] Nobby's sense of belonging and that of Ruby's other children comes from their exposure to oral history whilst growing up predominantly in Sydney. In making journeys back to Bundjalung country Ruby realigns herself with kin, not only at an individualistic level, but also as daughter, granddaughter and niece of others.

For Nobby, his initial acceptance at Box Ridge relies almost exclusively on his position as Ruby's son. Ruby introduces him to her elders and her contemporaries as Nunyars jarjum, or my child. She uses the same form of address in the out-of-country urban context, amongst a predominantly non-Bundjalung audience when opening his first art exhibition when she says 'Then I called out in my lingo, '*Balugan nunyars jarjum!* [Handsome young man my child] Welcome back to your Dreaming.'[34] The term Balugan or handsome young man is not purely descriptive. It is originally the name of a Bundjalung ancestor figure. Balugan's mother-in-law Dirrangun, was a clever woman, who because of her jealousy of Balugan suppressed the local water with her body. Eventually the force of the water caused a flow from both legs. In this way the Clarence and Richmond Rivers that are central to many Bundjalung Dreaming tracks were formed.[35] Significantly, Dreaming Tracks do not only relate to the movement of ancestor figures from what the West would term antiquity. They may

---

31. Huggins, Huggins, and Jacobs, 'Kooramindanjie', 243–4.
32. Langford Ginibi, *My Bundjalung People*, 106.
33. Langford Ginibi, *My Bundjalung People*, 106.
34. Langford Ginibi, *My Bundjalung People*, 160.
35. Langford Ginibi, *My Bundjalung People*, 7–8.

also be roads along which repetitive journeys or one journey of great significance, were made.[36]

Of the examples discussed on children making their first visit to their country, a consistent feature is that they are 'welcomed to country' by family members. It doesn't matter if, as with Nobby or Jackie, this occurs as an adult, they are entitled to welcome, to the public acknowledgement of his or her belonging; the introduction to country and kinship network in body and spirit and enfranchisement in kinship history. While today, these often occur without the stringent formality of ritual that many anthropologists would recognise, there is no doubt that they meet the core requirements of cultural continuity for Aboriginal people.

In a broader sense, the notion of 'Welcome to Country', expressed in a variety of ways, has formed an integral part of many Indigenous ceremonies for thousands of years. All areas of the continent have had large gatherings of different Indigenous groups. These gatherings served a number of purposes. First, they allowed for participation in ceremony for the purposes of required ritual, spiritual renewal, storytelling, and teaching of law.[37] Second, they were often related to abundant natural resources, particularly those that were seasonal. This meant that the local area could support large numbers of people without damaging the ecosystem. Third, although rarely acknowledged by the academy, they acted as a site for trade. Fourth, they allowed for the arrangement of intermarriage between groups and for the complexities of the kinship system to be continued.[38] A common feature of ceremony was the welcome and acknowledgement of participating groups. The spirits were also recognised, with the dual purpose of respect, but also to ask for protection to the participants from any malevolent spiritual forces.

In mainstream Australian institutional practice, the adoption of 'Welcome to Country' or 'Acknowledgement of Country' shows the dynamism of Indigenous cultures. An elder from the local country

---

36. P Baines, 'Seeking justice: Traditions of social action among Indigenous women in the south-west of Western Australia', in *Words and Silences: Aboriginal Women, Politics and Land*, edited by P Brock (Crows Nest: Allen and Unwin, 2000).
37. Rose, *Nourishing Terrains*.
38. T Dingle, *Aboriginal Economy* (Ringwood: McPhee Gribble/Penguin Books, 1988), 17–21.

generally performs a 'Welcome to Country'. Alternatively, a custodial elder, someone accepted by the local community as an elder whose country is elsewhere or designated person may be the speaker. As part of both these processes, the audience is given welcome to the area on behalf of the Aboriginal people, past and present. In an acknowledgement of country, respect is paid to the 'traditional owners' of the local area. Again, this acknowledges the past and present. The potential tokenism of this practice is discussed by Jane Haggis who recognises the practice of Welcome to Country being performed within the Academy but questions her own commitment to its deeper meaning.

> Having enacted such acknowledgements of Indigenous ownership on numerous occasions, I now experience a growing sense of ambivalence about my iteration of the protocol. I wonder what my words actually do? It seems to me that as I speak, I both reveal and disguise my complicity in a continuing colonising moment in the production of knowledge. Apart from paying respect to the prior and continuing presence of First Nations, I do not engage with the ways of knowing and being embedded in that Indigenous presence.[39]

Haggis' preoccupation here resonates with what I have noted where Welcome to Country occurs in wider settings, at formal gatherings, in schools or in public lectures and events. It is often used as an opportunity to teach about local history, but not to explicitly acknowledge that non-Indigenous people have just been included in an Indigenous cosmology. In not clearly giving voice to the import of this practice its power as both a spiritual experience and as a reconciliatory mechanism are undermined.

Non-Aboriginal people sometimes articulate that they have little knowledge about Aboriginal culture and no direct experience of it. Getting them to understand their place as participants in Indigenous culture through the continuity of Dreaming practice can give them

---

39. J Haggis, 'Thoughts on a politics of whiteness in a (never quite post) colonial country: abolitionism, essentialism and incommensurability', in *Whitening Race: Essays in Social and Cultural Criticism,* edited by A Moreton-Robinson (Canberra: AIATSIS, 2004), 48–49.

both a personal connection to Indigenous spirituality and the understanding of why Welcome to and Acknowledgement of Country is performed.

Spirituality embodied in the Dreaming is an integral element of Aboriginal cultures with Lyons arguing that for Indigenous people 'Spirituality is the highest form of politics'.[40] This chapter has shown that the Dreaming is indeed a politicised in many arenas. Secondly, it alerts us that historical revisionism is both possible and I would argue desirable. History, and our understandings of it, can be rethought from a perspective of distance and a broader data selection than might have been possible earlier. This holds as true for Indigenous specific issues, as for macro-agendas such as nationalism. The task of an inclusive National Dreaming is to find those stories that speak to multiple audiences according to shared values.

This National Dreaming cannot be exclusively limited to Indigenous participation and must have the potential to enfranchise a national reconciliatory position. A case in point is the Wave Hill Walkout, widely acknowledged as the beginning of the modern Land Rights movement.[41] Consistent with the national imaginary of the underdog, the Walkout of Gurindji people from Wave Hill, a cattle station owned by powerful British peer, Lord Vestey, posed the under-class struggle against the aristocracy and brought to international public attention the second-class citizenship of Indigenous Australians generally.[42] Further, the Wave Hill Walkout received support from 'ordinary decent Australians'[43] and can be linked to the foundational mythic tradition of Australian unionism, which provided both financial support for strikers and penalised Vestey's through the refusal of waterside workers to load beef from his stations at the docks.[44]

---

40. O Lyons, cited in M Stewart-Harawira, 'Cultural Studies, Indigenous Knowledge and Pedagogies of Hope', in *Policy Futures in Education*, 3/2 (2005): 155.
41. L Burney, 'Into the Light', *The Seventh Vincent Lingiari Memorial Lecture*, 2006, <http://freedomday.info/VLlectures/VLlecture7-LBurney.html>. Accessed 17 March 2009.
42. W Deane, 'Some Signposts from Daguragu', *The Inaugural Lingiari Lecture*, 1996, <http://freedomday.info/VLlectures/VLlecture1-WDEane.html>. Accessed 23 April 2004.
43. L Burney, 'Into the Light'.
44. L Burney, 'Into the Light', 16.

In the current debate on the crisis in Aboriginal communities, two paradigms on Aboriginal empowerment are advanced.[45] The first of these focuses on economic sustainability and an improvement of the Aboriginal statistical profile to one that is comparable to mainstream Australians. Identified as a 'Bread' discourse, this continues to empower the existing regimes of governmentality to improve their efficiency thus solving the Aboriginal problem. The second model for Aboriginal empowerment concerns the discourse of 'Freedom', that argues for the recognition of sovereign Aboriginal rights and the need for Aboriginal cultural autonomy to be central to any capacity building initiatives. The history of Aboriginal activism in Australia, which is exemplified in the Wave Hill Walkout recognises the centrality of Freedom within many Aboriginal agendas. The annual celebration of Wave Hill is aptly named Freedom Day.

Additionally, the return of Gurindji land also shows the intersection of two forms of law, Australian and Gurindji. As Kev Carmody's and Paul Kelly's song *From Little Things, Big Things Grow* concludes:

> That was the story of Vincent Lingiari
> But this is a story of something much more.
> How power and privilege cannot move a people
> Who know where they stand and stand in the law.[46]

Viewed through a lens of Indigeneity, as part of Gurindji law and Dreaming the hand back of Wave Hill forms a part of the specific story of Lingiari a 'Kadijeri man—the man in charge of the secret and chief male ceremony—of the Gurindji people'.[47] One of the best-recognised Australian photographs of the twentieth century shows Gough Whitlam pouring dirt into the hand of Vincent Lingiari incorporating the symbolic and actual return of land.[48] Lingiari's comment 'They took our country away from us, now they have

---

45. L Irabinna-Rigney, 'Bread versus Freedom: Treaty and the Stabilising of Indigenous Languages', *National Treaty Conference,* Canberra, 2002, <http://www.treatynow.org/conference.asp>. Accessed 12 September 2011.
46. Paul Kelly and Kev Carmody, *From Little Things Big Things Grow,* 1992, <http://unionsong.com/u036.html>. Accessed 7 February 2011.
47. Deane, 'Some Signposts'.
48. M Bishop, *Photograph of Gough Whitlam and Vincent Lingiari by Mervyn Bishop 1975,* 1975, <http://www.powerhousemuseum.com/collection/database/?irn=344580>. Accessed 15 May 2010.

brought it back ceremonially'[49] speaks to the importance of ceremony in processes of reconciliation and reparation.

It is from this basis that new dynamics of interaction can be developed as evidenced in the fortieth anniversary celebrations of the Walkout where Victor Lingiari, in a 're-enactment' with Gough Whitlam, reversed the power relations of the original image by pouring the dirt into Whitlam's hands. It is significant to note that the symbolism of this interaction requires both Aboriginal and non-Aboriginal participation. As a metaphor for reconciliation this strongly attests to the necessity of the process involving both the Aboriginal and non-Aboriginal in a way that is fluid, empowering and inclusionary.

The Gurindji and many other Aboriginal land rights claims can be linked to the intrinsic values of land as 'sacred'.[50] Even viewed through the dominant Judeo-Christian culture, the Aboriginal concern for the protection of sacred sites should resonate to a much greater degree than it seems to.[51] Far more readily there has been an eagerness within the public sphere to deny the continuity and importance of Aboriginal connections to land. For those Aboriginal claimants that succeed in the return of land or the cessation of land damaging practices of capital, there are accusations of being anti-progress and 'un-Australian'. In contrast, those who receive monetary compensation or who attempt to use land to allow for capital ventures that will generate economic self-sufficiency are branded fraudulent on a flawed conception that spiritual connection to land negates any other form of usage. The academy appears to have had a greater vested interest in furnishing 'experts' to adjudicate on the authenticity of Aboriginal land claims than addressing the no-win situation that Aboriginal claimants are subjected to. The promotion of understanding within both the academy and public sphere is paramount for the future.

---

49. Deane, 'Some Signposts.'
50. H Wooten, 'Resolving disputes over Aboriginal sacred sites: some experiences in the 1990s', in *Negotiating the Sacred: Blasphemy and Sacrilege in Multicultural Society*, edited by EB Coleman and K White (Canberra: Australian National University, E Press, 2006).
51. *Andronicus*, 16, 2003, 254.

The current interest in debate regarding an inclusive Australia offers a significant space for giving voice to those groups previously marginalised from nationalist tropes. The ongoing Dreaming and connection to country intersects with the Dreaming of repatriated country and cultural recognition for Indigenous peoples and mainstream Australian traditions seeking a socially just society. This stands in stark contrast to the model of 'progress' in the celebration of national history where the Indigenous presence is primarily at the beginning, moving in a linear progression through the colonial period to the present. If however, we can celebrate the Indigenous and non-Indigenous as concurrent, Indigeneity could begin to assume its rightful place as integral part of the national imagination. Mick Dodson described the possibility as follows:

> We have extended our hand to other Australians. Those Australians who take our hand are those who dare to dream of an Australia that could be. In true reconciliation, through the remembering, the grieving and the healing, we become as one in the dreaming [sic] of this land. [52]

---

52. P Dodson, cited in Australian Museum. 'Reconciliation: Towards the Future', *Social Justice*, 2004, viewed on 2 March 2014 http://www.dreamtime.net.au/indigenous/social.cfm.

10
'They asked for bread and you gave them a stone, for fish a snake': The Future of Worship in Oceania

Gerard Moore

What underpinning principles of worship did the missionaries introduce to the peoples of Oceania? Were these bread or stone, fish or snake? There is a sense that they were bread and fish, given the power of worship in these lands and islands, and the ongoing centrality of liturgy to the lives of many communities. Yet they also were stone in some communities and snake in others. General patterns are hard to pin down, as the variety of cultures, in multiple ways, absorbed the Christian principles and integrated them into their cultural framing. Along with this is the constant of change. The communities and peoples of the South Pacific have and are undergoing change, and with they are reinterpreting their worship in new ways and under new paradigms. What then is the future of worship in Oceania?

In taking up this question the chapter has a broad remit, and will make sweeping statements. The intention is to open up the debate, while reflecting on the effect on peoples and cultures, of liturgical and theological principles which have been imposed without regard to the contextual and sometimes indigenous roots of those principles.[1]

---

1. An early explanatory note is required here. Many of the examples that follow come from conversations, discussions and observations with men and women from Oceania, missionaries from the first world, and my own experiences and theological reflections. Little of this is documented, though when this work has been presented, the Oceania members of the audiences have been in agreement with the lines of approach and have recognised the patterns and problems. Given the unpublished nature of much of what will be said, there will be few footnotes across the paper. I have also resisted the temptation, in most cases, of drawing parallels between some of the points being made and similar situations that have arisen across the breadth of Christian history. Though there are many, they mainly serve to show how narrow was the sense of Christianity introduced by the missionaries.

And with this come some dangers, more easily named than avoided. Is the paper driven by the author's self-interest, by questions I am interested in but which are written onto the canvas of Oceania and seen as indigenous problems. Can such a re-colonising be avoided? The diversity of culture and language and land-form across Oceania and Australia is vast, so as already stated there will be some sweeping generalisations paired with particular anecdotes paired with sweeping statements, necessarily made with a small broom!

Three Sub-cutaneous 'Heresies'

The missionaries to Oceania brought with them the out-workings of three long and multifaceted theological debates that had traction in almost every aspect of ecclesial life. The results were orthodoxies that were virtually unassailable, yet in fact closely approximated 'heresies.' Unsurprisingly, one was around the scriptures, another around the sacraments; the first more at home in the trunks of Protestant missionaries, the second in the satchels of their Catholic counterparts. The third is concerned with tradition. I will deal with issues around the scriptures and sacraments before turning to the question of tradition.

Stone and Snake: The Scriptures as 'Bible'

The heretical prospect around the scriptures lies in the ability of ministers and churches to reduce the living Word, who is Christ, to the words of the Hebrew Bible/Old Testament and New Testament texts.[2] The living Word and these words are inextricably united, but the priority lies with the risen Christ. In this, the sacred texts are a 'sacrament' of the Word, and indeed a necessary sacrament. The reduction of the Word of God to the word of the sacred texts also loses sight of the ways in which the sacred texts themselves point beyond words themselves and apply language as an analogous concept. Here it is worth noting Psalm 19:4 which sings of the 'silence' and 'speechlessness' in which creation speaks words of praise.

---

2. For an extended discussion see Charles Sherlock, *Words and the Word: Case Studies in Using Scripture* (Eugene: Wipf and Stock, 2013), 17–21.

What then is lost when the Word of God is known through the prism of script and bible? This is one question in European context, but another in Pacific indigenous contexts. It is worth examining our common language. The Word of God is a script/ure, an en/scripted piece, something written. This is effective and intelligible in cultures where writing is a commonplace and essential aspect of society and culture. Not that in such societies all can read and write, but it is enough that officials in government, business and religious sites can keep records and hold transactions and agreements as scripts. Consequently, education is closely associated with learning to read and write, and becoming familiar with the literature. What is forgotten is that there is nothing inherent in the metaphor of 'word', far less divine 'Word', that presupposes 'script'. The primary repository of Word is not script, which is visual, but actualising memory, which is oral and corporeal, held in communities of narrative, dance, song and dreams. The European missionaries to the regions of Oceania did not bring an oral tradition but a written tradition. As a Fijian woman, Ini Foiakau, reminded when commenting on a version of this paper, there is a saying in the Pacific that the missionaries came with a pen! To engage with the peoples the missionaries had to impose a new form of the transmission of knowledge, while reverting to oral forms only as a lesser option. The indigenous peoples had then to take up a new way to authorise knowledge—reading—while leaving the oral practices on the margins of emerging Christian identity.

This predominance of script was exacerbated by the production of the scriptures as a 'biblio', a book, with the helpful connotation to being a library of books. In and of themselves, books are primary artefacts of Western culture, never more so than after the invention of the printing press. To bring a book to Tonga, Samoa, Parramatta was to bring a quintessential reminder of the differences between European and Indigenous societies, showcasing the superiority of the one while reminding all that access to knowledge was restricted to the 'educated.' Further the nature of the bible as book, as cultural artefact, also reduced the bible to being one book amongst other books—books of law, science, military and naval tactics, and literature—that dominated the societies of the South Pacific and Australasia.

Efforts were made to ameliorate this relegation of the Bible to one amongst other imposed books through the process of translation, but this remained within the paradigm of the word of God being held in a book, and unlocked only by those who could read. Indigenous ministers, as leaders in faith, necessarily became leaders in literacy. They also became alternate sources of authority and power in the community, and open to collusion with the intruders and their imperial ambitions. In some situations a counterbalance between the emerging power of the ministers and the threatened power of the regnant leaders was set in place through the process of translation itself. For example, particular languages differentiated between the speech of nobles and that of others. Which form was the most appropriate for the scriptures? Choices by translators could reinforce the 'divine' claims of the nobility. Theologically there still remains the question of whether it does honour to God to translate the scriptures into the language of the ordinary people. According to Tongan minister Rev Kamaloni Tu'iono from a student essay in 2006: *In Tonga there are some special languages which are only used for the King. So when all the Psalms were translated into the Tongan bible, the translators used the kingly language: in such a way as to express our respect for God.* There is some irony here. The question of the necessary nobility of liturgical language has a long tradition, with discussions by Lactantius (240–320) and then Hilary of Poitiers (300–368), who opines that a beautiful and dignified style gives honour to God.[3] Yet the biblical authors themselves do not use classical Greek, but rather the common Greek of the empire. And were the psalms written by David the king, or David the poet or even in the language of the royal court?[4]

The presentation of the Word of God as a western script, albeit translated, led to Christians prizing the written text over oral tradition. It was easy, and perhaps a missional strategy, to denigrate indigenous ways of knowing, a method that had successfully transmitted knowledge/law for centuries through the range of means available to oral traditions, and yet now was treated as inferior. It could no longer

---

3. The development of a sacral liturgical language is taken up in Christine Mohrmann, *Liturgical Latin: Its Origins and Character* (Washington: Catholic University of America Press, 1957), 30–59. For Hilary see 49.
4. It is difficult to see the lament psalms as composed in the language of the royal court; however Psalm 21, with its references to the coronation of the king, may well be composed within a courtly register.

match the 'book', nor the overwhelming technologies and superior power of the cultures that had books.

This fixation with the bible as the sole source of revelation meant there was little missionary interest in evaluating local custom and belief for signs of the ongoing presence of the Spirit. Theologically this excluded indigenous culture and faith from contributing to the interpretation of revelation, impoverishing the breadth of current Christian thought and understanding. It also means that the Word of God has been unable to dialogue with deeper layers of indigenous thought, layers which remain at play in the culture and are only accessible through oral tradition. With this in mind we turn to the second of our 'heresies.'

Stone and Snake: The Sacraments as Fixed

Prominent in the theology and practice of the missionaries was that the number of sacraments was fixed, whether at two or seven, and that the sacramental economy was a completed system, biblically warranted, under ecclesial discipline, and able to be imposed in any place and time. It was a sacramental system whose roots in the sacramentality of creation, the incarnation, and the ongoing mystery of grace as revealed in the Spirit had been obscured. The Catholic missionaries brought their ritual books, and were preoccupied with the post-Tridentine obsessions with validity and uniformity. In parallel, Protestant missionaries carried the Bible, worship texts and hymn books, themselves pillars of right worship.

What was lost sight of with this wholesale importation of ritual forms and expectations was the sacramentality of faith itself. This sacramentality has a number of pre-suppositions which can be set out as follows. The number of sacraments is not closed. New sacraments may be required, while present ones may fall into disuse. The language of sacramentality is ritual, however it only remains a living and viable language as long as it facilitates cultural engagement. In this, each culture is a sacramental expression of humanity in grace. Sacraments acquire their ecclesial authority when they arise out of a community of critical practice.

There are profound expressions of sacramentality across Oceania. There is the religious and cultural importance of the woven mats of the South Pacific, which mark significant milestones in life, belonging and death. Mats of different types and quality are used on specific occasions, particularly the much prized 'fine' mats. The work of the women mat weavers is not merely decorative, but rather speaks into the life situations they commemorate, defines the participants, and allows for particular ritual engagement, all the while rendering the space sacred. Setting mats in place for worship is far different from carpeting the church or sweeping the vestry. The mats establish and define the space, and in turn offer belonging and a place for all while bringing an element of critique. As cultural creations they also have a devotional layer in the way they are produced by the women. However once used to define Christian ritual space they take on aspects of sacramentality, and without them worship is severely deficient since the worship space remains undefined and from a cultural perspective foreign. Mats have a significant place in establishing community meetings, rituals of reconciliation, marriage rites, and funerals.

Another expression of sacramentality is 'land'. For many of the cultures and peoples of Oceania, the land itself is demarcated and often sacred. This takes a range of forms, and there is no single constant construct of the meaning of land. However we can be sure that the Western notion of land as a form of property which can be owned, alienated and sold has little validity. Two cases give evidence of the centrality of land, and the diversity of meanings.

One emerges out of the chaos of the rebellion in Bougainville (1989–99). The rebellion itself erupted out of grievances around the Rio-Tinto-run Panguna copper mine, described as a hole six kilometres wide and four kilometres deep.[5] At the centre was that the mountain 'disappeared', and the compensation was adjudged as inadequate. Yet the compensation was always going to be insufficient, since what was lost, this piece of earth that was owned by people, was their past, their present and their future. It also symbolised the potential for any piece of land to be alienated from its longstanding owners. One feature of the ten-year rebellion was the burning of churches. This was commonly blamed on inter-denominational strife and there is some sense to this. But another feature was that the

---

5. For some background see Anouk Ride, 'The Rebel Peace,' *New Internationalist*, 1 April 1999 <http://newint.org/features/1999/04/01/png/#sthash.6ZlCRQWK.dpuf>.

missionary churches had bought and built on land that 'belonged' to others, and was an inalienable possession. The troubles allowed an opportunity for families to regain their land, and reaffirm their future. In terms of worship, there needs to be an ongoing negotiation with the culture as to where is the appropriate place for worship, and who has proprietary over the space. Is it possible to worship on land wrongly acquired? Does it give honour to God when people are faced with worshipping on land that now belongs to the church, but which the people feel still remains part of their own God-given patrimony?

A second view of 'land' reflects more directly the sacramentality of land itself. Australian indigenous peoples understand land as the central locus of religious identity. The spiritual powers that shaped the land and all the creatures of the land are themselves revealed in and through the land, from where they continue to nurture all life. In this, the land is 'mother.' As mother, the landscape is filled with sacred sites and networked through songlines and trade routes. The people have a role to 'sing' the land, to keep it in harmony and enable increase of animals and plants. There is continuous sacramentality in sites and landscape, celebrated in rites and songs, mapped through sacred objects (such as the *tjuringa*), and joined by songlines. We gain a sense of this in Shirley Purdy's painting *Ngambuny Ascends*, depicting the ascension of Jesus as he is taken into the earth.[6] Our focus here is on sacramentality, and indigenous Christianity wishes to engage the sacramentality of the faith in ways far transcending the limitations of the two or seven rites and practices.

In passing it is worth noting that openness to new forms of sacramentality goes hand in hand with a reappraisal of Western sacramental practices. Again we can turn to indigenous Australia. The sacramentality of land and its ritual celebration has an effect on two particular liturgical centrepieces. One is the meaning of time, which in Australian indigenous society is immediately related to the renewal of the earth, the migration of animals, birds and fish, the seeding and flowering of plants, the availability of secure water, the seasons of burning and refreshing. In face of this, the Sunday-based, seven-day-week liturgical calendar makes little sense. The second is around the ownership of ritual power, which is diffused across indigenous society. In Australian indigenous society there are no

---

6. See <http://www.artway.eu/content.php?id=1777and lang=enand action=show.>

overarching ordained ministers, and religious power is owned and wielded by individuals, women and men, at different times and for different ceremonies. There is little room for, nor need of, a set of ordained ministers with jurisdiction over all official rites. There is a deep challenge here to the current state of the sacrament of orders.

In sum, sacramentality and its sacramental forms are effective when they successfully incorporate the three deep structures of symbolic activity: attention to body, language and time. Of their nature, the sacraments and sacramentality itself are essentially open, not closed. They also reflect many of the ways of knowing that are treasured in oral society: narrative, dance and song. There is much to be learnt from the peoples of Oceania.

Snakes and Stones: Snake Charmers, Snake Handlers and Stonemasons

We are already past two hundred years of Christianity in Oceania. There are now upwards of seven generations of faithful in some communities, living proof of the power of the Spirit expressed in worship. The scriptures are available in a plethora of languages, literacy has grown, indigenous churches with strong denominational affiliation have developed. If inadvertently the missionaries introduced snakes, some snake charmers and snake handlers have emerged to work with the situation. If stones have been brought, stonemasons have taken the opportunity to build. What are the ways in which the indigenous peoples take up the theological and liturgical offerings of the missionaries? My intention here is not to write a treatise on inculturation, but to show that the receiving cultures were active in a variety of ways, not always appreciated nor understood by the missionaries.

Snake Charming: Collusion, Complicity, Complexity

Soon enough there is collusion and complicity. It is worth beginning with a non-theological example. In late nineteenth-century Maori thought, women were not allowed to be in war canoes. It was not their place, and highly inappropriate, even 'taboo.' Yet the earlier late eighteenth-century records of navigators venturing to the shores of

Aotearoa mention times when their ships were under attack from swarms of canoes, filled with warriors female and male. It was not until the influence of Victorian values on the remembering of history that women were wiped from the record, and a new era of indigenous male superiority was created. The same shift in indigenous values is apparent in different parts of Oceania. Only in relatively more recent times have (male) anthropologists taken seriously the ritual power of Australian indigenous women, their ownership of country and ceremony, and their custodial rights and place in law. This late recognition was to the advantage of indigenous men.

The situation of the Protestant churches in Tonga shows a complex interaction and collusion between faith and culture. The introduction of ordained ministers offered an alternative power structure to that of the hierarchical organisation around king, nobles and warriors. At the same time, ordained ministers took on/were expected to have the qualities of leaders in the culture: disciplined, strong, fit, resistant to the lure of alcohol and gambling, highly proficient public speakers. With this new type of 'order', recognisable to the people in part due to its appropriation of cultural values of leadership, the church ritual allowed for an alternative platform for authority and leadership in the island communities.

Yet this situation became more complex as the king took up/was granted a role in faith. We have seen something of this above in the use of 'royal' language in the translation of the scriptures. As well, amongst the liturgical furnishings in some contemporary Tongan churches there is a throne in place for the king, even in churches of the Tongan diaspora, effectively creating a state church, under the patronage of the king. An interesting dynamic emerges in this case. The badging of a church as a state church allows for the ordained ministry, itself an alternate form of power, to act as an alternate hierarchy within society but still under the authority of the royal family. As the noble families held sway over the law, the ministers held tightly to the alternative 'law', the gospel as brought by the missionaries. Yet to maintain this position, the ministers took it as their duty to maintain the theological constructs introduced by the missionaries, to hold fast to the theology, teaching and practices introduced by the missionaries. It was not to their advantage to develop and authorise the inculturation of faith, the re-oralisation of the Word of God, and the development of new forms of sacramentality. The presence in the worship space of a throne for the king brought this second form of authority into partnership with the cultural and political leadership. As a consequence, the collusion of faith and culture in the arena of leadership, as well as in the forms and rites of belief brought by the missionaries and upheld as the staple of authority to the minister class, were closed off from the processes of inculturation.

Snake Handling: Accretion

Something different, more snake handler than snake charmer, can be seen in attempts at adding indigenous features to received rites. At first glance, this can appear to be merely decorative. Yet there are serious attempts to redefine the worship space itself, re-orienting the ownership over the imposed rites, and re-casting the influence of imported ministers and practices. The laying of 'fine' mats in the churches, especially at funerals in the diaspora, allows the foreign rituals to speak into indigenous experience and open the way for deeper expressions of faith in culture.

Also of interest are the Maori ceremonies welcoming strangers onto the marae for the celebration of a Christian rite. These indigenous rites bruit that there is no guaranteed rite of passage: entry is at the will of the community, and remains their prerogative. It is the land owners who provide for the warrant to enter the place, even for the performance of a sacred duty. In effect, any rite that is performed on this land is carried out in consultation with the people of the land. The ritual may reflect its western origins in every way, but the context for celebrating the rite belongs to the original inhabitants. And so while at one level the indigenous ceremonies of welcome may seem like an accretion, a frivolous addition that weighs upon the rite, at a deeper level some additions re-orient the event in its entirety, allowing for the recognition of indigenous authority and offering a place for indigenous expression and experience.

Stonemasons: Acceptance

Sometimes snakes can be fish, and stones bread. A central Australian indigenous language group considers it a high honour when another people offers them the gift of a sacred ritual. The acceptance and treasuring of rites is one of their deepest traditions, in which they see the exchange of rituals as a very high form of gift-giving and offering respect. On accepting Christianity, this people gratefully received, pure and unchanged, the liturgy for Sunday eucharist. They celebrated it exactly as it was given them, replete with all the European adornments and affectations that the prayer book exemplified. To satisfy their curiosity as to the provenance of the gift, they even sent a member of the group into the nearest town centre, to ensure that the ritual they were given was the same as that celebrated by the Europeans. They were fully satisfied on learning that the rite they had been given was exactly the same as that celebrated in the churches of the white settlers. In this case, the acceptance of a rite and its celebration strictly according to the book was one of the highest forms of inculturation.

Receiving cultures should not be seen as passive. The intrusion of the missionaries into the practices and rites of worship was not a disruption in all things. The new power and wisdom and truth was received within culture and through time honoured politics of collusion, accretion and acceptance, all which need to be read from within the culture.[7]

Stone and Snake: The Tradition

The third sub-heresy that the churches brought to the lands, peoples and languages of Oceania was that the present is based in the past, and the future is grown from the present. It is clearly contentious to question this point, given the nature of the scripturally-based, tradition-infused western churches and similarly the attachment to custom of the deeply traditional indigenous societies, with their sophisticated sets of beliefs, legislation and practices wrapped in an overwhelming consciousness of the power and necessity of 'law.' Yet Christianity cannot reduce the future to just another outgrowth of the present. There can be new ruptures, new expressions of revelation, new discoveries of the salvation wrought by the God incarnate, new

---

7. I will leave aside here the question of what it was the missionaries thought was happening, and how those expectations were conditioned culturally and theologically.

responses in worship, new unveilings of grace. In a faith built upon the ongoing revelation of God in Christ, the role of the past ought not to be to control the future.

Churches, missionaries and ministers are unsettled by the prospect of a future that is more open than closed. The intent of the missionaries in bringing the gospel to these unknown indigenous worlds was to bring the peoples into unity with a past. The mission movement would have been much more healthy if, rather, it had intended to invite the past of Christianity into a new future with the indigenous people.

There are two aspects of the future orientation of this interaction between gospel, church and culture that require consideration. One is historical. Do we want historians in the year 3015, when life, culture, science and the environment will be radically different from now, to look at this period of interaction and see it as an opportunity lost? Or do we want them to marvel at our boldness to face the question of unity of worship and belief in a region like Papua New Guinea where there are over 700 languages and traditional entrenched distrust of the 'other'? Do we want them to be inspired by our willingness to explore the integration of creator and created as we pursue the question of the place of the divine as Australian indigenous theology sets God within a unity of earth and sky, not above it as in a celestial heaven as in the current, though scientifically outdated, Christian religious imagination? Do we want those historians from the future to be inspired by the models for reconciliation amongst quite small clusters of families living within islands demarcated by sea which of necessity need to resolve disputes and maintain equilibrium and promote harmony?

The second is eschatological. The scriptures, which open with the word of God actively creating (Gen 1), close with the vision of a new heaven and a new earth (Rev 21). Too often our liturgical understanding is fixed on the practices of the past. It would be good to hold it accountable to the vision of what is to come, with what it is like when the dwelling of God is with humanity, and the divine is at home among us (Rev 21:3). Some of that future for the church, its liturgy, theological questions, methods of biblical interpretation, is found in the traditions and practices of the indigenous peoples, and this process of recovering possible futures has not yet begun in earnest.

Concluding Remarks

The missionaries could only offer the faith to the peoples of Oceania in light of their formation in worship, theology and ecclesiology, all of which took place within a particular time in western culture: the time of the book, the time of the post-Reformation need for denominational discipline, and more broadly the time of empires and colonies, the time of the idea of the 'noble savage' and an interest in 'primitive' peoples. The missionaries brought a 'book' which contained the living Word of God. They carried set rituals, open to revision but closed in nature and purpose. They offered a vision of the future that was based in their European past and exclusive of the present of the indigenous peoples. Through this presentation of the Bible, the sacraments and the tradition, the indigenous peoples came in contact with the living word, the living presence of Christ and the history of grace in cultures. These gifts were not received uncritically. There were ways of subverting this message, ways of appropriating it, and ways of accepting it and incorporating it into indigenous society.

The intention of this paper has been to seek a fresh dialogue between church and indigenous peoples. There are ways of 'hearing' and interpreting the living word which reach beyond and behind the use of pen, script and book. There are ways of relating grace to culture beyond the two and seven sacraments. There are ways of reframing theology and ecclesiology beyond models from the past, looking instead to new understandings of the way the sacred is found in creation. The Christians of Oceania offer the wider church the challenge of accompanying them on their journey of faith, a journey begun in the Spirit long before the arrival of those bold but constrained missional servants of the gospel.

11
Everywhere and Nowhere: Experiencing God in a Decentred Context

David Ranson

I am a sixth-generation Tasmanian. My family, both on the side of my mother and my father, came to the island in the 1840s, farming the area around Longford, and then in the north east and north west. Though I left home quite early at the age of seventeen, never returning to live in Tasmania for more than a few months over the subsequent nearly forty years, being Tasmanian is something ingrained within my consciousness.

Some twenty-five years ago I undertook something of an intellectual pilgrimage about the meaning of being Tasmanian through the discovery of literary studies about the Tasmanian experience, especially that of Germaine Greer and Peter Conrad. Independently of each other, both were in Tasmania in 1986 struggling with the question about Tasmanian identity.[1] In my own quest to understand the Tasmanian psyche, Conrad's recollection of his experience as a young boy at the Hobart Show has struck me particularly. As Conrad ruminates,

> Where am I? is the first demand the wailing infant makes of the world he arrives in. Calmed and comforted, you stop asking after a while, and are so soon so adjusted to reality (an adult invention) that you forget the question. I continued, inconveniently and unappeasably, to ask it in Tasmania. I remember a Sunday afternoon when I must have been four or five years old. My parents had taken me to gymkhana at the agricultural showground near our house. From up there,

---

1. Germaine Greer, *Daddy, We Hardly Knew You* (New York: Harper and Row, 1990), and Peter Conrad, *Down Home: Revisiting Tasmania* (London: Chatto and Windus, 1988).

on the dusty raised race-track, you could see the closed circle of our world: Mount Wellington to one side, to the other—behind the loops of bitumen and the bright weatherboard cartons of our suburb, set down on a hill only a few months before—glum, hunched Mount Direction; the choppy waters of our bay with its rank mud flats, the frayed grass of the rifle range, the smoking skyline which was the zinc works. A northerly wind whipped up small tornadoes of grit. The sky, overcast and opaque, stifled the scene as if beneath glass. There were cheers from the track: someone or other had won a race. Wandering through the sparse crowd holding my father's hand, I began suddenly, inexplicably to cry. I remember the heat of the tears, and my gasping for breath in order to wail some more. My parents were mystified, embarrassed, finally annoyed. What was the reason? they asked. I was too busy bellowing to say. They were with another couple, who also had an only son. He too looked on, aghast at the exhibition. 'Graeme isn't crying,' they pointed out. Well, no, of course he's not, I suppose I thought: how could he be? The tantrum was my own exclusive means of self-expression. My parents had no choice but to bundle me home, their day ruined; and I think they were a little suspicious of me ever after, afraid of the inordinate demands I'd make on life, and of the dissatisfaction and frustration dramatised by my outburst on the showground.

My silly fit of misery in the grey afternoon repeated that first cry of the displaced infant. Where *am* I? it insisted on knowing. The mountains told me that I was in Tasmania, which only made things worse. This was not the life I wanted; somehow I'd been given the wrong one. My tears raged at the injustice—or incompetence—of it. What continued to terrify me was the rawness, the shivering vulnerability of the place.[2]

This remarkable self-reflection by Conrad, engaging such vivid geographical description, highlights with personal poignancy a fundamental tension in the experience of place: experience is invariably centripetal in its tendency, whilst subsequently centrifugal in its impulse.

---

2. Peter Conrad, *Down Home: Revisting Tasmania*, 7–8.

On the one hand, place lends structure, contextuality and vividness of memory to the narrative of experience. We remember 'where' things happened rather than 'when.' And further, the place in which we live deeply affects consciousness. As Jung observed,

> The soil one stands on transmits its morphology into one's soul. Just as, in the process of evolution, the mind has been moulded by earthly conditions, so the same process repeats itself under our eyes today. Imagine a large section of some European nation transplanted to a strange soil and another climate. We can confidently expect this human group to undergo certain psychic and perhaps also physical changes in the course of a few generations, even without the admixture of foreign blood. Certain Australian primitives assert that one cannot conquer foreign soil, because in it there dwell strange ancestor-spirits who reincarnate themselves in the new-born. There is a great psychological truth in this. The foreign land assimilates its conqueror . . . Everywhere the virgin earth causes at least the unconscious of the conqueror to sink to the level of its indigenous inhabitants.[3]

The French scholar of spirituality, Michel de Certeau, whom I wish to focus on extensively below, was intensely aware of the role of context in spirituality, such that he would propose, 'mystical literature relates first of all to a certain topography.'[4] In a landmark essay on the importance of culture to spiritual experience, he wrote,

> The structures of society, the terms in which it voices its aspirations, the objective and subjective forms of the common conscience, build up the religious conscience, which in turn manifests them. A particular type of society and a particular social balance (including the essential elements of the significance of power . . .) are reflected in the problems of spiritual experience. Experience is always defined in cultural terms, even when it is religious . . . it is in the very cultural situation that [a person's] yearnings and [their] predicament

---

3. Carl Jung, 'Mind and Earth' in *Civilisation in Transition*. Collected Works (Princeton: Princeton University Press, 1970), Volume X.
4. Michel de Certeau, 'Mystic Speech', in *Heterologies: Discourse on the Other*, translated by Brian Massumi, *Theory and History of Literature* (Minneapolis: University of Minnesota Press, 1986), 17:83.

'take flesh', it is through this medium that [they] find God yet ever seek him, that [they] express [their] faith, that [they] carry] on simultaneous experiments in colloquy with God and with [their] actual [fellows] . . . A culture is the language of a spiritual experience. The very history of spirituality demonstrates this fact, unless we are determined to look at it in blinkers which would exclude its context. And by 'context' I mean not only a framework or external trappings, but the very element from which the experience takes its form and expression . . . Spiritual experience replies to the questions of the moment, and always replies in the terms of those questions, for these are what the [people] of a particular society talk about and live by . . . Because it is often describing an experience, and because in any case it has in mind the difficulties of actually living out any practice of religion, every spiritual movement is essentially historical in character. It is less concerned with elaborating a theory than with showing how to live in dependence on the Absolute in the conditions actually laid down by a given situation. It is therefore expressed in terms of the experiences, ambitions, fears, sicknesses and greatnesses proper to [people] who are caught up with contemporaries in a world conditioned by a particular kind of exchange and a particular type of consciousness.[5]

Yet, as Conrad's bleak experience under Mount Wellington at the end of the earth illustrates, the tension between place and 'no place' is a vigorous one. Experience is a tension of both emplacement and displacement. Place can never fully contain our experience—especially our experience of the divine. We are sent forth from the place of our experience, beyond it, to take with us something that affects every new place in which we find ourselves. This is even more acute when our very topography is one of displacement. 'So far did I seem from somewhere, anywhere' suggested Conrad.

It may be argued that we live, in fact, in an age of displacement, occasioned, firstly because we increasingly bear the outcome of widespread patterns of modern migration, and, secondly, because of the more radical experience of dislocation inherent to the emergence of postmodernity. As Cruz identifies, the issue of human mobility

---

5. Michel de Certeau, 'Culture and Spiritual Experience', in *Concilium* 9 (November 1966): 3–16.

today is in the process of redefining and transforming the human condition, proposing,

> At no other point in the history of humanity has the number of people on the move been at such a large scale that the current period is being referred to as the age of migration. A 2013 United Nations (UN) report, for example, states that there are currently 232 million international migrants compared with 175 million in 2000 and 154 million in 1990. Estimates by the International Organisation of Migration even indicate that the number of migrants worldwide could rise to as much as 405 million by 2050. Today, one in 33 people and migrants and more than three per cent of the world's population is comprised of migrants . . . In fact, if all migrants in the world were to come together to constitute a country, theirs would be the world's fifth most populous. This immense movement of peoples is not only rearranging human geography but also transforming the economic, religious and cultural landscapes of many countries in positive but, oftentimes, politically divisive ways.[6]

As an eloquent expression of how these figures translate into personal experience, Cruz quotes the Cuban-American theologian Ada Maria Isasi-Diaz

> I am caught between two worlds neither of which is fully mine, both of which are partially mine . . . As a foreigner in an alien land I have not inherited a garden from my mother but rather a bunch of cuttings. Beautiful but rootless flowering plants—that is my inheritance. Rooting and replanting them requires extra work . . . it requires much believing in myself.[7]

---

6. Gemma Tulud Cruz, 'Migration as *Locus Theologicus*', in *Colloquium* 46/1 (2014): 88–89.
7. Ada Maria Isasi-Diaz, 'A Hispanic Garden in a Foreign Land,' in *Inheriting our Mothers' Gardens*, edited by Letty Russell *et al* (Philadelphia: Westminster Press, 1988), 22, cited in Cruz, 'Migration as *Locus Theologicus*,' 96. See also Greg A Madison, *The End of Belonging: Untold Stories of Leaving Home and the Psychology of Global Relocation* (London: Unpublished Manuscript, 2009, revised 2010). Madison's work is 'based upon individual stores of leaving home; autobiographies of homelessness by unsettled people who move from place to place, country to country, in search of fulfilment.'

Permeating this phenomenon of migration, threads the curious postmodern paradox though, that whilst, on the one hand, perhaps as never before, have we had the opportunity to celebrate diversity and autonomy yet, on the other hand, perhaps as never before have we been less sure about who we are. WS Gilbert once suggested—rather prophetically I think of our own time—in the 1889 Gilbert and Sullivan musical *The Gondoliers* when, 'Everybody is somebody, *nobody* is anybody; if everybody is abnormal, we don't need to worry about anybody'. The postmodern celebration of diversity can easily slip into a type of fragmentation, a disconnection from cohesive sources of meaning, leaving us in independent compartments. The freedom of apparent autonomy, prized by Western culture, comes, however, at a price. The diminishment of the relationships that, ultimately, bear meaning for us, creates a radical insecurity. We can feel lost, small islands in a vast ocean that threatens to swamp us. We becomes anxious about who we are. This cultural anxiety is further exacerbated by the social experience of people living alone. In Australia, the number of single households has dramatically increased. In 1996 just over twenty-two per cent of all households had single occupancy; in 2006 it was just below twenty-thee per cent.[8] In 2011, lone-person households had increased to twenty-four per cent of households, meaning that 1.9 million or 1 in 10 Australians lived alone. According to Mackay, lone households are predicted to exceed thirty per cent by 2030.[9] It was these types of figures that, as an example of social research on the theme, Michael Flood and the Australia Institute to issue the report, *Mapping Loneliness in Australia.*[10] However, as the Australian Bureau of Statistics highlights,

---

8. These figures are taken from the Australian Bureau of Statistics 2006 national census. See David Dale, 'We're richer but lonelier as old-style family fades,' *Sydney Morning Herald*, Thursday 28 June 2007: 9. See also Hugh Mackay, *Advance Australia—Where?* (London: Hachette, 2007), 210–236.
9. See Hugh Mackay, *The Art of Belonging: It's Not Where You Live, It's How You Live* (Sydney: Pan Macmillan Australia, 2014), 156.
10. Michael Flood, *Mapping Loneliness in Australia*, The Australia Institute Discussion Paper Number 76, February 2005, <http://www.melbourneinstitute.com/hilda/Biblio/ophd/Flood_Loneliness%20in%20Australia.pdf>. Accessed 16 July 2010. See also Adrian Franklin and Bruce Tranter, 'Loneliness in Australia', Paper No. 13, Housing and Community Research Unit, School of Sociology and Social Work, University of Tasmania (2008), <http://families.org.au/article_files/Marriage/Loneliness%20in%20Australia%202008.pdf>. Accessed 30 October

While 24 per cent of households having one resident may seems a lot, it is not particularly large by international standards. De Vaus and Richardson found that the percentage of lone-person households was largest in Scandinavian countries. For example, around 46 per cent of households in Sweden have one person living in them. A high rate of lone-person households is also apparent in Western European countries at around 30 per cent.[11]

What then are the implications of such dislocation for our sense of ecclesiality? How does such a social topography shape our sense of Church, and what are the implications for our way of being Church in such a context?

To address these questions I turn to the scholarship of Michel de Certeau.[12] Much of de Certeau's scholarship was focused on sixteenth- and seventeenth-century French and Spanish mysticism, the period in which he identifies that the more precise historical formation of the Christian mystical tradition became understood in a modern way.[13] Importantly, he notes that the mystics of this period,

> were for the most part from regions or social categories which were in socio-economic recession, disadvantaged by change, marginalised by progress, or destroyed by war. The memory of past abundance survived in these conditions of impoverishment, but since the doors of social responsibility were closed, ambitions were redirected toward the open spaces of utopia, dream, and writing.[14]

2014.

11. See <http://theconversation.com/australian-census-one-in-ten-live-alone-but-that-doesnt-mean-theyre-lonely-7674>. Accessed 11 September 2014.
12. For what follows is taken in large part from a fuller treatment of the social implications of de Certeau's perspective in David Ranson, *Between the 'Mysticism of Politics' and the 'Politics of Mysticism': Interpreting New Pathways of Holiness within the Roman Catholic Tradition* (Adelaide: ATF Press, 2013).
13. De Certeau, 'Mystic Speech', 82–83. See also Michel de Certeau, *The Mystic Fable: Volume I, The Sixteenth and Seventeenth Centuries*, translated by Michael B Smith (Chicago and London: University of Chicago Press, 1992), 16. For useful commentary on de Certeau's contribution to spirituality, see Philip Sheldrake, 'Unending desire: de Certeau's 'mystics', in *The Way Supplement* 102 (2001): 38–48.
14. De Certeau, 'Mystic Speech', 84.

In other words, it was a context of a certain social dislocation, a time reacting to what he refers to as the 'humiliation of the Christian tradition' and to the very decline of institutions of meaning, such that they were experiencing the disintegration of a sacred world. De Certeau's framework, however, is not simply a commentary of the sixteenth and seventeenth century. It is a commentary equally on our modern experience. In the very last paragraph of the first volume of *The Mystic Fable*, de Certeau brings into superb summary his own biographical experience, his historical scholarship, and his insight for a contemporary context:

> He or she is mystic who cannot stop walking and, with the certainty of what is lacking, knows of every place and object that it is *not that*; one cannot stay *there* nor be content with *that*. Desire creates an excess. Places are exceeded, passed, lost behind it. It makes one go further, elsewhere. It lives nowhere. It is inhabited, Hadewijch also said, by a noble *je ne sais quoi*, neither this nor that, that leads us, introduces us and absorbs us in our Origin, On that self-surpassing spirit, seduced by an impregnable origin or end called God, it seems that what for the most part remains, in contemporary culture, is the movement of perpetual departure . . . Unmoored from the 'origin' of which Hadewijch spoke, the traveller no longer has foundation or goal. Given over to nameless desire, he is the drunken boat. Henceforth this desire can no longer speak to someone. It seems to have become *infans*, voiceless, more solitary and lost than before, or less protected and more radical, ever seeking a body or poetic locus. It goes on walking, then, tracing itself out in silence, in writing. [Italics in the original][15]

De Certeau thus brings us to the very dilemma of the modern Christian: the loss of place within a secularised context. In his enigmatic essay, 'The Weakness of Believing: From the Body to Writing, a Christian Transit,' he brings to bear his historical insights

---

15. De Certeau, *The Mystic Fable*, 299. The image of the drunken boat is taken from the best-known work of Arthur Rimbaud (1854–91), *Le Bateau Ivre* ('The Drunken Boat'), which appeared in 1871. In the poem Rimbaud sent a toy boat on a journey, seeing in it an allegory for a spiritual quest. See 'Arthur Rimbaud', <http://www.kirjasto.sci.fi/rimbaud.htm>, accessed 26 September, 2008.

on the nature of the relationship between the Christian at the end of the twentieth century and their society.¹⁶ De Certeau begins his complex essay by naming the dislocation of the ecclesial body in the modern context. Now Christian experience,

> as though it had fallen from the sinking ecclesial ship . . . is lost in the vast and uncertain poem of an anonymous reality which comes and goes; it renounces the appropriation of a sense which the hull and portholes conditioned, and instead receives from this indeterminate history a life which fulfils everyone by going beyond them. There is no body other than the body of the world and the mortal body.¹⁷

He remarks how, for a time, in the face of this, there was a tendency to seek an alternative 'site', another space, from which the Church could speak, consequent to its displacement from the centre of society, just as there have been efforts to replicate a past. Yet, as he traces, such alternate 'sites'—the 'worker-priest movement', emergent marginal communities of one kind or another—in the end, fail as their referent becomes less and less the ecclesial community itself:

> The institutions to which the groups refer are no longer religious and are less and less ideological. There remains the gesture of taking a distance from institutions, but without the ground which it was related to; an instrument adapted to work on one system survives the corpus it has traversed. The function can no longer find the place where it used to be applied.¹⁸

In de Certeau's mind, different initiatives to re-locate a social body inevitably face a choice: they either create only what he calls 'scriptural sites', that is, ways of discourse which are entirely subjective, lacking any objective exteriority—such as 'charismatic' or Pentecostal groups—or

---

16. Michel de Certeau, 'The Weakness of Believing: From the Body to Writing, a Christian Transit', translated by Saskia Brown, in *The Certeau Reader*, 214–243. The themes are also developed, though in slightly different ways, in Michel de Certeau, *The Practice of Everyday Life* (1984), translated by Steven F Rendall. See in particular chapters 9 and 13.
17. De Certeau, 'The Weakness of Believing', 229.
18. De Certeau, 'The Weakness of Believing', 220.

they become enmeshed into a network of social practices, 'anybody's, anonymous, stripped of distinctive rules or marks,' which, in the end, situates them elsewhere than the ecclesial community.[19] Yet, as de Certeau points out the mystics of the sixteenth and seventeenth centuries, such as Teresa of Avila and Ignatius of Loyola, do not desert the Church. Rather they enter 'the ruins' of both the Churches and the Scriptures, 'considered equally corrupt' because they 'represented in their minds the state of the contemporary Christianity and, like the cave of rejection at Bethlehem, were *where* they were to seek a repetition of a founding surprise.' [Italics in the original.][20] De Certeau wishes to maintain that Christian experience 'can [indeed] introduce changes within the social sites where it intervenes'.[21]

This possibility of 'founding surprise' drives home to de Certeau the question of, '[h]ow can a Christian reference be marked in social practices, since, for Christians, there are no longer sites of production which are properly their own?'[22] In a situation in which the ecclesial 'body of sense' has lost its effectiveness and in which 'civil society has replaced the Church in the role of defining tasks and positions, leaving the Church with only a marginal possibility of correcting or going beyond the delimitation of domains,' the task will fall more and more to the individual Christian, as de Certeau writes, to 'do' faith.[23] For de Certeau, this requires a New Testament combination of 'following' and of 'conversion'—'a going beyond which the name of Jesus opens up . . . [and] a corresponding transformation of consciousness and of conduct.'[24] He will call this 'evangelical sense'. It is not a new site, itself, but that which 'expresses itself in terms of instituting and going beyond, relative to the effective sites of our history which yesterday were religious, today civil'.[25] In other words, it is the vital component

---

19. This has a direct bearing on such current pastoral questions as the maintenance of Catholic identity of ecclesial agencies in the provision of social service delivery within a pluralist and secular context. As an Australian example of such a pastoral problem, see *Identity and Mission in Catholic Agencies,* edited by Neil Ormerod (Strathfield: St Paul's Publications, 2008).
20. De Certeau, 'Mystic Speech', 86.
21. De Certeau, 'The Weakness of Believing', 224.
22. De Certeau, 'The Weakness of Believing', 224.
23. De Certeau, 'The Weakness of Believing', 226.
24. De Certeau, 'The Weakness of Believing', 226.
25. De Certeau, 'The Weakness of Believing', 228.

of the Christian's effectiveness in the world. This twofold response is for de Certeau is not compromised by the 'weakening, dissemination and even disappearance of the (ecclesial) sites which it has traversed'.[26] After all, according to him, these in the end but constituted a space for the development of such a response.

The stance, or style, or profile, (which is the outcome) will have no single concrete expression in de Certeau's perspective because of the essentially dynamic character of the call to follow and the possibility of change:

> This principle is in fact an evanescent event. It is 'mythical' in a double sense: the event has no site, except for the writings which narrate it, and it generates speech and action and yet more 'writings,' while remaining itself unobjectifiable. This beginning point is a vanishing point. That which opens possibility is also that which goes beyond, withdraws or escapes.[27]

De Certeau is talking here about an entirely 'responsive' attitude, always relative to site, now required by the contemporary Christian. It is an attitude 'mad about loving,' deeply attentive 'to all the "calls" to which many reply by turning round, discrete invitations to excesses which punctuate normal procedures with risk'.[28] It is a response that is quintessentially mystical:

> The 'follow me' comes from a voice which has been effaced, forever irrecuperable, vanished into the changes which echo it back, drowned in the throng of its respondents . . . It is no longer anything except the tracing of a passage—made possible by it—a relation between an arrival (birth) and a departure (death), then between a return (resurrection) and a disappearance (ascension), indefinitely. Nothing but a name without a site. Writings which initially set out to respond, then, themselves develop as a series of 'listening—following—changing,' already inflected in a hundred different ways, and never with a stable term before them. The Name which institutes this series designates at once (and only) the different

---

26. De Certeau, 'The Weakness of Believing', 228.
27. De Certeau, 'The Weakness of Believing', 227.
28. De Certeau, 'The Weakness of Believing', 229.

> elements which it allows to emerge after it and whatever refers it to its other I a movement of listening to and following the Father. Jesus is the vanishing unknown factor of this relation 'call-conversion' which he names. He himself enters into this relation which posits terms which are indeterminate: he is yes (2 Corinthians 1:19), a response relative to an Unnameable who calls, and he is the continually 'converted' son of the inaccessible Father who says to him 'come'.[29]

Such is what de Certeau understands as the 'excess of belief'. It brings with it particular conditions by which Christian faith can work on social practices. That effect will no longer be a consequence of Christian experience unifying itself as one body. Rather now, it will be more and more relegated to the private sphere, in the sense that it calls for individual discernment and action, and in its responsiveness, is destined to lose itself in history, that is, it is always situated before something other than the self. This brings about what de Certeau calls 'the violence of the instant'.[30] There is an enormous loss as one feels the once firm Christian ground disappear, but precisely in the loss, animated by this two-fold response, something 'begins': an in-fancy. Movement is instigated. An initial non-site, what de Certeau suggests analogously as 'the empty tomb,' gives rise to new writings'—which de Certeau earlier defines as the inscription of a desire into the system of a language, and not simply literary—'a language without force, structured by the absence of a body, the renunciation of proximity, and the obliteration of the proper.'[31] Thus, in the sixteenth and seventeenth centuries it is not surprising for de Certeau that groups emerge which are at the extremes, at least, vacillated 'between ecstasy and revolt—*mysticism and dissent*'.[32] For de Certeau it is no accident that the 'Machiavellian Moment' and the 'mystic invasion' coincide.[33]

The outcome for de Certeau is what he calls the 'evangelical fable'. It is the response, from a distance, 'to texts encountered along the way, dispersed, without any unity which one might grasp or seek, but nevertheless productive, because of the 'turmoil' or . . . the

---

29. De Certeau, 'The Weakness of Believing', 227.
30. De Certeau, 'The Weakness of Believing', 230.
31. De Certeau, 'The Weakness of Believing', 234.
32. De Certeau, 'Mystic Speech', 85. Italics in the original.
33. De Certeau, *The Mystic Fable*, 153–156.

'crisis' which, like dreams, they first provoke in us'.³⁴ Subsequently, the discourse that is possible must remain in the interrogative—'like dream, it has no sense except for what comes to it from elsewhere and from an other . . .'³⁵ Belief is, through and through, a 'coming' and 'following'.

> The fable remains always in the distance, as the poetic other of historical effectivity, as a utopia which articulates with social topographies only through private risk . . . A fragile and floating text, witness to itself alone, yet lost in the innumerable murmur of language, and hence perishable. But this fable heralds the joy of obliterating itself in what it figures, of returning to the anonymous work out of which it was born, of converting itself to this other which it is not.³⁶

I think what de Certeau is suggesting by the 'evangelical fable' is that from this place, a 'siteless site' as he names it—related both to the fragility of social position or the uncertainty of institutional referents—that a new language is born.³⁷ For de Certeau there is an inherent 'weakness' in the evangelical fable—weakness in the sense of the opposite of the apparent strength provided by something which might appear more sure, more lasting. Yet, this very 'weakness' becomes the foundation for a new way of being. No longer can we enjoy the litany of past strengths—ecclesial property with cultural prestige, nor 'ideological substitutes for this body of sense—communities of utterance, historical facts, 'anthropological' positivities'. Rather what we now have, and all we now have, is what emerges in the interaction between 'the effective sites of our social belonging' and the possibility inherent in the evangelical fable.³⁸ In this interaction is a constant beginning. This requires in de Certeau's words, 'a contract of language which, because it has no property, takes the form of the lack and desire of the other.'³⁹ De Certeau recognises that ordinary Christian discourse is supported by its relation to its originating community for

---

34. De Certeau, 'The Weakness of Believing', 234.
35. De Certeau, 'The Weakness of Believing', 231.
36. De Certeau, 'The Weakness of Believing', 237.
37. De Certeau, 'Mystic Speech, 90.
38. De Certeau, 'The Weakness of Believing', 237.
39. De Certeau, 'Mystic Speech,' 92. See also de Certeau, *The Mystic Fable*, 25, and particularly 157–76.

'social belonging founds linguistic "competence".[40] But what becomes of this language, he asks, when the body with which it is articulated is disseminated? 'What happens when a language is no longer articulate with a body, no longer supported and held by it?'[41] It is the mystical figure, particularly as he or she emerges in de Certeau's study of the sixteenth and seventeenth century, who makes 'readable an absence that has multiplied the productions of desire'.[42]

For de Certeau we see this particularly exemplified in the dynamic of the poem—the special utterance of mysticism: received, that which comes from beyond, containing that excess which names but remains unnameable. 'It says nothing. It permits saying. For that reason, it is a true "beginning". It is a liberating space, where yesterday's readers—but "we" also—can find speech'.[43] The mystical poem speaks of the absence of what it designates. This is its mystical character:

> [t]he establishment of a space where change serves as a foundation and saying loss is an other beginning. Because it is always *less* than what *comes* through it and allows a genesis, the mystic poem is connected to the *nothing* that opens the future, the time to *come*, and more precisely, to that single word, 'Yahweh,' which forever makes possible the self-naming of that which induces departure.[44]

This idea that mystical discourse represents rupture, departure, ever new beginnings leads to the fundamental paradox in mystical discourse, and that which renders it with a radical destabilising capacity:

> That is why the text is destabilised: it is at the same time *beside* the authorised institution, but outside it and *in* what authorises that institution, i.e., the Word of God. In such a discourse, which claims to speak on behalf of the Holy Spirit and attempts to impose that convention on the addressed, a particular assertion is at work, affirming that what is said in this *place*, different from the one of magisterium language, is

---

40. De Certeau, 'The Weakness of Believing', 216.
41. De Certeau, 'The Weakness of Believing', 217.
42. De Certeau, *The Mystic Fable*, 13.
43. De Certeau, 'Mystic Speech', 97–99.
44. De Certeau, 'Mystic Speech', 100. Italics in the original.

the *same* as what is said in the tradition, or else that these two places amount to the same.⁴⁵

Yet, for de Certeau, such mystical discourse lends itself to social practice that is, itself, subversive, acting as critique to accepted norms of behaviour. As Sheldrake observes, 'the language of movement implies a continual transgression of fixed points'.⁴⁶ As such, in de Certeau's perspective, the mystic defines a different treatment of the Christian tradition:

> Accused (with good reason) of being 'new', caught up in and 'bound to' circumstances, yet founded on faith in a Beginning that must come about in the present, they institute a 'style' that articulates itself into *practices* defining a *modus loquendi* and/or a *modus agendae*.⁴⁷

It is precisely ways of acting that organise the invention of a mystic body, according to de Certeau. In time, this 'labour of transcending limits' begins to shape the tradition that 'has deteriorated and opacified'.⁴⁸ De Certeau traces the traditions of the 'idiot woman' of the fourth century, and the sixth century's 'laughter of madmen' to demonstrate such a point.⁴⁹ Both speak of the repressed Other; they disrupt that which would suffocate the Other, forcing by their very madness, their silence, and their marginal witness, 'a turning aside toward another county, in which [they] . . . create the challenge of the unbound'.⁵⁰ Thus, the mystic, both in language and in practice, critiques the status quo, calling it beyond its innate tendency to complacency and ossification and to once again be surprised by the potential within a new rupture, a new beginning. Mysticism, even in its silence, thus has within itself a politically subversive dimension.

Given that the Christian place is now dependent on the encounter with alterity, the genuine Christian response in a contemporary context must always involve rupture for de Certeau.

---

45. De Certeau, 'Mystic Speech', 92–93. Italics in the original.
46. Sheldrake, 'Unending desire', 40.
47. De Certeau, *The Mystic Fable*, 14.
48. De Certeau, *The Mystic Fable*, 15.
49. De Certeau, *The Mystic Fable*, 31-48.
50. De Certeau, *The Mystic Fable*, 32.

> Practice, always relative to a site, is indefinitely 'responsive' and believing, on the move, like Jacob who 'went on his journey' after having erected a stele at Bethel, the unexpected and awesome place of his vision (Genesis 28:18–29). It always has to take risks further on, always uncertain and fragmentary.[51]

This is critical for de Certeau who recognises that in Christian spirituality there is always the temptation 'to transform the conversion into establishment . . . or . . . as in evangelical transfiguration (a metaphoric movement) to take the "vision" as a "tent" and the word as a new land.'[52] Genuine spirituality within the Christian tradition, however, resists this trap:

> In its countless writings along many different trajectories, Christian spirituality offers a huge inventory of difference, and ceaselessly criticises the trap; it has insisted particularly on the impossibility for the believer of stopping on the moment of the break—a practice, a departure, a work, an ecstasy—and of identifying faith with a site. Today we are even more radically obliged, due to history, to take this lesson seriously.[53]

In the topography of displacement learning this lesson will hold our future.

---

51. De Certeau, 'The Weakness of Believing', 228.
52. De Certeau, 'The Weakness of Believing', 236.
53. De Certeau, 'The Weakness of Believing', 236.

12
Are There Really Angels in Oceania? Forging a New Mysticism of Place, Time and History Through Dialogue Among Oceanic Peoples and Traditions

Gerard Hall

Introduction

Whether in Oceania or elsewhere, practical theology does not tend to focus on angels or mysticism.[1] Nonetheless, all theology, practical or otherwise, needs to acknowledge the importance of the experience of God, the Divine or the Sacred. And, as Terry Veling argues, practical theology needs to embrace both mystical and prophetic imaginations.[2] Such a practical-mystical-prophetic theology is not an otherworldly disengagement from social concerns; nor is it particularly concerned with so-called extraordinary mystical experiences.[3] Rather, the mystical dimension of practical theology is concerned with what Karl Rahner termed the 'mysticism of everyday life'[4] *and* what Johann Metz termed 'political mysticism' or 'mysticism of open or opened

---

1. Claire Wolfteich explicitly states that practical theology 'rarely engages with mystical texts or experience' even as she advocates the need to 'traverse this divide between mysticism and practical theology.' See her 'Practices of Unsaying', in *Spiritus: A Journal of Christian Spirituality*, 12 (2012): 161.
2. Terry Veling, *Practical Theology: On Earth as it is in Heaven* (Maryknoll: Orbis Books, 2005), 204–211. He builds on the words of German political theologian, Johannes Metz: 'the radical nature of following Christ is mystical and political at one and the same time', 204.
3. Claire Wolfteich, 'Catholic Voices and Visions in Practical Theology,' in *Invitation to Catholic Theology*, edited by Claire Wolfteich (New York: Paulist Press, 2014), 338–339.
4. Karl Rahner, 'The Mysticism of Everyday Life,' in *The Practice of the Faith: A Handbook of Contemporary Spirituality* (New York: The Crossroad Publishing Company, 1986), 84.

eyes'.⁵ The argument of this chapter is that, if practical theology is to play its role in the recovery of an ecclesial sense of place and purpose in Oceania,⁶ then it needs to give impetus to an understanding of religious experience, or what is here called a new mysticism of place, time and history.⁷

Writing some twenty years ago on theology in a postmodern world, Noel Rowe wrote an incisive article entitled 'Are there really angels in Carlton?'⁸ For the followers of Australian football, Carlton had just won the 1992 Premiership which, along with ANZAC Day, represents perhaps the highest annual secular liturgy on the Australian calendar.⁹ The purpose of the article was to provoke a new kind of dialogue between Christian theology and a predominantly secular Australian society in which, to use Rowe's language, neither church nor society is totally aligned with either angels or demons. Specifically, he challenges theology to be genuinely inculturated. For Rowe, 'inculturation'¹⁰ is not simply a matter of interpreting the Word of God for other people, which is more an act of translation, but also involves breaking open the Word in the self-emptying (*kenotic*) manner of Christ's own Crucifixion so that the Christian tradition is itself transformed through deep dialogue with cultures. This is what is sometimes termed the process of 'acculturation.'¹¹

---

5. Johann Baptist Metz, *A Passion for God: The Mystical-Political Dimension of Christianity* (New York: Paulist Press, 1997), 162–163.
6. For the purposes of this paper, reference to Oceanic peoples includes all who inhabit our lands and oceans, including Indigenous, European, Asian and others.
7. For Raimon Panikkar, mysticism 'belongs to human nature itself, inviting us to take part consciously—that is to say, humanly—in the adventure of reality.' See his *Mysticism and Spirituality* (New York: Orbis Books, 2014), xxv.
8. Noel Rowe, 'Are There Really Angels in Carlton? Australian Literature and Theology', in *Pacifica*, 6/2 (1993): 141-164.
9. Both these events—Australian Football Premiership and Anzac Day—while unknown in most parts of the world will be generally recognised for their national importance in Australia, New Zealand and many other places in South-Western Oceania.
10. *Inculturation* emerged as a theological term in the 1970s referring to the process by which Christian faith is genuinely incarnated in a particular culture, transforming it into a new creation. Gerald Arbuckle, *Culture, Inculturation and Theologians* (Collegeville: Liturgical Press, 2010), 167. Inculturation was given prominence in Catholic theology following Paul VI's Apostolic Letter on *Evangelisation* (Vatican City: Sacred Congregation for Evangelisation, 1975).
11. *Acculturation* is the other side of the *inculturation* process noted, for example,

Consequently, if practical theology is to speak of forging a new mysticism of place, time and history, this involves interreligious and intercultural engagement. Specifically, it challenges the hegemony of any single cultural or religious worldview. Likewise, it acknowledges the ambiguous phenomenon of globalisation: positively, a deepened sense of human interdependence and an extended awareness of religious, cultural and ethnic diversity; negatively, the homogenisation of human traditions or, alternatively, a tribal, even militant, fundamentalism.[12] As part of this globalised world, Oceania is still in the process of unshackling itself from its colonial past. Here, too, our theologising must confront the reality that the Gospel has been largely transmitted in words, rituals and symbols that presumed the superiority of European culture. An Oceanian practical theology will be sensitive to these and similar issues in seeking a mystical and prophetic way forward for our lands, seas and peoples.

Raimon Panikkar and Depth-Dialogue Among Traditions

In the visionary thought of intercultural and interreligious scholar, Raimon Panikkar, the call for depth-dialogue among traditions has become the existential imperative of our times.[13] Panikkar (1918–2010), a Catholic priest of Catalan and Indian descent, is known as an apostle and pioneer of interreligious dialogue especially among Christians, Hindus, Buddhists and Secular Humanists. In later life, he became increasingly convinced of the urgency of dialogue with Indigenous traditions.[14] The goal of such dialogue is the creation of

---

in the way that the post-Constantinian Church not only Christianised Europe but, equally, Christianity was Europeanised. For definition of acculturation, see *Global Dictionary of Theology*, edited by WA Dyrness and V-M Kärkkäinen (Westmont: InterVarsity Press, 2008), 1–2; also Arbuckle, *Culture*, 167–168.

12. For insightful discussion on the ambiguity of globalisation, note the dedicated issue on 'Theology and Globalisation', in *Theological Studies* 69/2 (2008).
13. He states for example: 'No single human or religious tradition is today self-sufficient and capable of rescuing humanity from its present predicament.' Raimon Panikkar, *Essays on Contemplation and Responsibility* (Minneapolis: Fortress Press, 1995), 175.
14. For this purpose, he organised a series of seminars over a three year period (2006–09) which included the presence of Aboriginal Australian Elder, Aunty Joan Hendriks. Proceedings published as *Spirit of Religion: A Program for Meeting and Dialogue directed by Raimon Panikkar*, edited by M Carrara et al

a 'new innocence', 'new myth', 'new praxis' and/or a 'new mystical way' of thinking, acting and being which celebrates one's identity in relationship with, rather than in opposition to, other traditions.[15] While always being aware of the dangers of relativism (a particular concern of Pope Benedict XVI),[16] Panikkar is nonetheless adamant that only in-depth 'intra-religious dialogue'[17] among the traditions will enable us to confront the moral, spiritual, social and political quagmire of our times.

With specific reference to the Australian situation, and as far as I am aware the final public statement of Panikkar prior to his death, were these following remarks to a gathering of Indigenous peoples and interreligious scholars at the 2010 Brisbane 'Indigenous Theology Symposium':

> I am deeply convinced that the situation of the inhabitants of Australia today, after two centuries of suffering and tension, can now give birth to a new culture and civilisation as it happened some four thousand years ago when the Arians met with the ancient Indigenous population in India and the Vedic experience arose. But in order to have a fruitful fecundation, love is essential: only through love can I know my neighbour and be enriched.[18]
>
> In Australia the Western approach to reality, which is more masculine and based on the intellect power, meets with a more feminine approach to life open to the voice of the Spirit who inspires dreams and sacred stories and makes humans recognise the sacredness of nature. Humankind's life on earth is at a serious risk: the survival of humanity is possible

---

(Milan: Servitium, 2011).

15. This is what Panikkar calls 'The Catholic Moment'. Raimon Panikkar *The Cosmotheandric Experience: Emerging Religious Consciousness* (Maryknoll: Orbis Books, 1993), 46–53.
16. For Pope Benedict's critiques of relativism, see G Jankunas, *The Dictatorship of Relativism: Pope Benedict XVI's Response* (Staten Island: St Paul's Book Center, 2011).
17. Raimon Panikkar, *The Intra-Religious Dialogue*, revised edition (New York: Paulist Press, 1998).
18. Proceedings published as *Dreaming a New Earth: Raimon Panikkar and Indigenous Spiritualities*, edited by Gerard Hall and Joan Hendriks (Preston: Mosaic Press, 2012).

only through a real fecundation of these two approaches and Australia has this important opportunity.[19]

What this brings to light, and was celebrated at the Brisbane symposium, is the utmost importance of dialogue with and learning from the cosmic, earth-centred spiritualities of Indigenous traditions. Moreover, such dialogue needs to be highlighted in our approach to practical theology noting, as Panikkar states, Australia/Oceania is in a privileged situation to be a catalyst to 'give birth to a new culture and civilisation.' Panikkar also provides us with a possible vision and language which may aid our endeavours for the kind of depth-dialogue between Indigenous and other voices that he believes is required for the 'very survival of humanity.' In particular, he asks if there is an emerging global myth capable of providing a ground for dialogue among diverse cultures and traditions?[20]

An Emerging Global Myth? Cosmotheandric Experience and Transhistorical Consciousness

When Panikkar speaks of myth or *mythos*, he is speaking of the ever-elusive horizon of understanding that precedes its articulation in rational thought or *logos*.[21] This is not to decry the use of reason, but to admit that in meetings of persons, cultures and religions, which often enough espouse 'mutually irreconcilable worldviews or ultimate systems of thought,'[22] there is need for a fundamental trust in 'reality' itself. Now, for Panikkar—and for human traditions generally—reality is cosmic (*cosmos*), divine (*theos*) and human (*andros*), hence his word *cosmo-the-andric*.[23] So one does not trust

---

19. Panikkar, cited in *Dreaming a New Earth*, iii.
20. Panikkar explicitly states: 'I would like to fathom the underlying myth, as it were, and be able to provide elements of what may be the emerging myth for human life in its post-historical venture.' Raimon Panikkar, *The Rhythm of Being* (Maryknoll: Orbis Books, 2010), xxvi.
21. For example, Panikkar states that 'pluralism does not stem from the *logos*, but from the *mythos*.' Raimon Panikkar, *Myth, Faith, and Hermeneutics* (New York: Paulist Press, 1979), 102; see also his 'The Myth of Pluralism,' in Raimon Panikkar, *Invisible Harmony: Essays on Contemplation and Responsibility* (Minneapolis: Fortress Press, 1995), 52–91.
22. *Invisible Harmony*, 153.
23. Panikkar states that 'envisioning all of reality in terms of three worlds is an

in oneself alone, even less in one's ideas, but *in reality*. Consequently, such human cosmic trust does not proceed on the basis of an agreed set of propositions, a universal theory, or any other set of doctrines or beliefs; it is an act of faith that Panikkar also calls 'cosmotheandric confidence' and may be expressed in vastly diverse belief systems.[24] Importantly, this cosmic trust is first and foremost expressed through *symbol* rather than thought, since symbols are carriers of meaning linking subject to object, *mythos* to *logos*, darkness to light, understanding to interpretation, and faith to belief. Neither symbol nor myth can be artificially conceived, but must be allowed to emerge from the life-world of human experience—noting that, for Panikkar, human experience is also three-fold (body, mind and spirit).

Panikkar presents his cosmotheandric vision or intuition as belonging to the order of myth[25] which, he proposes, is capable of providing an horizon of meaning under which people of diverse cultural and religious systems may effectively communicate. Given that the human person is effectively a 'triad of senses, reason, and spirit in correlation with matter, thought, and freedom,'[26] an authentic approach to reality needs to encompass body (cosmic-dimension), mind (consciousness-dimension) and spirit (depth-dimension). Clearly, what Panikkar calls 'the Western approach to reality'—and the predominant Christian one—privileges the *logos*, rationality and intellectual knowledge. But as he elsewhere reminds us: 'Reality is not mind alone, or *cit*, or consciousness, or spirit. Reality is also *sat* and *ananda*, also matter and freedom, joy and being.'[27] Moreover, human knowledge is not reducible to the intellect, but needs to include

---

invariant of human culture, whether this vision is expressed, spatially, temporally, cosmologically or metaphysically.' *Cosmotheandric Experience*, 55. See also, Gerard Hall, 'Trusting the Other: Raimon Panikkar's Contribution to the Theory and Praxis of Interfaith Dialogue', in *Paths to Dialogue in Our Age: Australian Perspectives*, Volume 1 Edmund Chia and Fatih Tuncer (Fitzroy: Australian Catholic University, 2014), 136–149.

24. See Panikkar, 'A Universal Theory of Religion or a Cosmic Confidence in Reality,' in *Invisible Harmony*, 145–182.
25. *Cosmotheandric Experience*, 15.
26. *Rhythm of Being*, 244.
27. Panikkar, 'Religious Pluralism: The Metaphysical Challenge', in *Religious Pluralism*, collective work (South Bend: University of Notre Dame Press, 1984), 112.

body/sense perception and mystical experience.[28] Integral to this cosmotheandric experience is the need to awaken to 'the voice of the Spirit who inspires dreams and sacred stories' and reconnects us to 'the sacredness of nature.'[29]

Little wonder, then, that Panikkar turns to Indigenous traditions that have so much to teach in regard to a more holistic experience of life in which *logos*, matter and spirit—or human, cosmic and divine—are seen and experienced more integrally. In particular, Indigenous traditions exhibit in diverse and concrete ways what has been called a *biocosmic* spirituality or foundational religious experience in which the cosmos itself is experienced as something ultimate and sacred—'"something" in which everything participates.'[30] Panikkar calls such consciousness 'non-historical', by which he means that time is measured by the rhythms of nature and the seasons as distinct from the clock and advanced technologies.[31] For non-historical consciousness, 'the divine permeates the *cosmos*' and the world is 'full of gods'.[32]

Panikkar is not advocating a return to pre-historical consciousness, admitting that, even if desirable, such a venture is no longer possible for those who have encumbered the 'myth of history' identified as Western, scientific, rational, technological consciousness.[33] Rather, with the advent of historical consciousness and the ensuing 'crisis of history',[34] Panikkar speaks of the emergence of a new kind of consciousness— 'trans-historical'—capable of gathering together 'all the fragments of the scattered cultures and religions . . . for an ever better shaping of reality.'[35] While the cosmotheandric experience

---

28. See, for example, Panikkar's essay entitled 'The Contemplative Mood: A Challenge to Modernity' in *Invisible Harmony*, 1–19; and Panikkar, *The Experience of God: Icons of the Mystery* (Minneapolis: Fortress Press, 2006). The insight of course is recognised by the mystics of all traditions.
29. Panikkar's words cited above, *Dreaming a New Earth*, iii; note also the inclusion of Pope Francis in this discussion below.
30. See Philip Gibbs who develops this with particular reference to Melanesians of Papua New Guinea, 'Indigenous Spirituality: Expanding the View', in *Dreaming a New Earth*, 54–66; citation, 55.
31. *Cosmotheandric Experience*, 93–99.
32. *Cosmotheandric Experience*, 95–96.
33. *Cosmotheandric Experience*, 100–107.
34. *Cosmotheandric Experience*, 108–119.
35. *Invisible Harmony*, 175. See also *Cosmotheandric Experience*, 120–133; and 'The

is more specifically identified with transhistorical consciousness, its roots are deeply embedded in the biocosmic spiritualities of Indigenous traditions especially in their appreciation of the sacredness of the earth, their sense of the interrelationship of all realities, and their openness to the world of symbols.[36]

The Natural Mysticism of Indigenous Spiritualities

It may seem strange that when Panikkar speaks of the 'three eyes' of knowledge—senses, reason and spirit—he does not equate the 'third eye' (realm of the spirit) with mysticism.[37] Rather, he describes mysticism as 'the experiential awareness of the whole' which is beyond the field of consciousness.[38] If we are to equate mysticism with a form of knowledge, Karl Rahner's notion of 'unthematic knowledge' of God provides a helpful clue since such 'knowledge' is not 'consciousness of' an object beyond ourselves, but the 'unobjective grasp' or 'participative knowledge' of the divine mystery.[39] In similar fashion, we may imagine or employ metaphor to speak of Indigenous spiritualities exhibiting a type of cosmic or natural mysticism.[40]

The natural or cosmic mysticism of Indigenous traditions is not to be confused with the 'nature mysticism' of nineteenth-century Romanticism which is the personal, ecstatic experience of unity with nature accompanied by intense, *sui generis* visionary moments.

Emerging Mythos,' in *Rhythm of Being*, 368–404.
36. As Francis D'Sa notes, 'the cosmotheandric world is a world of symbols.' See his 'The call to get in touch with our origins', in *Dreaming a New Earth*, 12.
37. *Rhythm of Being*, 247.
38. *The Rhythm of Being*, 244. He adds that 'the locos of the mystical is not knowledge, not even knowledge of Being, but the realm of *śunyatā*, of emptiness', *Rhythm of Being*, 248.
39. See Karl Rahner, *Foundations of Christian Faith* (New York: The Seabury Press, 1976), 51–71. Rahner's 'unobjective grasp' or 'participative knowledge' is equivalent to Bernard Lonergan's notion of 'authentic subjectivity' as noted by Anthony Maher; information to the author.
40. For development of the idea of 'natural mysticism,' with particular focus on Aboriginal Australia, see Joan Hendriks and Gerard Hall, 'A Dialogue between Indigenous Australian Experience and Panikkar's Cosmotheandric Vision', in *Dreaming a New Earth*, 41–53. Philip Gibbs also speaks of Indigenous spiritualities having 'natural appreciation for the mystical and relational', in *Dreaming a New Earth*, 65.

Rather, Indigenous peoples' experience of nature is more cosmic, more communal, more natural.⁴¹ It is not the ecstatic, unrepeatable experience of a chosen individual, but the ordinary, every-day abiding experience of the sacred and the unity of all beings with the earth, cosmos and ultimate reality. One is not separate from this reality since there is no one—for that matter no Other—separable from creation and the natural world.⁴² The importance that Indigenous peoples give to symbol, ritual and ceremony through dance, movement and song highlights a bodily way of knowing that mediates an entire cosmology 'beyond the reach of explicit consciousness and thought.'⁴³ Such knowledge is sensory, affective, aesthetic, practical and exhibits its own kind of life-celebrating intelligence evidenced, for example, in the Aboriginal Corroboree which connects the participants to ancestral myths and laws of the Dreaming.⁴⁴ In so doing, the Corroboree celebrates the cosmic reality of the human community and the sacred reality of the cosmos.⁴⁵

A more poetic and existential expression of this 'natural mysticism' is presented by Ngangikurungkurr woman (Australian Northern Territory) Miriam Rose Ungunmerr-Baumann. In the language of her people, she tells us of the importance of *Dadirri*.⁴⁶ She calls it 'our most unique gift ... perhaps the greatest gift we can give to our

---

41. For an understanding of 'natural mysticism'—and its application to Indigenous peoples—see Wayne Teasdale, 'The Mysticism of the Natural World', in *Mystic Heart* (Novato: New World Library, 2001), 173–210.
42. Panikkar notes: 'The experience of the divine in nature is not reducible to an earthly numinous feeling regarding a *mysterium fascinans et tremens*. The relationship is a great deal more intimate. ... "Creation" is inseparable from the "Creator".' *Experience of God*, 128.
43. This is connected to Pierre Bourdieu's notion of *habitus* which recognises a particular form of embodied intelligence beyond the realm of discursive knowledge. Mark Wynn, 'Knowledge of God, Knowledge of Place, and the Aesthetic Dimension of Religious Understanding', in *Australian Ejournal of Theology* 11/1 (2008).
44. Hendriks and Hall, 'Indigenous Experience and Cosmotheandric Vision', 45, 50–51.
45. Panikkar states: 'Although humans become so in community, the human community is not limited to its fellow human creatures. The human community is also cosmic since the human is an integral, even, constitutive part of the cosmos.' *Experience of God*, 127.
46. '*Dadirri*: A Reflection by Miriam Rose Ungunmerr-Baumann', in *Dreaming a New Earth*, 4–8.

fellow Australians.' Emphasising the more feminine approach to life, of which Panikkar spoke, she describes *dadirri* as deep inner listening and quiet still awareness; or as a form of contemplation which is turned outward to the land and things about us as well as being deeply aware of the living springs within.[47] There is a sense of the whole that includes the sacred reality of land or country and the realisation that human community is itself dependent on one's shared connection to place and cosmos. While the emphasis of *dadirri* is on listening, it also includes story-telling, corroborees, smoking ceremonies, sounds of the didgeridoo and clapsticks. *Dadirri* 'makes us feel whole again,' part of tribe and country, and connects us to Mother Earth, Sacred Spirit or whatever words we use to describe the ultimate mystery of all life.[48]

If we were to describe this natural, cosmic mysticism in terms of the divine mystery or the God of nature, we need to understand this in the manner that Panikkar describes:

> The experience of God in nature is not primarily the experience of the one who makes it, whether creator or artist. Nor is it the experience of another force that sustains or gives existence to what is called the natural order. It is not what our aesthetic sense or calculation discovers, what the microscope, the telescope, or even rational thought may reveal. It is not a question of raising ourselves to the level of nature's author or penetrating the mysterious depths of the cosmos. It is primarily an experience more simple and more profound, not an experience of immanence or transcendence, nor an experience of an Other, but the experience of a Presence, of the most real presence of the actual thing in itself, from which we are not absent. To repeat, the experience of God is the total experience of the human being, in which nature is not absent.[49]

---

47. Miriam Rose Ungunmerr-Baumann, paraphrased by Rod Cameron, *Alcheringa: The Australian Experience of the Sacred* (Homebush: St Paul's, 1992), 24.
48. As with all things Aboriginal, there is a plurality of names for this Sacred Spirit: *Baiame* is the great Spirit of the south-eastern areas; *Nooralie* dwells in the heart of the Murray River region; in the West, we hear of the call of *Wandjina*. Information from Aunty Joan Hendriks.
49. *Experience of God*, 128–129.

This cosmic 'experience of a Presence' is both within time and beyond time, or where the eternal touches time, or what Panikkar also calls 'tempiternity'.⁵⁰ For Rod Cameron, this is what 'Aborigines called *Alcheringa* . . . Sacred Dreaming . . . Eternal Now'.⁵¹ Other Indigenous traditions will have their own *sui generis* experiences, modes of consciousness and ways of expressing their interrelatedness with the 'whole'. What is being emphasised is that this 'experiential awareness of the whole' is a spiritually heightened, 'total experience of the human being' which, in theological terms, is a genuinely mystical experience of the divine mystery within the cosmos.⁵²

So, are there Really Angels in Oceania? Implications for Practical Theology

The issue of Oceania's future cannot be the sole responsibility of any single people, culture, religion or tribe. We need first of all to call upon the angels of interreligious and intercultural dialogue. Clearly, this has not been a strength of our colonial past. There are still many prejudices against the worthwhileness or even possibility of genuine dialogue between peoples of such vastly diverse experiences and worldviews.⁵³ However, if we accept the reality of what Panikkar calls the 'crisis of history' and the increasingly recognised 'ecological crisis' facing our planet, it becomes clearer we need to draw on insights of all our various traditions. It is the task of practical theology not only to promote such dialogue, but to see its own discipline as an intercultural and interreligious activity.

---

50. *Cosmotheandric Experience*, 124–125.
51. *Alcheringa*, 77. See also anthropologist Tony Swain who speaks of 'Abiding events' and 'rhythmic events' in Aboriginal life which are designed to transcend time. Cited in *Dreaming a New Earth*, 48.
52. Panikkar notes that 'true religiousness is not bound to theisms' and that the "divine dimension" should not be identified with a monotheistic God.' *Rhythm of Being*, 322. The question of whether or not, or to what extent, we can interpret biocosmic spiritual traditions in 'theistic' terms is discussed by Philip Gibbs with reference to Melanesian spirituality in *Dreaming a New Earth*, 54–56.
53. There is also the danger of appropriating the other according to one's own experience, rather than authentically meeting the 'other' as 'other' in dialogue. This is a concern Panikkar shares with others, notably Jewish-French philosopher Emmanuel Levinas.

Second, we need to listen to angels that speak to us of the earth's wisdom. This is not merely a matter of reducing carbon emissions and being more generally ecologically aware. While this may be a positive start, it amounts to a continuation of the same 'colonising' approach to the earth.[54] What is required, Panikkar insists, is radical transformation if we are to effectively respond to the cries of the earth and the poor.[55] Such a call for a fundamental change of attitude is evident in Pope Francis' recent encyclical on the environment which proposes an 'ecological conversion'.[56] In a manner reminiscent of Panikkar's cosmotheandric vision, Francis reminds us that 'everything in the world is connected' and that 'human life is grounded in three fundamental and closely intertwined relationships: with God, with our neighbour and with the earth itself'.[57] Specifically, Francis tells us Indigenous peoples should be our 'primary dialogue partners' because, for them, 'land is not a commodity but rather a gift from God and from their ancestors.'[58]

In Panikkar's terminology, the call for an 'ecological conversion' represents a change of focus from 'ecology' (the science of the earth) to what he terms 'ecosophy' (the wisdom of the earth).[59] In different language, Francis proposes an 'integral ecology' which is respectful of human, social, cultural and economic concerns as well as environmental ones.[60] Both Panikkar and Francis are critical of the 'dominant technocratic paradigm' which they hold responsible for the crises besetting humanity and the environment.[61] However, neither is

---

54. This is what Panikkar calls the 'ecological interlude' which 'will do no more than delay some of the damage, and rationalise some of the exploitation.' *Rhythm of Being*, 353; see also *Cosmotheandric Experience*, 38–46.
55. *Cosmotheandric Experience*, 46.
56. Pope Francis, Encyclical Letter *Laudato Si'* on 'Care for our Common Home,' 24 May 2015, esp. nn 216–221.
57. *Laudato Si'*, nn 16 and 66.
58. *Laudato Si'*, n 146. For an example of dialogue with Indigenous Maori peoples, see Charlotte Šunde, 'Ecosophy and Indigenous Spiritualities,' in *Dreaming a New Earth*, 158–170.
59. Ecosophy is nowhere better expressed than in the feminine spirit of *dadirri* which is responsive to cosmic life and open to the voice of the Spirit within creation. Note Panikkar's reflections on *Anima Mundi* in *Cosmotheandric Experience*, 137–139.
60. *Laudato Si'*, chapter 4.
61. *Laudato Si'*, chapter 3; *Cosmotheandric Experience*, 108–118.

naïvely suggesting a return to a pre-modern worldview; rather they seek an integration of the positive aspects of science and technology with the spiritual, cultural and religious insights of humanity. Both call for a 'more integral and integrating vision' capable of responding to 'every aspect of the global crisis'.[62] In turn, this requires more extensive engagement with Indigenous spiritualities in order to develop a more practical-mystical-prophetic theology of creation, the environment and the natural world.

Conclusion

If we are to forge this new mysticism of place, time and history in Oceania this clearly requires our engagement with all Oceanian peoples, cultures and traditions. This includes being open to angels of secular humanism who inspire political commitment for justice, peace and freedom. Nor should we ignore other modern angels of science, technology and human reason which have an indisputable role to play. Equally, this emerging mysticism has much to learn from the world's classical theistic traditions with their insistence on a transcendent reality without which there would be neither world nor humanity. However, the until now much neglected angels of our Indigenous traditions are speaking to us of a more integral experience of life in which place, time and history are not merely fields for scientific and technical enquiry, but earth-bound and earth-transcending realities pointing us to a more mystical-prophetic vision of a 'new heaven and a new earth' (Rev 21:1).

Certainly, in Oceania as elsewhere, there are many demons and other negative forces which threaten humanity, our planet and life itself. In Panikkar's words, 'nothing short of a radical *metanoia*, a

---

62. *Laudato Si'*, chapter 4; citations N's 141 and 137 respectively. For Panikkar, this is the 'cosmotheandric vision' whose centre is neither the heavens above (theocentrism), nor the earth below (cosmocentrism), nor the human ego (anthropocentrism), but on the whole divine-human-cosmic reality. Panikkar also speaks of 'three kairological moments of consciousness': (1) Ecumenic Moment (Man *of* Nature); (2) Economic Moment (Man *above* Nature); (3) Catholic Moment (Man *with* Nature). These can be equated with what he terms prehistorical, historical and transhistorical consciousnesses. See his *Cosmotheandric Experience*, 20–53.

complete turning of mind, heart and spirit will meet today's needs.'[63] Practical theology today needs to encourage such transformation at all levels, personal and communal, mystical and political, cultural and religious. Naturally, such a task requires our attendance to the experience and understanding of the divine mystery at work in the Christian tradition. Particularly in Oceania, this also requires us to engage with Indigenous traditions that, despite the often negative experience of colonisation, have engaged with European ways of being and acting in the world. However, we need to acknowledge that, in the hermeneutic task of intercultural and interreligious dialogue, it is the Indigenous peoples who have done most of the accommodating to the non-Indigenous other.[64] If for no other reason than the crisis of our times, practical theology is called upon to engage in a genuinely mutual dialogue in which the experience of Indigenous peoples, especially their appreciation of the sacredness of the earth and the interdependence of all realities, inspire mystical consciousness and prophetic praxis.[65]

---

63. *Cosmotheandric Experience*, 46.
64. Tony Swain acknowledges there can be no place for a 'naïve assimilation' of the other's experience and worldview but insists, nonetheless, in the language of Hans-Georg Gadamer, there is need for a 'fusion of horizons'. Cited in *Dreaming a New Earth*, 46.
65. It should be noted that this should be achieved through consultation with Aboriginal communities and does not mean that outsiders should have access to secret and sacred knowledge.

Forum for Theology in the World Vol 2 No 2/2015

Contributors

Kathleen Butler-McIlwraith is Associate Professor at Newcastle University, NSW and the Node Leader for the Yuraki Aboriginal and Torres Strait Islander Histories and Cultures node in the ARC funded National Indigenous Research and Knowledges Network (NIRAKN). Her most recent publication is *Exploring Urban Identities and Histories* (AIATSIS, 2013).

Neil Darragh is a New Zealand theologian who has taught theology in the Auckland Consortium for Theological Education and in the School of Theology of the University of Auckland. He is a Catholic priest with many years of pastoral and community development experience in urban issues, particularly those relating to immigration, housing, education, and poverty. Current research and publishing interests include eco-theology and contextual theology. He is the coordinator of the Auckland Theology Research Unit which promotes New Zealand theological research. His most recent publication is an edited book entitled *But is it fair? Faith communities and social justice,* (2014).

Chris Duthie-Jung is Director of the National Centre for Religious Studies and Head of Partnerships at the Catholic Institute of Aotearoa New Zealand (TCI). His recent doctoral research explored the Catholic religious identity of pakeha young adult Catholics and considered the findings in view of contemporary studies of secularisation. Chris now works in the ongoing development of Religious Education curricula and Catholic Special Character in New Zealand Catholic Schools. With extensive experience in youth and young adult ministry his research and teaching continues to focus on the contemporary situation of Catholic young people. Chris is married and has three children.

Gerard Hall SM is a Marist priest and Associate Professor in the Faculty of Theology and Philosophy at the Australian Catholic University. His theological interests include foundational theology, Christology, anthropology, practical theology, interfaith dialogue and the theology of mission. As a student of Raimon Panikkar, he was an invited member of the International Spirit of Religion Project (2006–2009) and serves on the Academic Board of the Intercultural Centre dedicated to Raimon Panikkar. He is a member of various interfaith committees and, in 2010, received Queensland Intercultural Society's 'Building Bridges Award'. He was an invited member of the University of Heidelberg's
Scholar Board for the John Templeton Award for Theological Promise [2006–10]. As former Head of School, he was instrumental in founding the Australian eJournal of Theology. He engages in workshops on mission and evangelisation, especially for Catholic religious and teachers. Gerard is the inaugural Fellow of APTO.

Gerard Kelly is a Catholic priest of the Archdiocese of Sydney and the President of the Catholic Institute of Sydney, which is a member institute of the Sydney College of Divinity. His Theological interests are focused on Christian unity and sacramental theology. He is currently the co-chair of the Lutheran–Roman Catholic Dialogue in Australia, and is a member of the Faith and Unity Commission of the National Council of Churches in Australia. He is also the editor of the *Australasian Catholic Record*.

Anthony Maher is the Coordinator of Christian Life and Ministry at the Catholic Institute of Sydney. He is a Fellow of the Higher Education Academy (London) and the current President of the Association of Practical Theology in Oceania (APTO). His most recent publication with Bob Hanley is *Educating Hearts: Seven Characteristics of A Good School* (2013); the edited monograph *Theology For Pastoral Ministry* (Forthcoming, 2016); and *The Forgotten Jesuit* (Forthcoming, 2016).

Katharine Massam is a historian whose writing focuses on Australian religion and cross-cultural encounter. She teaches within the ecumenical University of Divinity, Melbourne, and 'on-location' at the former Aboriginal mission town of New Norcia in Western Australia. Latest article includes: *Spirituality Hidden in the Heart of the Uniting Church*. In: *An Informed Faith*.

Gerard Moore is Associate Professor and Head of the School of Theology at Charles Sturt University. His area of speciality is worship, particularly around ritual, translation and culture. He is a member of the CSU Public and Contextual Theology Research Centre. His most recent publications are *Earth Unites with Heaven: an introduction to the Liturgical Year* (2014), and *The Disciples at the Lord's Table: Prayers over Bread and Cup across 150 Years of Christian Church (Disciples of Christ)* (2015).

Stephen Pickard is a Bishop in the Anglican Diocese of Canberra & Goulburn and Executive Director of the Australian Centre for Christianity and Culture. He was Head of Charles Stuart University's School of Theology from 1998 to 2006. Since then he has served as a bishop in the Archdiocese of Adelaide and as a professorial fellow at Ripon College, Cuddesdon, Oxford. Professor Pickard is the author of several books, most recently *Seeking the Church: an Introduction to Ecclesiology* (2012) and *In-Between God: Theology, Community and Discipleship* (2011).

Catherine Playoust is a Lecturer at Catholic Theological College, Melbourne, University of Divinity, working in New Testament and related areas. At the time of the 2014 APTO Conference she was a lecturer at Jesuit Theological College in the United Faculty of Theology, University of Divinity. Her research interests include early Jewish and Christian apocalypticism and the transformation of Jewish and Christian traditions in early Christian literature.

David Ranson is the Parish Priest of Holy Name, Wahroonga, and Vicar General of the Diocese of Broken Bay. He is Senior Lecturer in the Sydney College of Divinity, teaching in Spirituality at the Catholic Institute of Sydney. For many years he was a member of the

Cistercian Order at Tarrawarra Abbey, Yarra Glen, Victoria where he was ordained in 1992. David is the author of *Across the Great Divide: Bridging Spirituality and Religion Today* (2002); *Living in the Holy Spirit: Elements of Catholic Spirituality* (2008); The Contemporary Challenge of Priestly Life: A meditation on the paschal paradox (2009); and Between the *Mysticism of Politics and the Politics of Mysticism* (2013).

ATF Press Style Guide

1. Indented material: Indented quotations, of over 5 lines of material, or 30 words, should be indented on both sides. There should be a space of one line before and after the quotation. Quotations should not have quotation marks at the beginning or end and within the quotation there should be single quotation marks (exception: where *within* the indented quote there is a quote that is also quoting (. . . '. . . " . . . " . . . ' . . .).

2. Headings: Headings should not be numbered unless there is a particular need (for example, cross-referencing within the text, scientific or text-book style presentation. Capitals should be used for the initial letters only of headings and subsections (unless using proper nouns). Headings and subsections do not have punctuation at the end.

3. Spelling: The general guide to spelling will be taken from *The Macquarie Dictionary*. We use '-ise' forms for words (and not '-ize') (so: realise, globalisation, modernise . . .). Hyphens should be used in words such as 'co-operate' and 'co-ordinate', except where the mathematical 'coordinate' is used. *The Australian Writers Dictionary* is a valuable tool for assisting with the use of hyphens. We prefer World War 1 (and not First World War). All Latin, Greek and all foreign words should be in italics and have an English translation. We prefer transliterations of biblical languages but if biblical languages are used then the English must be given in brackets.

4. Abbreviations and contractions
Abbreviations are generally not used: editor (rather than ed.), translated by (rather than trans.), volume (rather than vol.), number (rather than no.), for example (not e.g.). Those such as USA or UN do not have full points between the letters. Contractions, which end in the last of the whole word, should not be given a full point: Dr (Doctor), St (Saint).

5. Personal initials Do not insert a stop or space between personal initials, as for example: AN Simple.

6. Dates and numbers Avoid unnecessary punctuation: 24 June 1999 (and not 24 June, 1999, or June 24th , 1999). 1990s (not 1990's). Twentieth century (not 20th century). When referring to the age of a person, 'she was in her eighties', use the spelt-out form, but use figures in the hyphenated form when writing of an '80-year-old woman'. In text use of year span: 1991–8 with an en rule (not hyphen and no space) (not 1991-8), 1902–3 (and not1902-03), 1878–83. When in headings or subsections, use 1990–1992. Financial years are 1991/92. Spans of numbers: use as few digits as possible, with the exception of 11–19, where 1 is repeated. So: 112–13, 103–8, 34–9, 145–53. Numbers up to ninety-nine are spelt out in the text, except where figures are needed in a string of hyphenated words (35-hour week) or where figures will assist with clarity (when several numbers are compared). Numbers over ninety-nine are usually written in numerals but can be spelt out (about a thousand people) where figures seem inappropriate in the text. When a date is the first word of the sentence, use the spelt out form. Use figures for sums of money, $1.24, but three cents. Times should be in words rather than numerals when precision is not intended. So: 'They had to leave at three o'clock'. But where a precise time is intended: 'The bus leaves at 10.23am'. Percentages should be spelt out in the text: ninety-three per cent (note 'per cent'). But 93% in footnotes and tables.

7. Hyphens and dashes: En rules (a short dash) should be used for spans of numbers: 182–3; for Christian biblical references for the verses: Mk 3:12–13; for expressions of time: May–June; expressions of distance: Adelaide–Melbourne; and where 'and' is meant. Em rules (a long dash) are used in parenthetical statements, with no gap either side. For example, 'To have wide lawns—and not any garden—is not necessary for a happy life'.

8. Quotations: Indented quotes do not have opening and closing quotation marks. Short extracts of less than 5 lines (or 30 words) may appear within the text, enclosed in single quotation marks. Quotation marks should go inside the final full point if there is any authorial comment within the sentence; that is, the full point belongs to the author as part of her/his sentence. Time and time again, 'people do not speak' was quoted by authors. Or Sally was known to have said that 'the weather at the Cape is fine all year round'. If the quotation begins within a sentence containing authorial comment but runs to more than one sentence, it is acceptable to place the closing quotation mark after the final full point. George Stephens wrote with glee 'about fifty men broke out of the prison yesterday evening. We expect to have them rounded up before the week is past.' When a sentence is entirely quoted material, then all punctuation belongs to the quotation; therefore, the final full point goes inside the closing quotation mark. Mary received the telegram at 10 am. 'I never knew a darker moment than when I read of John's death.' Double quotation marks are only used for quotes within quotes. Eggs were thrown at the 'vote "No" for a republic' banner.

Indicate any omission from a quotation by the use of an ellipsis (. . .), with a single space keyed in before and after each point. Do not insert an additional full point if the ellipsis occurs at the end of a sentence. Do not use editorial caps within square brackets as in '[I]t is then . . . ', but leave the lower close letter, or adjust the way the quote is used.

9. *Footnotes*

Notes should be used for sources you have used, published or unpublished, to a brief discussion of the sources, to develop a point out of the text, or to cross reference to other parts of the text. Footnotes in the text should be used as a superscript text and in Times.

9.1Books: First name (not initials) and surname, title of the book (in italics), place of publication, publisher and year (all in brackets), followed by page numbers. We do not use p or pp for footnote entries or in the text. In the text write word 'page' if necessary. In footnotes there is minimal punctuation: First reference:
Victor Pfitzner, *The Islands of Peru* (Adelaide: ATF Press, 1999), 21.

Second and subsequent references copy and paste name (surname only) and title of book (or abbreviated title), followed by page number. Where a title is long a suitable shorter version should be used in second and subsequent references.
Pfitzner, *The Islands of Peru*, 28.

9.2 Articles in journals: First name, surname, title of article, (with single inverted commas), title of the journal (in italics), volume and number, year (year in brackets), followed by a colon and then the pages of the article. We do not uses p or pp in footnotes or in the text. First reference: Victor Pfitzner, 'Where To From Here?', in *Interface: A Pyschology Review*, 1/2 (1998): 22–3.
Second and subsequent references: Pfitzner, 'Where to From Here?', 38.

9.3 Articles in books: First name, surname, title of article (with single inverted commas), edited by, with first name first, title of the book (in italics), place of publication, publisher and year (all in brackets), followed by a colon and then page. Victor Pfitzner, 'Yesterday, Today And Tomorrow', in *Readings in Contemporary History*, edited by Victor Pfitzner (Adelaide: ATF Press, 2002), 22–56. *9.4 Web references*: First name, surname, title of article, web address enclosed in <...>, access date. Victor Pfitzner, 'Today and Not Tomorrow' at <www.newspoll.com.apost-au>. Accessed 20 July 2010. (No underlining).

10. Bibliography: We do not normally have a bibliography included with texts. But if one is to be used then, authors surname first, followed by initials and in alphabetical order of surname. Title of the book is in italics and with place of publisher, publisher and year in brackets. Pfitzner, V, *History of The New Time* (Adelaide: ATF Press, 2002).

Lightning Source UK Ltd.
Milton Keynes UK
UKHW011251020920
369216UK00001B/88